350
TWO-STORY
HOME PLANS

Source

350 TWO-STORY HOME PLANS
DreamHOMESource
hanley▲wood

Published by Hanley Wood
One Thomas Circle, NW, Suite 600
Washington, DC 20005

Distribution Center
PBD
Hanley Wood Consumer Group
3280 Summit Ridge Parkway
Duluth, Georgia 30096

Vice President, Home Plans, Andrew Schultz
Associate Publisher, Editorial Development, Jennifer Pearce
Managing Editor, Hannah McCann
Editor, Simon Hyoun
Assistant Editor, Kimberly Johnson
Publications Manager, Brian Haefs
Production Manager, Melissa Curry
Director, Plans Marketing, Mark Wilkin
Senior Plan Merchandiser, Nicole Phipps
Plan Merchandiser, Hillary Huff
Graphic Artist, Joong Min
Plan Data Team Leader, Susan Jasmin
Marketing Director, Holly Miller
Marketing Manager, Brett Bryant

Most Hanley Wood titles are available at quantity discounts with bulk purchases for educational, business, or sales promotional use. For information, please contact Andrew Schultz at aschultz@hanleywood.com.

VC Graphics, Inc.
Creative Director, Veronica Vannoy
Graphic Designer, Jennifer Gerstein
Graphic Designer, Denise Reiffenstein

Photo Credits
Front Cover, Main: HPK2700319, for details see page 295. Photo © Steve Gorum/ "Studio G," Mobile, Alabama, courtesy of Chatham Home Planning Inc. Front Cover, Inset: Photo courtesy of Stephen Fuller, Inc. See plan HWEPL05648 on eplans.com. Back Cover, Left: Photo by Sam Gray. Back Cover, Top: Design HPK2700114, for details see page 87. Photo by Raef Grohne Photography, courtesy of Select Home Designs. Page 14: Top courtesy of Andersen Windows. Bottom by Sam Gray. Page 15: Jessie Walker. Page 64: Top by Mark Samu. Bottom by Sam Gray. Page 65: Top by Mark Samu. Bottom by Sam Gray. Page 158: Peter Loppacher. Page 159: Sam Gray. Page 242: Top courtesy of Alan Mascord Design Associates, Inc. Bottom by Mark Samu. Page 243: Top by Ahmann Design, Inc. Bottom courtesy of Studio Becker. Page 328: Left by Getty Images. Right by Mark Samu. Page 329: Top left by Getty Images. Top right courtesy of Tropitone.

10 9 8 7 6 5 4 3 2 1

Printed in the United States of America

Library of Congress Control Number: 2006925914

ISBN-13: 978-1-931131-66-7
ISBN-10: 1-931131-66-X

350 TWO-STORY HOME PLANS

DreamHOMESource

CONTENTS

Build Up

Two-story homes suit families of any size, at any stage of life, and are often cost-efficient alternatives to sprawling one-level designs. Their flexibility stems from the way these designs vary the room placement and architectural structure of the home, accommodating multiple needs and preferences.

MASTER OF THE HOUSE

Two-story plans have the advantage of a second floor to help separate bedrooms from common living spaces or other bedrooms. Parents who seek privacy from children may prefer to have the master bedroom on the first floor. This is also an ideal choice for those planning to live in the home through retirement or with aging parents. The bedroom's location is often on the opposite side of the home from common areas such as the kitchen or family room, and sometimes includes a hallway for a foyer-like transition. For added distance from noisy living spaces, locate the bedroom upstairs for a quiet retreat. Also consider designs with dual suites—one upstairs, one down—so that the lower level can serve as guest space while you enjoy the elevated views from the second floor. In later years, the second suite can become the primary master.

ONWARD AND UPWARD

The thought of two stories on a home may sound like an overwhelming amount of square footage and cost, especially to those moving up from single-level living, but that second floor can in fact be a space-efficient and cost-efficient design choice. If you have a small lot or prefer a large yard, a two-story home will add the square footage upward instead of outward. And because it does not increase the design's footprint, a two-story plan reduces the expense of additional foundation and roofing materials that come with sprawling home style.

ROOMS WITH A VIEW

An aesthetic benefit of building upward is the access to scenic vantage points, both inside and out. Interior balconies, lofts, and railed walkways add elegance, as does a graceful staircase or two. Exterior second-floor decks and balconies provide breathtaking views of the surrounding countryside—and a convenient gathering space for guests to mingle.

Of course, just because you want to see views from your home doesn't mean you

DORMERS provide second-floor bedrooms with stunning views while keeping down costs. See ordering information for this plan on page 134.

welcome views into it. A second floor will increase the privacy of your master suite, study, or any other room you choose to place upstairs.

A SHINGLED EXTERIOR AND PLAYFUL fenestration distinguish a simple design. The balcony is modest yet practical, and adds interest to the facade. See more of this home on page 87.

GET PERSONAL
Almost all predrawn house plans can be modified at time of purchase, which makes it easy to give a stock design your own personal touch. Do you need more rooms for your large family or do you prefer fewer, larger rooms to entertain guests? Would you rather have a side- or back-loading garage instead of the front-loading unit specified in your plan? This is your home—make it your own! More information on house plan customization can be found on page 378.

HOW TO USE THIS BOOK
The featured homes beginning on the next page will guide you through some of the options and advantages described above. Imagine yourself and your furnishings in one of these homes. Consider the adjustments that would make it truly yours, and flip through the pages of the plans sections. We've collected 350 excellent designs

that will help you maximize your living space with style. And that's not all: our 43 pages of landscape and garage plans will help you beautify your outdoor spaces, as well.

The final step is to turn your dreams into reality! Any of the homes in this book could one day be yours, so turn to page 376 for details on the ordering process and what you will receive with your purchase. A materials list, customization, home automation, and other options are also explained in this section, followed by the list of prices on page 382. Please note that the plans are organized by page number, not plan number. Any time you have a question or simply would like a second opinion about a home, please feel free to contact our representatives at 1-800-521-6797.

Going Coastal

A cottage gains inspiration from the homes of the Gulf shores

This quaint, two-story cottage speaks volumes for the advantages of Gulf Coast-style living and design. The central eyebrow dormer, flanked by two gabled dormers, crowns the entrance beyond the full-length front porch. Supporting columns recall the Southern Colonial style while a carved railing brings a touch of country charm to the facade.

Inside, the floor plan welcomes in the outdoors with multiple windows and sliding glass doors; access the rear yard from either the master bedroom or the great room. A formal dining room lies at the front of the home and is adjacent to an open, island kitchen, which overlooks a welcoming great room. The master bedroom is on the lower level, making the design ideal for empty-nesters or those looking to retire. Homeowners will feel pampered by the suite's long walk-in closet and a bath complete with separate tub, shower, and water closet. A double vanity helps ease the routine of nightly and morning rituals.

A staircase in the foyer leads upstairs, where two bedrooms share a full bath. Each room has wide reach-in closets. The open stairway allows for a two-story foyer and a second-floor overlook. Make use of the dormer in each bedroom, which provides a clever nook for a bed, or add a window seat from which to enjoy expansive views across the front yard. A second stairway from the utility room leads to a bonus room above the garage. This flexible space can easily convert to a rec room, guest apartment, or hobby room.

❶ A WHITE PICKET FENCE adds the final touch of southern charm to this coastal cottage. For more information on this home, turn to page 147.

Photos courtesy of: William E. Poole Designs, Inc. - Wilmington, NC

2 FRENCH DOORS
lead directly from the
great room to a back-
yard patio.

FIRST FLOOR ❶   SECOND FLOOR

3 AN OPEN LAYOUT BETWEEN THE KITCHEN, breakfast nook, and great room is a modern element in an otherwise traditional coastal home.

4 **THE DINING ROOM** off the foyer provides a formal setting for family meals and special occasions.

5 **SUNLIGHT** enters through French doors into the master bedroom that includes a walk-in closet, master bath, and private outdoor access.

Above and Beyond

The low-lying facade belies a hidden second floor with an outdoor treat

Low, hipped rooflines give the impression that this Mediterranean masterpiece is a single-story home, when in fact it contains two floors filled with worthwhile spaces. Hips and gables of varying height and width add depth and interest to the roofline. Columns supporting a keystone arch bring focus to the recessed entry.

Step inside the foyer for a closer look at this modern, attractive plan. The first floor includes the major living spaces and common areas of the home. To the left, double doors open to a study with walls of built-in shelves and cabinets. Just beyond, another set of doors lead to a master suite complete with a 17x15-foot bayed bedroom, walk-in closet plus built-in valet, luxurious master bath, and private garden.

Cross the living room to the right wing and find everything a homeowner needs for ultimate comfort and entertainment. An oval tray ceiling defines the dining room from the foyer and the living room. Nearby, a guest suite gives visitors the comforts of home. Pass the pool bath to the double-island kitchen, breakfast nook, and leisure room, which is sure to become the hub of family activity.

The second floor houses yet another guest suite, complete with private bath and walk-in closet. Just outside the room, a loft holds an entertainment center—a perfect computer corner. Beside the bay window, French doors open to the most exciting space on this level: the observation deck. Here, sunbathers can enjoy views and privacy from atop the lanai, and owners can host outdoor summer soirees.

1 **COLUMNS AND AN ARCH** frame the front entryway, adding an attractive centerpiece to the facade. See ordering information for this home on page 272.

2 AN OBSERVATION DECK on the second floor overlooks the expansive rear lanai.

3 POCKET GLASS DOORS open to the lanai (above), inviting in the outdoors on temperate evenings. Great for very-large gatherings, the second-floor observation deck is an extension of the leisure spaces on the first floor.

4 **A BAY WINDOW**, above, encircles a comfortable reading nook within the opulent master bedroom.

5 **FIND SHELTER** from the hot summer sun or cool spring drizzle beneath the observation deck (left) just outside the **6** **LEISURE ROOM** (right), near a built-in grill.

Downstairs, the lanai expands the width of the home and curves around an inviting spot for a pool or tropical landscaping. Both the living room and leisure room have pocket doors that open the rooms entirely to the outdoors, and the master suite has its own lanai access. To the far end, the above observation deck provides welcome shade and cover for the built-in outdoor grill.

7 THIS KITCHEN is fit for a gourmet, with stylish black appliances, artful cabinetry, a center work island, and a snack-bar island.

8 A HEXAGONAL SPA TUB occupies a corner opposite the glass shower in the lavish master bath.

FIRST FLOOR

© THE SATER DESIGN COLLECTION, INC.

SECOND FLOOR

Think Small—
Get More from Less

PERSONAL TOUCHES like this stained-glass window add character to smaller homes.

Ahome of this size is perfect for the young family building for the first time. Most of the common living space remains on the first floor, reserving the second floor for one or two bedrooms and a bath, or perhaps a bonus room.

In a home that's less than 2,000 square feet, the biggest concern is making the best use of existing space. A smaller home should feel snug, not cramped—a challenging balance. With that in mind, open layouts that combine living rooms with dining areas and kitchens are functional and feel spacious. Smartly built homes incorporate household elements that can perform "on demand." For example, a peninsula counter in the kitchen functions flexibly as a dining area, prep space, breakfast bar, and serving buffet for larger meals. Entries may forego the formal foyer in favor of opening straight to the living room. Separate this room into separate areas using rugs or vignette-style furniture placement to provide both formal and casual spaces, such as two chairs with an end table near the window or hearth for sitting space when guests arrive and a comfortable couch facing the entertainment center for laid-back evenings with the family. This will allow areas of the home to retain definition without being closed off.

MAKE GOOD USE of nooks and crannies, such as in this roofline alcove with an attractive storage bench.

Expanding outdoor space is also a cost-effective way to compensate for a smaller square footage. Turn unused garage space into a storage room, or invest in a deck plan (see page 380 for details) to extend your breakfast nook and kitchen. Decks and patios are inexpensive places for grilling and serving alfresco meals—an elegant substitution for a formal dining room.

Bonus rooms offer myriad options for smaller homes and are not included in the otal square footage, which means you basically get whole room for free! If storage is an issue, use this oom to keep off-season clothing and decorations; f there's a bathroom nearby, turn it into a guest edroom; working from home? Make it your own ome office or study. The possibilities for making he most of your smaller home are endless.

Lastly, put to work what you'll save by building small. Let your home communicate a sense of intimacy and regard for meaningful details by incorporating quality materials and artful touches. Whether you're building a primary residence or vacation home, you'll be amazed at how a smaller-than-average home can fit just right.

HAVING AN OPEN LAYOUT is a stylish way to ombine rooms and conserve space.

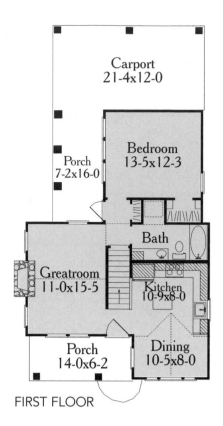

Carport
21-4x12-0

Porch
7-2x16-0

Bedroom
13-5x12-3

Bath

Greatroom
11-0x15-5

Kitchen
10-9x8-0

Porch
14-0x6-2

Dining
10-5x8-0

FIRST FLOOR

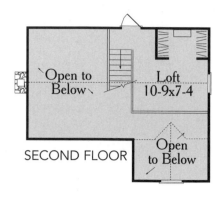

Open to Below

Loft
10-9x7-4

Open to Below

SECOND FLOOR

IN THE WILDERNESS OF EVERYDAY LIFE, wouldn't it be nice to come home to this cabin retreat? Perfect for retirees or a mountain getaway, this home is one of a kind. Nestle in front of the stone fireplace on a cold winter night, or enjoy the front and side porches on starry summer evenings. The L-shaped island kitchen opens to the dining area, which is framed by a Palladian window. Tucked in the back, the bedroom and bath are quite comfortable. On the second level you will find a loft with overlooks to the great room and dining room below.

HPK2700001

HOME PLAN

Style: Cottage

First Floor: 707 sq. ft.

Second Floor: 148 sq. ft.

Total: 855 sq. ft.

Bedrooms: 2

Bathrooms: 1

Width: 26' - 0"

Depth: 50' - 2"

Foundation: Crawlspace, Slab, Unfinished Basement

eplans.com

FIRST FLOOR

Nook

Kitchen

Family
13⁸ • 13⁰

Utility

Bath

Closet

storage

Foyer

Master Bedroom
14⁰ • 11⁰

Entry

HPK2700002

HOME PLAN

Style: Country

First Floor: 820 sq. ft.

Second Floor: 350 sq. ft.

Total: 1,170 sq. ft.

Bedrooms: 3

Bathrooms: 2

Width: 37' - 0"

Depth: 67' - 0"

Foundation: Slab

eplans.com

SECOND FLOOR

Bedroom 3
10⁰ • 10²

Bath

Bedroom 2
10⁰ • 11⁸

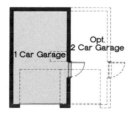

Opt.
2 Car Garage

1 Car Garage

THIS HOME IS DISTINGUISHED BY ITS TWO PROMINENT DORMERS—one facing front and the other on the left side. The dormer to the left boasts a sunburst window that spills light into the family room. Enter through a large covered porch to a foyer that looks into the family room. Beyond, a vaulted kitchen/nook area is graced with an abundance of windows and rear-door access. The master bedroom is located at the front of the plan and is accented with a full bath. On the second floor are two additional bedrooms, each with ample closet space.

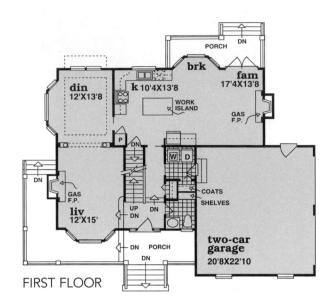

FIRST FLOOR

Labels in first floor plan: PORCH, DN, brk, fam 17'4X13'8, din 12'X13'8, k 10'4X13'8, WORK ISLAND, GAS F.P., P, DN, UP DN, DN, GAS F.P., liv 12'X15', COATS, SHELVES, W, D, two-car garage 20'8X22'10, DN, PORCH, DN

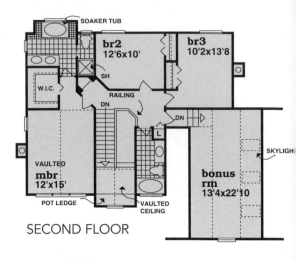

SECOND FLOOR

Labels in second floor plan: SOAKER TUB, br2 12'6x10', br3 10'2x13'8, W.I.C., SH, RAILING, DN, DN, L, SKYLIGHT, VAULTED, mbr 12'x15', POT LEDGE, VAULTED CEILING, bonus rm 13'4x22'10

THIS CHARMING COUNTRY EXTERIOR CONCEALS AN ELEGANT INTERIOR, starting with formal living and dining rooms, each with a bay window. Decorative columns help define an elegant dining room. The gourmet kitchen features a work island and a breakfast area with its own bay window. A fireplace warms the family room, which opens to the rear porch through French doors. Upstairs, two family bedrooms share a full bath and a gallery hall with a balcony overlook to the foyer. Also on this floor, a master suite boasts a vaulted ceiling, a walk-in closet, and a tiled bath.

HOME PLAN

HPK2700003

Style: Country

First Floor: 1,007 sq. ft.

Second Floor: 917 sq. ft.

Total: 1,924 sq. ft.

Bonus Space: 325 sq. ft.

Bedrooms: 3

Bathrooms: 2 ½

Width: 53' - 0"

Depth: 44' - 0"

Foundation: Crawlspace, Unfinished Basement

eplans.com

© 1991 Donald A. Gardner, Architects, Inc

A MOUNTAIN RETREAT, THIS RUSTIC HOME FEATURES COVERED PORCHES at the front and rear. Enjoy open living in the great room and kitchen/dining room combination. Here, a fireplace provides the focal point and a warm welcome that continues into the L-shaped island kitchen. A cathedral ceiling graces the great room and gives an open, inviting sense of space. Two bedrooms—one with a walk-in closet—and a full bath on the first level are complemented by a master bedroom on the second floor. This suite includes a walk-in closet and deluxe bath. Attic storage is available on the second floor.

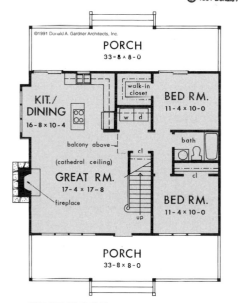

©1991 Donald A. Gardner Architects, Inc.

PORCH
33-8 x 8-0

KIT./
DINING
16-8 x 10-4

walk-in closet

w d

BED RM.
11-4 x 10-0

balcony above

bath

(cathedral ceiling)

cl

GREAT RM.
17-4 x 17-8

fireplace

BED RM.
11-4 x 10-0

up

PORCH
33-8 x 8-0

FIRST FLOOR

HPK2700004

HOME PLAN

Style: Country

First Floor: 1,002 sq. ft.

Second Floor: 336 sq. ft.

Total: 1,338 sq. ft.

Bedrooms: 3

Bathrooms: 2

Width: 36' - 8"

Depth: 44' - 8"

eplans.com

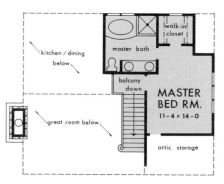

walk-in closet

master bath

kitchen / dining below

balcony down

great room below

MASTER BED RM.
11-4 x 14-0

attic storage

SECOND FLOOR

© 1996 Donald A. Gardner Architects, Inc.

HOME PLAN
HPK2700005

Style: Country
First Floor: 1,395 sq. ft.
Second Floor: 502 sq. ft.
Total: 1,897 sq. ft.
Bonus Space: 316 sq. ft.
Bedrooms: 3
Bathrooms: 2 ½
Width: 53' - 4"
Depth: 51' - 4"

FIRST FLOOR

SECOND FLOOR

HOME PLAN
HPK2700006

Style: Craftsman
First Floor: 1,012 sq. ft.
Second Floor: 556 sq. ft.
Total: 1,568 sq. ft.
Bedrooms: 3
Bathrooms: 2 ½
Width: 34' - 0"
Depth: 48' - 0"
Foundation: Crawlspace, Unfinished Basement

FIRST FLOOR

SECOND FLOOR

HOME PLAN

HPK2700007

Style: Colonial Revival

First Floor: 637 sq. ft.

Second Floor: 730 sq. ft.

Total: 1,367 sq. ft.

Bedrooms: 3

Bathrooms: 2 ½

Width: 37' - 6"

Depth: 34' - 0"

Foundation: Crawlspace, Unfinished Walkout Basement

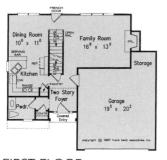

FIRST FLOOR

SECOND FLOOR

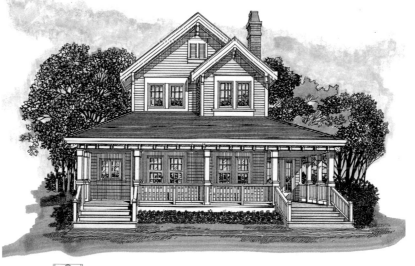

HOME PLAN

HPK2700008

Style: Victorian Eclectic

First Floor: 995 sq. ft.

Second Floor: 484 sq. ft.

Total: 1,479 sq. ft.

Bedrooms: 3

Bathrooms: 2 ½

Width: 38' - 0"

Depth: 44' - 0"

Foundation: Crawlspace, Unfinished Basement

FIRST FLOOR

SECOND FLOOR

HOME PLAN

HPK2700009

Style: Country

First Floor: 1,061 sq. ft.

Second Floor: 430 sq. ft.

Total: 1,491 sq. ft.

Bedrooms: 3

Bathrooms: 2 ½

Width: 40' - 4"

Depth: 36' - 0"

Foundation: Unfinished Walkout Basement

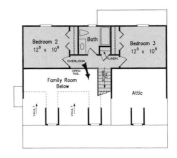

FIRST FLOOR

SECOND FLOOR

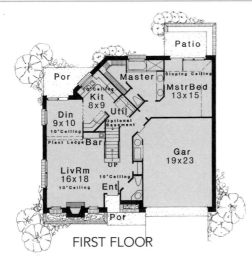

FIRST FLOOR

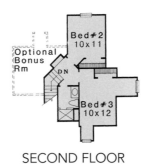

SECOND FLOOR

HOME PLAN

HPK2700010

Style: Norman

First Floor: 1,130 sq. ft.

Second Floor: 370 sq. ft.

Total: 1,500 sq. ft.

Bonus Space: 110 sq. ft.

Bedrooms: 3

Bathrooms: 2 ½

Width: 45' - 0"

Depth: 38' - 10"

Foundation: Crawlspace, Slab, Unfinished Basement

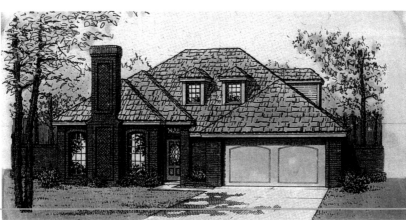

HOME PLAN
HPK2700011

Style: Country

First Floor: 767 sq. ft.

Second Floor: 738 sq. ft.

Total: 1,505 sq. ft.

Bedrooms: 3

Bathrooms: 2 ½

Width: 47' - 10"

Depth: 36' - 0"

Foundation: Crawlspace, Slab, Unfinished Walkout Basement

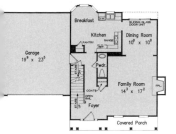

FIRST FLOOR

SECOND FLOOR

HOME PLAN
HPK2700012

Style: Country

First Floor: 1,050 sq. ft.

Second Floor: 458 sq. ft.

Total: 1,508 sq. ft.

Bedrooms: 3

Bathrooms: 2 ½

Width: 35' - 6"

Depth: 39' - 9"

Foundation: Pier (same as Piling)

FIRST FLOOR

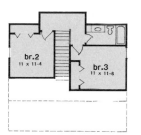

SECOND FLOOR

FIRST FLOOR

SECOND FLOOR

HOME PLAN
HPK2700013

Style: Tidewater

First Floor: 1,073 sq. ft.

Second Floor: 470 sq. ft.

Total: 1,543 sq. ft.

Bedrooms: 4

Bathrooms: 2

Width: 30' - 0"

Depth: 71' - 6"

Foundation: Pier (same as Piling)

HOME PLAN
HPK2700014

Style: Farmhouse

First Floor: 1,050 sq. ft.

Second Floor: 533 sq. ft.

Total: 1,583 sq. ft.

Bedrooms: 3

Bathrooms: 2

Width: 42' - 0"

Depth: 38' - 0"

Foundation: Crawlspace, Unfinished Basement

FIRST FLOOR

SECOND FLOOR

SECOND FLOOR

FIRST FLOOR

HOME PLAN

HPK2700015

Style: Cottage

First Floor: 1,094 sq. ft.

Second Floor: 492 sq. ft.

Total: 1,586 sq. ft.

Bedrooms: 3

Bathrooms: 2

Width: 46' - 0"

Depth: 44' - 4"

Foundation: Crawlspace, Slab, Unfinished Basement

HOME PLAN

HPK2700016

Style: Queen Anne

First Floor: 840 sq. ft.

Second Floor: 757 sq. ft.

Total: 1,597 sq. ft.

Bedrooms: 3

Bathrooms: 3

Width: 26' - 0"

Depth: 32' - 0"

Foundation: Unfinished Basement

FIRST FLOOR

SECOND FLOOR

FIRST FLOOR

SECOND FLOOR

HOME PLAN

HPK2700017

Style: Farmhouse

First Floor: 828 sq. ft.

Second Floor: 772 sq. ft.

Total: 1,600 sq. ft.

Bedrooms: 3

Bathrooms: 2 ½

Width: 52' - 4"

Depth: 34' - 0"

Foundation: Crawlspace, Slab, Unfinished Walkout Basement

FIRST FLOOR

HOME PLAN

HPK2700018

Style: New American

First Floor: 1,005 sq. ft.

Second Floor: 620 sq. ft.

Total: 1,625 sq. ft.

Bedrooms: 2

Bathrooms: 2 ½

Width: 30' - 0"

Depth: 44' - 6"

Foundation: Finished Walkout Basement

SECOND FLOOR

© 1995 Donald A. Gardner Architects, Inc.

FIRST FLOOR

SECOND FLOOR

HOME PLAN

HPK2700019

Style: Farmhouse

First Floor: 1,380 sq. ft.

Second Floor: 466 sq. ft.

Total: 1,846 sq. ft.

Bonus Space: 326 sq. ft.

Bedrooms: 3

Bathrooms: 2 ½

Width: 61' - 8"

Depth: 65' - 0"

HOME PLAN

HPK2700020

Style: New American

First Floor: 993 sq. ft.

Second Floor: 642 sq. ft.

Total: 1,635 sq. ft.

Bedrooms: 2

Bathrooms: 2 ½

Width: 28' - 0"

Depth: 44' - 0"

Foundation: Finished Walkout Basement

FIRST FLOOR

SECOND FLOOR

HOMES UNDER 2,000 SQUARE FEET

HOME PLAN

HPK2700021

Style: New American

First Floor: 897 sq. ft.

Second Floor: 740 sq. ft.

Total: 1,637 sq. ft.

Bedrooms: 3

Bathrooms: 2 ½

Width: 30' - 0"

Depth: 42' - 6"

Foundation: Unfinished Walkout Basement

FIRST FLOOR

SECOND FLOOR

FIRST FLOOR

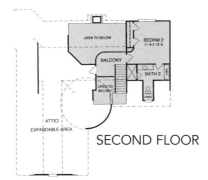

SECOND FLOOR

HOME PLAN

HPK2700022

Style: Tudor

First Floor: 1,276 sq. ft.

Second Floor: 378 sq. ft.

Total: 1,654 sq. ft.

Bedrooms: 2

Bathrooms: 2 ½

Width: 54' - 4"

Depth: 53' - 10"

Foundation: Crawlspace, Slab

HOME PLAN

HPK2700023

Style: New American

First Floor: 1,179 sq. ft.

Second Floor: 479 sq. ft.

Total: 1,658 sq. ft.

Bonus Space: 338 sq. ft.

Bedrooms: 3

Bathrooms: 2 ½

Width: 41' - 6"

Depth: 54' - 4"

Foundation: Crawlspace, Slab, Unfinished Walkout Basement

FIRST FLOOR

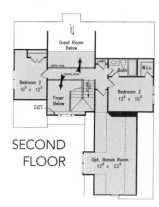

SECOND FLOOR

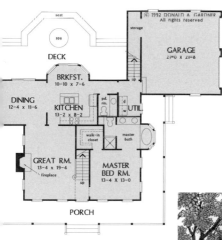

FIRST FLOOR

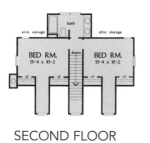

SECOND FLOOR

HOME PLAN

HPK2700024

Style: Farmhouse

First Floor: 1,145 sq. ft.

Second Floor: 518 sq. ft.

Total: 1,663 sq. ft.

Bedrooms: 3

Bathrooms: 2 ½

Width: 59' - 4"

Depth: 56' - 6"

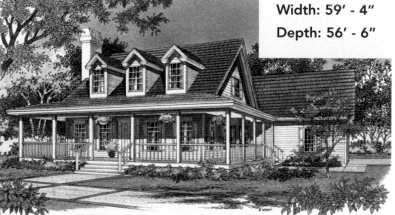

© 1997 Donald A. Gardner Architects, Inc.

FIRST FLOOR

SECOND FLOOR

HOME PLAN
HPK2700025

Style: Country
First Floor: 1,219 sq. ft.
Second Floor: 450 sq. ft.
Total: 1,669 sq. ft.
Bonus Space: 406 sq. ft.
Bedrooms: 3
Bathrooms: 2 ½
Width: 50' - 4"
Depth: 49' - 2"

HOME PLAN
HPK2700026

Style: Colonial Revival
First Floor: 882 sq. ft.
Second Floor: 793 sq. ft.
Total: 1,675 sq. ft.
Bonus Space: 416 sq. ft.
Bedrooms: 3
Bathrooms: 2 ½
Width: 49' - 6"
Depth: 35' - 4"
Foundation: Crawlspace, Slab, Unfinished Walkout Basement

FIRST FLOOR

SECOND FLOOR

© 1994 Donald A. Gardner Architects, Inc.

HOME PLAN

HPK2700027

Style: Country

First Floor: 1,100 sq. ft.

Second Floor: 584 sq. ft.

Total: 1,684 sq. ft.

Bedrooms: 3

Bathrooms: 2

Width: 36' - 8"

Depth: 45' - 0"

FIRST FLOOR

w d cl

UTILITY
8-4 x 7-8

PORCH

KIT.
8-0 x 11-4

DINING
10-4 x 11-2

bath

BED RM.
12-0 x 10-0

cl

balcony above

lin. cl

cl

GREAT RM.
17-4 x 17-0

fireplace

BED RM.
12-0 x 13-4

up

© 1994 DONALD A. GARDNER
All rights reserved

PORCH

SECOND FLOOR

LOFT/
STUDY
12-0 x 14-0

master
bath

walk-in
closet

railing   down

great room
below

MASTER
BED RM.
12-0 x 14-0

attic
storage

HOME PLAN

HPK2700028

Style: Vacation

First Floor: 1,046 sq. ft.

Second Floor: 638 sq. ft.

Total: 1,684 sq. ft.

Bedrooms: 3

Bathrooms: 3

Width: 25' - 0"

Depth: 65' - 6"

Foundation: Crawlspace

REAR EXTERIOR

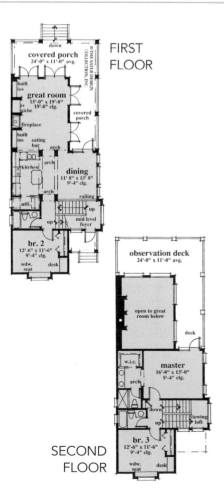

FIRST FLOOR

down

covered porch
24'-0" x 11'-0" avg.

built
ins

great room
15'-0" x 19'-0"
19'-0" clg.

tv
niche

covered
porch

fireplace

built
ins   eating
bar

arch

kitchen   arch

dining
11' 8" x 13' 0"
9'-4" clg.

arch

util.

railing

up   up

mid level
foyer

br. 2
12'-6" x 11'-6"
9'-4" clg.

wdw.
seat   desk

SECOND FLOOR

observation deck
24'-0" x 11'-0" avg.

open to great
room below

deck

w.i.c.

master
16'-0" x 13'-0"
9'-4" clg.

arch

down

up

viewing
loft

br. 3
12'-6" x 11'-6"
9'-4" clg.

wdw.
seat   desk

HOME PLAN

HPK2700029

Style: Cottage

First Floor: 1,230 sq. ft.

Second Floor: 477 sq. ft.

Total: 1,707 sq. ft.

Bonus Space: 195 sq. ft.

Bedrooms: 3

Bathrooms: 2 ½

Width: 40' - 0"

Depth: 52' - 10"

Foundation: Crawlspace

FIRST FLOOR

SECOND FLOOR

HOME PLAN

HPK2700030

Style: Cottage

First Floor: 1,292 sq. ft.

Second Floor: 423 sq. ft.

Total: 1,715 sq. ft.

Bedrooms: 3

Bathrooms: 2 ½

Width: 40' - 0"

Depth: 59' - 8"

FIRST FLOOR

SECOND FLOOR

HOME PLAN

HPK2700031

Style: Country

First Floor: 954 sq. ft.

Second Floor: 783 sq. ft.

Total: 1,737 sq. ft.

Bonus Space: 327 sq. ft.

Bedrooms: 3

Bathrooms: 2 ½

Width: 56' - 0"

Depth: 40' - 0"

Foundation: Crawlspace

FIRST FLOOR

SECOND FLOOR

HOME PLAN

HPK2700032

Style: Cottage

First Floor: 879 sq. ft.

Second Floor: 869 sq. ft.

Total: 1,748 sq. ft.

Bedrooms: 3

Bathrooms: 2 ½

Width: 37' - 6"

Depth: 47' - 10"

Foundation: Crawlspace,
Unfinished Basement

FIRST FLOOR

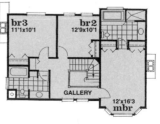

SECOND FLOOR

HOMES UNDER 2,000 SQUARE FEET

HOME PLAN

HPK2700033

Style: French Country

First Floor: 941 sq. ft.

Second Floor: 819 sq. ft.

Total: 1,760 sq. ft.

Bedrooms: 3

Bathrooms: 3

Width: 50' - 0"

Depth: 44' - 6"

Foundation: Crawlspace

FIRST FLOOR

SECOND FLOOR

FIRST FLOOR

SECOND FLOOR

HOME PLAN

HPK2700034

Style: Cottage

First Floor: 1,211 sq. ft.

Second Floor: 551 sq. ft.

Total: 1,762 sq. ft.

Bonus Space: 378 sq. ft.

Bedrooms: 3

Bathrooms: 2 ½

Width: 64' - 4"

Depth: 39' - 4"

Foundation: Crawlspace, Unfinished Basement

HOME PLAN
HPK2700035

Style: French Country

First Floor: 1,144 sq. ft.

Second Floor: 620 sq. ft.

Total: 1,764 sq. ft.

Bedrooms: 3

Bathrooms: 2 ½

Width: 41' - 0"

Depth: 46' - 4"

Foundation: Crawlspace, Unfinished Walkout Basement

FIRST FLOOR

SECOND FLOOR

FIRST FLOOR

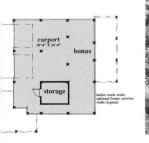

SECOND FLOOR

REAR EXTERIOR

HOME PLAN
HPK2700036

Style: Cracker

First Floor: 1,136 sq. ft.

Second Floor: 636 sq. ft.

Total: 1,772 sq. ft.

Bedrooms: 2

Bathrooms: 2

Width: 41' - 9"

Depth: 45' - 0"

Foundation: Pier (same as Piling), Slab

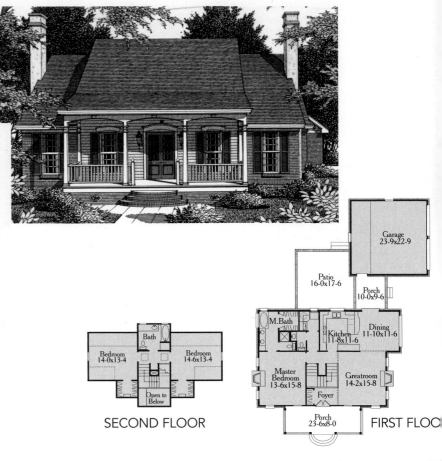

HOME PLAN

HPK2700037

Style: Cottage

First Floor: 1,173 sq. ft.

Second Floor: 602 sq. ft.

Total: 1,775 sq. ft.

Bedrooms: 3

Bathrooms: 2 ½

Width: 51' - 5"

Depth: 69' - 6"

Foundation: Crawlspace, Slab, Unfinished Basement

SECOND FLOOR

FIRST FLOOR

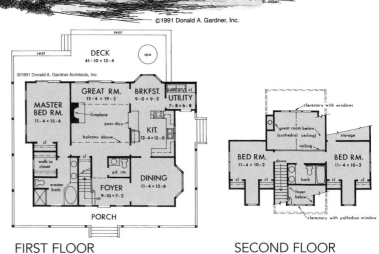

HOME PLAN

HPK2700038

Style: Tidewater

First Floor: 1,325 sq. ft.

Second Floor: 453 sq. ft.

Total: 1,778 sq. ft.

Bedrooms: 3

Bathrooms: 2 ½

Width: 48' - 4"

Depth: 51' - 10"

©1991 Donald A. Gardner, Inc.

FIRST FLOOR

SECOND FLOOR

HOME PLAN

HPK2700039

Style: Mediterranean

First Floor: 1,230 sq. ft.

Second Floor: 649 sq. ft.

Total: 1,879 sq. ft.

Bedrooms: 3

Bathrooms: 2 ½

Width: 38' - 0"

Depth: 53' - 6"

Foundation: Slab

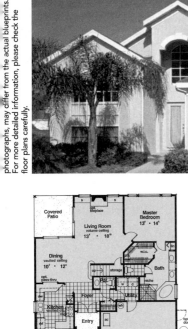

FIRST FLOOR

SECOND FLOOR

HOME PLAN

HPK2700040

Style: Italianate

First Floor: 1,143 sq. ft.

Second Floor: 651 sq. ft.

Total: 1,794 sq. ft.

Bonus Space: 476 sq. ft.

Bedrooms: 2

Bathrooms: 2 ½

Width: 32' - 0"

Depth: 57' - 0"

Foundation: Slab

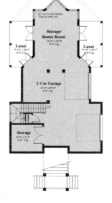

FIRST FLOOR

SECOND FLOOR

FIRST FLOOR

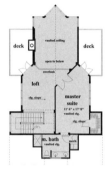

SECOND FLOOR

HOME PLAN

HPK2700041

Style: Gothic Revival

First Floor: 1,143 sq. ft.

Second Floor: 651 sq. ft.

Total: 1,794 sq. ft.

Bedrooms: 2

Bathrooms: 2 ½

Width: 32' - 0"

Depth: 57' - 0"

Foundation: Island Basement

HOME PLAN

HPK2700042

Style: Contemporary

First Floor: 1,143 sq. ft.

Second Floor: 651 sq. ft.

Total: 1,794 sq. ft.

Bonus Space: 651 sq. ft.

Bedrooms: 2

Bathrooms: 2 ½

Width: 32' - 0"

Depth: 57' - 0"

Foundation: Unfinished Walkout Basement

FIRST FLOOR

SECOND FLOOR

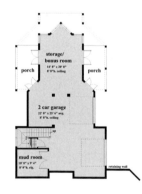

©The Sater Design Collection, Inc.

REAR EXTERIOR

© 2002 Donald A. Gardner, Inc.

HOME PLAN
HPK2700043

Style: French Country

First Floor: 1,345 sq. ft.

Second Floor: 452 sq. ft.

Total: 1,797 sq. ft.

Bonus Space: 349 sq. ft.

Bedrooms: 3

Bathrooms: 2 ½

Width: 63' - 0"

Depth: 40' - 0"

FIRST FLOOR

SECOND FLOOR

HOME PLAN
HPK2700044

Style: Country

First Floor: 916 sq. ft.

Second Floor: 895 sq. ft.

Total: 1,811 sq. ft.

Bonus Space: 262 sq. ft.

Bedrooms: 3

Bathrooms: 2 ½

Width: 44' - 0"

Depth: 38' - 0"

Foundation: Crawlspace, Slab, Unfinished Walkout Basement

FIRST FLOOR

SECOND FLOOR

HOMES UNDER 2,000 SQUARE FEET

HOME PLAN #

HPK2700045

Style: New American

First Floor: 972 sq. ft.

Second Floor: 843 sq. ft.

Total: 1,815 sq. ft.

Bonus Space: 180 sq. ft.

Bedrooms: 3

Bathrooms: 2 ½

Width: 45' - 0"

Depth: 37' - 0"

Foundation: Crawlspace

FIRST FLOOR

SECOND FLOOR

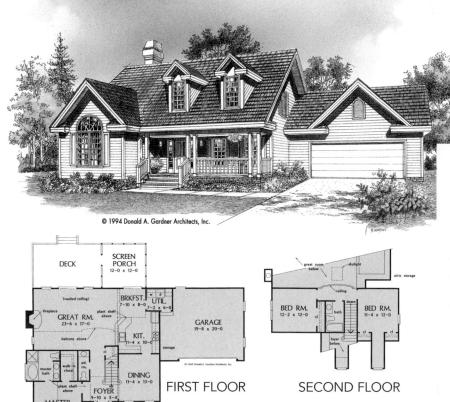

© 1994 Donald A. Gardner Architects, Inc.

FIRST FLOOR

SECOND FLOOR

HOME PLAN #

HPK2700046

Style: Country

First Floor: 1,335 sq. ft.

Second Floor: 488 sq. ft.

Total: 1,823 sq. ft.

Bedrooms: 3

Bathrooms: 2 ½

Width: 61' - 6"

Depth: 54' - 0"

© 1990 Donald A. Gardner Architects, Inc.

HOME PLAN

HPK2700047

Style: Country

First Floor: 1,289 sq. ft.

Second Floor: 542 sq. ft.

Total: 1,831 sq. ft.

Bonus Space: 393 sq. ft.

Bedrooms: 3

Bathrooms: 2 ½

Width: 66' - 4"

Depth: 40' - 4"

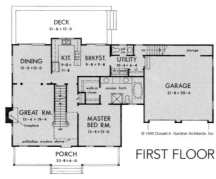

FIRST FLOOR

© 1990 Donald A. Gardner Architects, Inc.

SECOND FLOOR

FIRST FLOOR

REAR EXTERIOR

ECOND FLOOR

HOME PLAN

HPK2700048

Style: Victorian Eclectic

First Floor: 1,290 sq. ft.

Second Floor: 548 sq. ft.

Total: 1,838 sq. ft.

Bedrooms: 3

Bathrooms: 2 ½

Width: 38' - 0"

Depth: 51' - 0"

Foundation: Crawlspace, Unfinished Basement

FIRST FLOOR

SECOND FLOOR

HOME PLAN

HPK2700049

Style: Mediterranean

First Floor: 1,342 sq. ft.

Second Floor: 511 sq. ft.

Total: 1,853 sq. ft.

Bedrooms: 3

Bathrooms: 2

Width: 44' - 0"

Depth: 40' - 0"

Foundation: Island Basement

©The Sater Design Collection, Inc.

HOME PLAN

HPK2700050

Style: Cottage

First Floor: 1,342 sq. ft.

Second Floor: 511 sq. ft.

Total: 1,853 sq. ft.

Bedrooms: 3

Bathrooms: 2

Width: 44' - 0"

Depth: 40' - 0"

Foundation: Pier (same as Piling)

REAR EXTERIOR

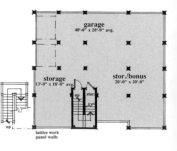

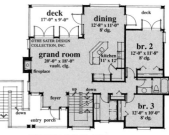

FIRST FLOOR

SECOND FLOOR

HOME PLAN

HPK2700051

Style: Cottage

First Floor: 1,342 sq. ft.

Second Floor: 511 sq. ft.

Total: 1,853 sq. ft.

Bedrooms: 3

Bathrooms: 2 ½

Width: 44' - 0"

Depth: 44' - 0"

Foundation: Island Basement

FIRST FLOOR

SECOND FLOOR

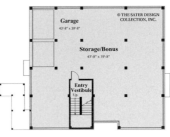

HOME PLAN

HPK2700052

Style: New American

First Floor: 1,342 sq. ft.

Second Floor: 511 sq. ft.

Total: 1,853 sq. ft.

Bedrooms: 3

Bathrooms: 2

Width: 44' - 0"

Depth: 40' - 0"

Foundation: Unfinished Basement

FIRST FLOOR

SECOND FLOOR

HOME PLAN #

HPK2700053

Style: New American

First Floor: 836 sq. ft.

Second Floor: 1,107 sq. ft.

Total: 1,943 sq. ft.

Bedrooms: 3

Bathrooms: 2 ½

Width: 32' - 4"

Depth: 35' - 8"

Foundation: Unfinished Basement

FIRST FLOOR

SECOND FLOOR

HOME PLAN #

HPK2700054

Style: Country

First Floor: 1,103 sq. ft.

Second Floor: 759 sq. ft.

Total: 1,862 sq. ft.

Bedrooms: 4

Bathrooms: 3

Width: 50' - 4"

Depth: 35' - 0"

Foundation: Crawlspace, Slab, Unfinished Walkout Basement

FIRST FLOOR

SECOND FLOOR

HOME PLAN
HPK2700055

Style: Cottage

First Floor: 1,314 sq. ft.

Second Floor: 552 sq. ft.

Total: 1,866 sq. ft.

Bonus Space: 398 sq. ft.

Bedrooms: 3

Bathrooms: 2 ½

Width: 44' - 2"

Depth: 62' - 0"

Foundation: Crawlspace

FIRST FLOOR

SECOND FLOOR

FIRST FLOOR

SECOND FLOOR

HOME PLAN
HPK2700056

Style: Federal - Adams

First Floor: 1,028 sq. ft.

Second Floor: 843 sq. ft.

Total: 1,871 sq. ft.

Bonus Space: 304 sq. ft.

Bedrooms: 3

Bathrooms: 2 ½

Width: 40' - 0"

Depth: 61' - 0"

Foundation: Crawlspace, Unfinished Basement

FIRST FLOOR

SECOND FLOOR

HOME PLAN

HPK2700057

Style: Traditional

First Floor: 870 sq. ft.

Second Floor: 1,007 sq. ft.

Total: 1,877 sq. ft.

Bonus Space: 263 sq. ft.

Bedrooms: 4

Bathrooms: 2 ½

Width: 40' - 0"

Depth: 49' - 0"

Foundation: Crawlspace

HOME PLAN

HPK2700058

Style: Colonial Revival

First Floor: 946 sq. ft.

Second Floor: 933 sq. ft.

Total: 1,879 sq. ft.

Bedrooms: 4

Bathrooms: 2 ½

Width: 55' - 4"

Depth: 35' - 0"

Foundation: Slab, Unfinished Basement

FIRST FLOOR

SECOND FLOOR

FIRST FLOOR

SECOND FLOOR

HOME PLAN

HPK2700059

Style: Neoclassical

First Floor: 1,347 sq. ft.

Second Floor: 537 sq. ft.

Total: 1,884 sq. ft.

Bedrooms: 3

Bathrooms: 2 ½

Width: 32' - 10"

Depth: 70' - 10"

Foundation: Crawlspace

HOME PLAN

HPK2700060

Style: Cottage

First Floor: 1,408 sq. ft.

Second Floor: 476 sq. ft.

Total: 1,884 sq. ft.

Bedrooms: 3

Bathrooms: 2 ½

Width: 41' - 8"

Depth: 56' - 4"

FIRST FLOOR

SECOND FLOOR

HOME PLAN #

HPK2700061

Style: Cape Cod

First Floor: 1,182 sq. ft.

Second Floor: 708 sq. ft.

Total: 1,890 sq. ft.

Bedrooms: 4

Bathrooms: 2

Width: 44' - 0"

Depth: 64' - 0"

Foundation: Unfinished Basement

FIRST FLOOR

SECOND FLOOR

HOME PLAN #

HPK2700062

Style: Farmhouse

First Floor: 1,032 sq. ft.

Second Floor: 870 sq. ft.

Total: 1,902 sq. ft.

Bonus Space: 306 sq. ft.

Bedrooms: 3

Bathrooms: 2 ½

Width: 66' - 0"

Depth: 38' - 0"

Foundation: Crawlspace

FIRST FLOOR

SECOND FLOOR

HOME PLAN

HPK2700063

Style: Bungalow

First Floor: 1,097 sq. ft.

Second Floor: 807 sq. ft.

Total: 1,904 sq. ft.

Bedrooms: 3

Bathrooms: 2 ½

Width: 40' - 0"

Depth: 45' - 0"

Foundation: Crawlspace

FIRST FLOOR   SECOND FLOOR

FIRST FLOOR

SECOND FLOOR

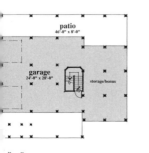

REAR EXTERIOR

HOME PLAN

HPK2700064

Style: Cottage

First Floor: 1,302 sq. ft.

Second Floor: 602 sq. ft.

Total: 1,904 sq. ft.

Bedrooms: 3

Bathrooms: 2 ½

Width: 48' - 0"

Depth: 45' - 0"

Foundation: Pier (same as Piling)

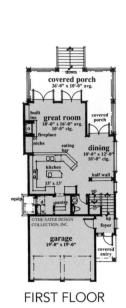

FIRST FLOOR

© The Sater Design Collection, Inc.

SECOND FLOOR

HOME PLAN #

HPK2700065

Style: Cottage

First Floor: 873 sq. ft.

Second Floor: 1,037 sq. ft.

Total: 1,910 sq. ft.

Bedrooms: 3

Bathrooms: 2 ½

Width: 27' - 6"

Depth: 64' - 0"

Foundation: Crawlspace

HOME PLAN #

HPK2700066

Style: French Country

First Floor: 1,398 sq. ft.

Second Floor: 515 sq. ft.

Total: 1,913 sq. ft.

Bonus Space: 282 sq. ft.

Bedrooms: 3

Bathrooms: 2 ½

Width: 48' - 0"

Depth: 50' - 10"

Foundation: Crawlspace, Slab, Unfinished Walkout Basement

FIRST FLOOR

SECOND FLOOR

HOME PLAN

HPK2700067

Style: Cottage

First Floor: 1,396 sq. ft.

Second Floor: 523 sq. ft.

Total: 1,919 sq. ft.

Bedrooms: 4

Bathrooms: 2 ½

Width: 44' - 0"

Depth: 51' - 0"

Foundation: Crawlspace

FIRST FLOOR

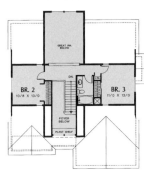

SECOND FLOOR

HOME PLAN

HPK2700068

Style: Country

First Floor: 1,082 sq. ft.

Second Floor: 838 sq. ft.

Total: 1,920 sq. ft.

Bedrooms: 3

Bathrooms: 2 ½

Width: 66' - 10"

Depth: 29' - 5"

Foundation: Crawlspace, Slab, Unfinished Basement

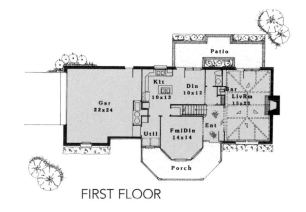

FIRST FLOOR

SECOND FLOOR

HOME PLAN #

HPK2700069

Style: Country

First Floor: 947 sq. ft.

Second Floor: 981 sq. ft.

Total: 1,928 sq. ft.

Bedrooms: 4

Bathrooms: 2 ½

Width: 41' - 0"

Depth: 39' - 4"

Foundation: Crawlspace, Slab, Unfinished Walkout Basement

FIRST FLOOR

SECOND FLOOR

HOME PLAN #

HPK2700070

Style: Victorian Eclectic

First Floor: 1,024 sq. ft.

Second Floor: 904 sq. ft.

Total: 1,928 sq. ft.

Bedrooms: 3

Bathrooms: 2 ½

Width: 65' - 0"

Depth: 35' - 5"

Foundation: Crawlspace, Unfinished Basement

FIRST FLOOR

SECOND FLOOR

© 1991 Donald A. Gardner Architects, Inc.

FIRST FLOOR

SECOND FLOOR

HOME PLAN

HPK2700071

Style: Country

First Floor: 1,025 sq. ft.

Second Floor: 911 sq. ft.

Total: 1,936 sq. ft.

Bonus Space: 410 sq. ft.

Bedrooms: 3

Bathrooms: 2 ½

Width: 53' - 8"

Depth: 67' - 8"

© 1993 Donald A. Gardner Architects, Inc.

FIRST FLOOR

SECOND FLOOR

HOME PLAN

HPK2700072

Style: Farmhouse

First Floor: 1,271 sq. ft.

Second Floor: 665 sq. ft.

Total: 1,936 sq. ft.

Bedrooms: 4

Bathrooms: 3

Width: 41' - 6"

Depth: 44' - 8"

HOMES UNDER 2,000 SQUARE FEET

© William E. Poole Designs, Inc.

HOME PLAN
HPK2700073

Style: Cottage

First Floor: 1,021 sq. ft.

Second Floor: 915 sq. ft.

Total: 1,936 sq. ft.

Bonus Space: 378 sq. ft.

Bedrooms: 3

Bathrooms: 2 ½

Width: 66' - 8"

Depth: 38' - 8"

Foundation: Crawlspace, Unfinished Basement

FIRST FLOOR

SECOND FLOOR

HOME PLAN
HPK2700074

Style: Cottage

First Floor: 911 sq. ft.

Second Floor: 1,029 sq. ft.

Total: 1,940 sq. ft.

Bedrooms: 3

Bathrooms: 2 ½

Width: 20' - 10"

Depth: 75' - 10"

Foundation: Crawlspace

© Larry E. Belk Designs

FIRST FLOOR

SECOND FLOOR

HOME PLAN
HPK2700075

Style: Country
First Floor: 968 sq. ft.
Second Floor: 977 sq. ft.
Total: 1,945 sq. ft.
Bedrooms: 4
Bathrooms: 2 ½
Width: 40' - 0"
Depth: 46' - 0"
Foundation: Crawlspace

FIRST FLOOR

SECOND FLOOR

HOME PLAN
HPK2700076

Style: Craftsman
First Floor: 1,082 sq. ft.
Second Floor: 864 sq. ft.
Total: 1,946 sq. ft.
Bonus Space: 358 sq. ft.
Bedrooms: 3
Bathrooms: 2 ½
Width: 40' - 0"
Depth: 52' - 0"
Foundation: Crawlspace

FIRST FLOOR

SECOND FLOOR

HOMES UNDER 2,000 SQUARE FEET

HOME PLAN

HPK2700077

Style: French Country

First Floor: 1,484 sq. ft.

Second Floor: 466 sq. ft.

Total: 1,950 sq. ft.

Bedrooms: 3

Bathrooms: 2 ½

Width: 42' - 6"

Depth: 53' - 9"

Foundation: Slab

FIRST FLOOR

SECOND FLOOR

FIRST FLOOR

SECOND FLOOR

HOME PLAN

HPK2700078

Style: Craftsman

First Floor: 1,352 sq. ft.

Second Floor: 605 sq. ft.

Total: 1,957 sq. ft.

Bonus Space: 285 sq. ft.

Bedrooms: 3

Bathrooms: 2 ½

Width: 60' - 0"

Depth: 43' - 0"

Foundation: Crawlspace

HOME PLAN
HPK2700079

Style: Craftsman

First Floor: 970 sq. ft.

Second Floor: 988 sq. ft.

Total: 1,958 sq. ft.

Bedrooms: 3

Bathrooms: 2 ½

Width: 40' - 0"

Depth: 43' - 0"

Foundation: Crawlspace

FIRST FLOOR

SECOND FLOOR

FIRST FLOOR

SECOND FLOOR

HOME PLAN
HPK2700080

Style: Neoclassical

First Floor: 904 sq. ft.

Second Floor: 1,058 sq. ft.

Total: 1,962 sq. ft.

Bedrooms: 3

Bathrooms: 2 ½

Width: 22' - 0"

Depth: 74' - 0"

Foundation: Crawlspace, Slab

HOMES UNDER 2,000 SQUARE FEET

HOME PLAN

HPK2700081

Style: Farmhouse

First Floor: 1,374 sq. ft.

Second Floor: 600 sq. ft.

Total: 1,974 sq. ft.

Bedrooms: 3

Bathrooms: 2 ½

Width: 51' - 8"

Depth: 50' - 8"

Foundation: Unfinished Basement

FIRST FLOOR

SECOND FLOOR

FIRST FLOOR

SECOND FLOOR

HOME PLAN

HPK2700082

Style: Mediterranean

First Floor: 1,383 sq. ft.

Second Floor: 595 sq. ft.

Total: 1,978 sq. ft.

Bedrooms: 3

Bathrooms: 2

Width: 48' - 0"

Depth: 42' - 0"

Foundation: Island Basement

HOME PLAN
HPK2700083

Style: New American

First Floor: 1,383 sq. ft.

Second Floor: 595 sq. ft.

Total: 1,978 sq. ft.

Bedrooms: 3

Bathrooms: 2

Width: 48' - 0"

Depth: 48' - 8"

Foundation: Unfinished Walkout Basement

FIRST FLOOR

SECOND FLOOR

FIRST FLOOR

SECOND FLOOR

REAR EXTERIOR

HOME PLAN
HPK2700084

Style: Cottage

First Floor: 1,383 sq. ft.

Second Floor: 595 sq. ft.

Total: 1,978 sq. ft.

Bedrooms: 3

Bathrooms: 2

Width: 48' - 0"

Depth: 42' - 0"

Foundation: Island Basement

FIRST
FLOOR

SECOND
FLOOR

HOME PLAN
HPK2700085

Style: Cottage

First Floor: 1,596 sq. ft.

Second Floor: 387 sq. ft.

Total: 1,983 sq. ft.

Bedrooms: 3

Bathrooms: 3

Width: 46' - 6"

Depth: 65' - 0"

Foundation: Crawlspace, Slab, Unfinished Basement

HOME PLAN
HPK2700086

Style: Cottage

First Floor: 803 sq. ft.

Second Floor: 1,182 sq. ft.

Total: 1,985 sq. ft.

Bedrooms: 4

Bathrooms: 2 ½

Width: 36' - 0"

Depth: 43' - 4"

Foundation: Crawlspace, Slab, Unfinished Walkout Basement

FIRST
FLOOR

SECOND
FLOOR

ORDER BLUEPRINTS ANYTIME AT EPLANS.COM OR 1-800-521-679

HOME PLAN

HPK2700087

Style: Farmhouse

First Floor: 1,480 sq. ft.

Second Floor: 511 sq. ft.

Total: 1,991 sq. ft.

Bonus Space: 363 sq. ft.

Bedrooms: 3

Bathrooms: 2 ½

Width: 73' - 0"

Depth: 51' - 10"

FIRST FLOOR

SECOND FLOOR

HOME PLAN

HPK2700088

Style: Bungalow

First Floor: 1,024 sq. ft.

Second Floor: 456 sq. ft.

Total: 1,480 sq. ft.

Bedrooms: 2

Bathrooms: 2

Width: 32' - 0"

Depth: 40' - 0"

Foundation: Finished Walkout Basement

FIRST FLOOR

SECOND FLOOR

HOMES UNDER 2,000 SQUARE FEET

HOME PLAN

HPK2700089

Style: Country

First Floor: 1,071 sq. ft.

Second Floor: 924 sq. ft.

Total: 1,995 sq. ft.

Bonus Space: 280 sq. ft.

Bedrooms: 3

Bathrooms: 2 ½

Width: 55' - 10"

Depth: 38' - 6"

Foundation: Crawlspace, Slab, Unfinished Walkout Basement

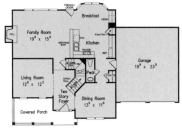

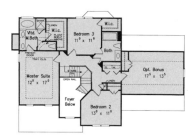

FIRST FLOOR

SECOND FLOOR

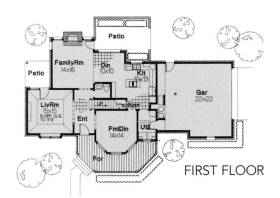

FIRST FLOOR

SECOND FLOOR

HOME PLAN

HPK2700090

Style: Victorian Eclectic

First Floor: 1,157 sq. ft.

Second Floor: 838 sq. ft.

Total: 1,995 sq. ft.

Bedrooms: 3

Bathrooms: 2 ½

Width: 66' - 10"

Depth: 36' - 11"

Foundation: Crawlspace, Slab, Unfinished Basement

HOME PLAN

HPK2700091

Style: Tudor

First Floor: 999 sq. ft.

Second Floor: 997 sq. ft.

Total: 1,996 sq. ft.

Bedrooms: 3

Bathrooms: 2 ½

Width: 60' - 0"

Depth: 28' - 10"

Foundation: Unfinished Basement

FIRST FLOOR

SECOND FLOOR

FIRST FLOOR

HOME PLAN

HPK2700092

Style: Neoclassical

First Floor: 1,078 sq. ft.

Second Floor: 921 sq. ft.

Total: 1,999 sq. ft.

Bedrooms: 3

Bathrooms: 3

Width: 24' - 11"

Depth: 73' - 10"

Foundation: Crawlspace

SECOND FLOOR

HOMES UNDER 2,000 SQUARE FEET

Movin' On Up—Designs for a New, More Spacious Home

THIS SPACIOUS MASTER BEDROOM incorporates built-in shelves for added storage and display space.

So, you've lived in a smaller home for several years and you're ready for an upgrade. Whether your family is growing, or your possessions are accumulating, or you can now afford a design that gives you a little room to spread out, a "family-sized" home will have all the space you need.

The plans in this collection are similar to those in the previous section, but it's amazing how much difference 100 to 500 square feet can make. Some designers apply the extra space to each room; others create additional rooms. The designs often include a foyer, for a more formal entry. They could have a formal dining room—if the open eating area in your previous home was not conducive to special occasions—or an extra bedroom for a new family member or for new-found guest space. While extra and formal rooms, like dens or offices, gain definition through walls or outlining columns, openness and room flow remain important design priorities.

Left: **WELCOME GUESTS** with an elegant dining room toward the front of the plan. Below: **A TWO-STORY HOME** in this size range allows for an impressive entry foyer to showcase a winding stairway.

Designers may also choose to add amenities to existing rooms. In this way, the master bedrooms tend to be more accommodating. You may have shared a common bath with another bedroom in your previous home, but a master suite will let you have the relaxing retreat all to yourself. Separate tubs and showers are sure to appear in these designs, as are walk-in closets. The master suite will also likely be secluded from the busier areas of the house and away from family bedrooms—a perfect family orientation.

So, for the growing family or the homeowners who would simply like a little extra room, a move-up house plan from this section will provide options and opportunities for both.

Left: **AN OPEN LAYOUT AND ROOM FLOW** are still important elements for making a 2,000- to 2,500-square-foot home feel comfortable.

A TRADITIONAL-STYLE HOME WITH A STORY-BOOK ENTRANCE offers today's family space to change and grow. The foyer features a powder room and a stairway to the second floor. The open living/dining room area is large enough for hosting both casual and formal affairs. A work island/snack counter, window sink, and breakfast nook highlight the kitchen. A fireplace warms the family room. Upstairs, four bedrooms include a master suite with a walk-in closet and private bath. Three family bedrooms share a compartmented bath that provides a double-bowl vanity. Bedroom 2 features a walk-in closet.

HPK2700093

Style: French Country

First Floor: 1,051 sq. ft.

Second Floor: 949 sq. ft.

Total: 2,000 sq. ft.

Bedrooms: 4

Bathrooms: 2 ½

Width: 44' - 0"

Depth: 38' - 8"

Foundation: Slab

eplans.com

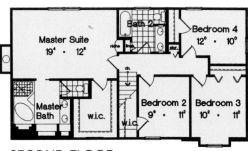

FIRST FLOOR

SECOND FLOOR

HOME PLAN

HPK2700094

Style: New American

First Floor: 1,500 sq. ft.

Second Floor: 518 sq. ft.

Total: 2,018 sq. ft.

Bonus Space: 248 sq. ft.

Bedrooms: 4

Bathrooms: 3

Width: 53' - 0"

Depth: 50' - 0"

Foundation: Crawlspace, Unfinished Walkout Basement

eplans.com

UROPEAN DETAILS ADD SPLASH TO THIS CHARMING OUNTRY EXTERIOR, while an arch-top clerestory rings in natural light. The heart of the home is the aulted family room, made cozy by a centered fireplace amed by tall windows. The first-floor master suite oasts a tray ceiling as well as a vaulted bath with twin anities, a walk-in closet with linen storage, and a win- owed whirlpool tub. An additional bedroom nearby ould serve as a quiet study. Upstairs, each of two family edrooms provides a walk-in closet.

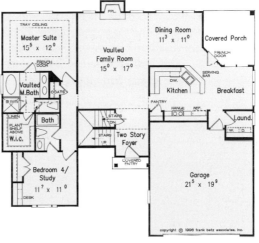

FIRST FLOOR

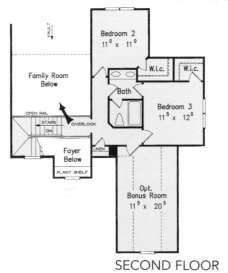

SECOND FLOOR

SECOND FLOOR

FIRST FLOOR

© William E. Poole Designs

WITH ALL OF THE SLEEPING QUARTERS LOCATED ON THE SECOND FLOOR, the first floor is ideal for family interaction and entertaining. The great room sits between the front and rear porches and opens to the adjacent breakfast area and kitchen. The bay-windowed dining room provides an option for formal meals. On the second floor, the master bedroom boasts a whirlpool tub, compartmented shower and toilet, dual-sink vanity, and his/her wardrobe. Two family bedrooms share a full bath. Future expansion space completes this plan.

HOME PLAN

HPK2700095

Style: Cottage

First Floor: 1,047 sq. ft.

Second Floor: 976 sq. ft.

Total: 2,023 sq. ft.

Bonus Space: 318 sq. ft.

Bedrooms: 3

Bathrooms: 2 ½

Width: 58' - 0"

Depth: 37' - 4"

Foundation: Crawlspace, Unfinished Basement Basement

eplans.com

© William E. Poole Designs, Inc.

HPK2700096

Style: Cottage

First Floor: 1,347 sq. ft.

Second Floor: 690 sq. ft.

Total: 2,037 sq. ft.

Bedrooms: 4

Bathrooms: 2

Width: 55' - 0"

Depth: 41' - 0"

Foundation: Unfinished Basement

HOME PLAN #

FIRST FLOOR

eplans.com

SECOND FLOOR

PERFECT FOR WATERFRONT PROPERTY, the home is designed for great views from the rear of the plan. Inside, open planning can be found in the living room, which offers a corner fireplace for cool evenings and blends beautifully into the dining and kitchen areas. For chores and storage, the laundry room is conveniently nestled between the kitchen and the two-car garage. The master suite features a walk-through closet and sumptuous bath. Upstairs, three uniquely shaped bedrooms share a full bath.

FIRST FLOOR

SECOND FLOOR

GRACEFUL CURVES WELCOME YOU INTO THE COURT-YARD of this Santa Fe home. Inside, a gallery directs traffic to the work zone on the left or the sleeping zone on the right. Straight ahead lies a sunken gathering room with a beamed ceiling and a raised-hearth fireplace. A large pantry offers extra storage space for kitchen items. The covered rear porch is accessible from the dining room, gathering room and secluded master bedroom. Luxury describes the feeling in the master bath with a whirlpool tub, a separate shower, a double vanity and closet space. Two family bedrooms share a compartmented bath. The study could serve as a guest room, a media room or a home office.

HPK2700097

HOME PLAN

Style: Santa Fe

First Floor: 1,055 sq. ft.

Second Floor: 981 sq. ft.

Total: 2,036 sq. ft.

Bedrooms: 3

Bathrooms: 2 ½

Width: 43' - 8"

Depth: 54' - 4"

Foundation: Unfinished Basement

eplans.com

© 1999 Donald A. Gardner, Inc.

 # HOME PLAN

HPK2700098

Style: Country

First Floor: 1,502 sq. ft.

Second Floor: 535 sq. ft.

Total: 2,037 sq. ft.

Bonus Space: 275 sq. ft.

Bedrooms: 3

Bathrooms: 2 ½

Width: 43' - 0"

Depth: 57' - 6"

eplans.com

THIS IMPRESSIVE HOME HAS AN ARRAY OF SPECIAL FEATURES, yet it's cost-effective and easy to build for those on a limited budget. Tray ceilings elevate the bedroom/study, dining room, and master bedroom. A bayed window illuminates the formal dining room. The great room features a cathedral ceiling and a striking fireplace. A smart angled counter is all that separates the great room, kitchen, and bayed breakfast area. The master bedroom suite remains a private getaway from the rest of the home. Note the tub, large separate shower, and double vanity.

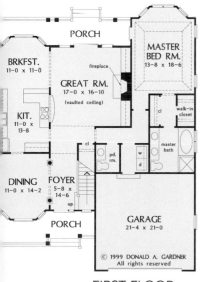

FIRST FLOOR

SECOND FLOOR

FIRST FLOOR

SECOND FLOOR

HOME PLAN

HPK2700099

Style: Greek Revival

First Floor: 1,370 sq. ft.

Second Floor: 668 sq. ft.

Total: 2,038 sq. ft.

Bonus Space: 421 sq. ft.

Bedrooms: 3

Bathrooms: 2 ½

Width: 71' - 8"

Depth: 49' - 4"

Foundation: Crawlspace

eplans.com

THIS CHARMING 2-STORY HOME OFFERS AN INVITING FRONT PORCH AND A REAR SCREENED PORCH, increasing the living space significantly. The foyer opens to the formal dining room and the great room, which in turn leads to the screened porch. The master suite is tucked away for privacy on the right—the sunny bedroom adjoins a luxurious private bath. The second-floor balcony, full bath, and lounge area separate the two family bedrooms.

© William E. Poole Designs, Inc.

HOME PLAN

◯# HPK2700100

Style: Colonial Revival

First Floor: 1,135 sq. ft.

Second Floor: 917 sq. ft.

Total: 2,052 sq. ft.

Bonus Space: 216 sq. ft.

Bedrooms: 4

Bathrooms: 3

Width: 52' - 4"

Depth: 37' - 6"

Foundation: Crawlspace, Slab, Unfinished Walkout Basement

eplans.com

THIS GRAND TWO-STORY HOME PROVES THAT TRIED-AND-TRUE TRADITIONAL STYLE IS STILL THE BEST! Thoughtful planning brings formal living areas to the forefront and places open, casual living areas to the rear of the plan. Bedroom 4 serves as a multipurpose room, providing the flexibility desired by today's homeowner. The second floor is devoted to the relaxing master suite, two secondary bedrooms, a full hall bath, and a balcony overlook.

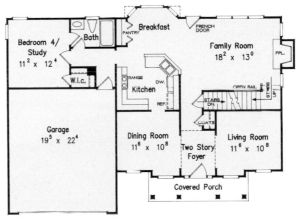

FIRST FLOOR

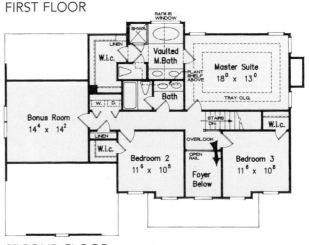

SECOND FLOOR

TRADITIONAL STYLING DISTINGUISHES THIS NARROW-LOT HOME. From the foyer, the large living room and dining room—both with volume ceilings—are visible beyond. A flex room that can be used as a guest suite or home office/study opens to the left. A roomy covered porch is accessed from the breakfast room and provides space for outdoor entertaining. Upstairs, the master suite has all the amenities, including access to a private second-story covered porch. Another bedroom and bath complete this efficiently designed plan.

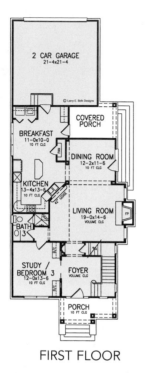

FIRST FLOOR

SECOND FLOOR

HOME PLAN

HPK2700101

Style: Colonial Revival
First Floor: 1,233 sq. ft.
Second Floor: 824 sq. ft.
Total: 2,057 sq. ft.
Bedrooms: 3
Bathrooms: 3
Width: 31' - 10"
Depth: 77' - 10"
Foundation: Crawlspace

eplans.com

© Larry E. Belk Designs

© 1999 Donald A. Gardner, Inc.

WITH ITS HIPPED ROOF, GABLES, COVERED ENTRY, AND BRICK AND SIDING EXTERIOR, this home possesses the enduring style of traditional elegance. The generous great room with a cathedral ceiling and fireplace is centrally located and open to the home's breakfast area and spacious island kitchen. A patio extends living space beyond the great room, while the breakfast area is expanded by a cozy back porch. The master suite is located on the first floor and features His and Hers walk-in closets and a private bath with a linen closet. Two more bedrooms and a bonus room share a full bath upstairs.

HPK2700102

Style: New American
First Floor: 1,588 sq. ft.
Second Floor: 487 sq. ft.
Total: 2,075 sq. ft.
Bonus Space: 363 sq. ft.
Bedrooms: 3
Bathrooms: 2 ½
Width: 60' - 1"
Depth: 50' - 11"

eplans.com

FIRST FLOOR

SECOND FLOOR

A PORTICO ENTRY, GRACEFUL ARCHES, AND BRICK DETAILING provide appeal and a low-maintenance exterior for this design. A half-circle transom over the entry lights the two-story foyer and a plant shelf lines the hallway to the sunken family room. This living space holds a vaulted ceiling, masonry fireplace, and French-door access to the railed patio. The nearby kitchen has a center prep island, built-in desk overlooking the family room, and extensive pantries in the breakfast area. The formal dining room has a tray ceiling and access to the foyer and the central hall. The master suite is on the first level for privacy and convenience. It features a walk-in closet and lavish bath with twin vanities, a whirlpool tub, and separate shower. Three family bedrooms, two of which feature built-in desks, are on the second floor.

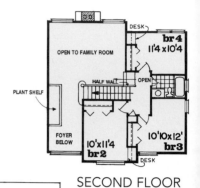

SECOND FLOOR

(#) HPK2700103

Style: New American

First Floor: 1,445 sq. ft.

Second Floor: 652 sq. ft.

Total: 2,097 sq. ft.

Bedrooms: 4

Bathrooms: 2 ½

Width: 56' - 8"

Depth: 48' - 4"

Foundation: Crawlspace, Unfinished Basement

eplans.com

FIRST FLOOR

ORDER BLUEPRINTS ANYTIME AT EPLANS.COM OR 1-800-521-6797

HOME PLAN

HPK2700104

Style: Queen Anne

First Floor: 1,492 sq. ft.

Second Floor: 607 sq. ft.

Total: 2,099 sq. ft.

Bedrooms: 3

Bathrooms: 2 ½

Width: 61' - 2"

Depth: 58' - 4"

Foundation: Crawlspace

eplans.com

DELICATE GINGERBREAD DETAILS embellish the inviting porches of this gracious Queen Anne home. A formal yet open floor plan makes entertaining a thrill; at the front of the home the living room flows right into the dining room for special occasions; while beyond the staircase, an airy arrangement of skylit family room, vaulted breakfast nook, and spacious kitchen can accomodate more casual family gatherings and everyday activities. The master suite hides in a secluded corner of the main level. Upstairs, two family bedrooms share a bath and a loft area for reading and studying.

FIRST FLOOR

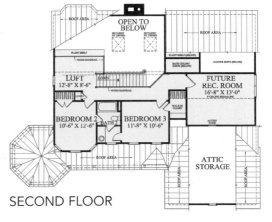

SECOND FLOOR

FIRST FLOOR

10'-0" X 18'-4"
3,00 X 5,50

12'-0" X 12'-8"
3,60 X 3,80

15'-0" X 16'-8"
4,50 X 5,00

12'-0" X 15'-0"
3,60 X 4,50

10'-0" X 12'-8"
3,00 X 3,80

16'-4" X 20'-4"
4,90 X 6,10

SECOND FLOOR

14'-8" X 12'-8"
4,40 X 3,80

12'-8" X 10'-8"
3,80 X 3,20

9'-4" X 20'-4"
2,80 X 6,10

THIS STURDY HOME WITH A BRICK EXTERIOR AND INTRIGUING GABLE LINES is well suited to make life comfortable and enjoyable for most any family. The huge island kitchen, with French-door access to the backyard, opens to a cozy dining area that will surely be a center for family socializing. A fireplace joins the dining area with the living room. A front study or home office is an especially attractive feature. The master suite with a lavish bath and a walk-in closet is also located on the first level. Above, on the second floor, two more bedrooms share a bath. Off the kitchen, a laundry and a half-bath are near the entry to the garage.

HPK2700105

HOME PLAN

Style: Gothic Revival

First Floor: 1,558 sq. ft.

Second Floor: 546 sq. ft.

Total: 2,104 sq. ft.

Bonus Space: 233 sq. ft.

Bedrooms: 3

Bathrooms: 2 ½

Width: 48' - 0"

Depth: 52' - 0"

Foundation: Unfinished Basement

eplans.com

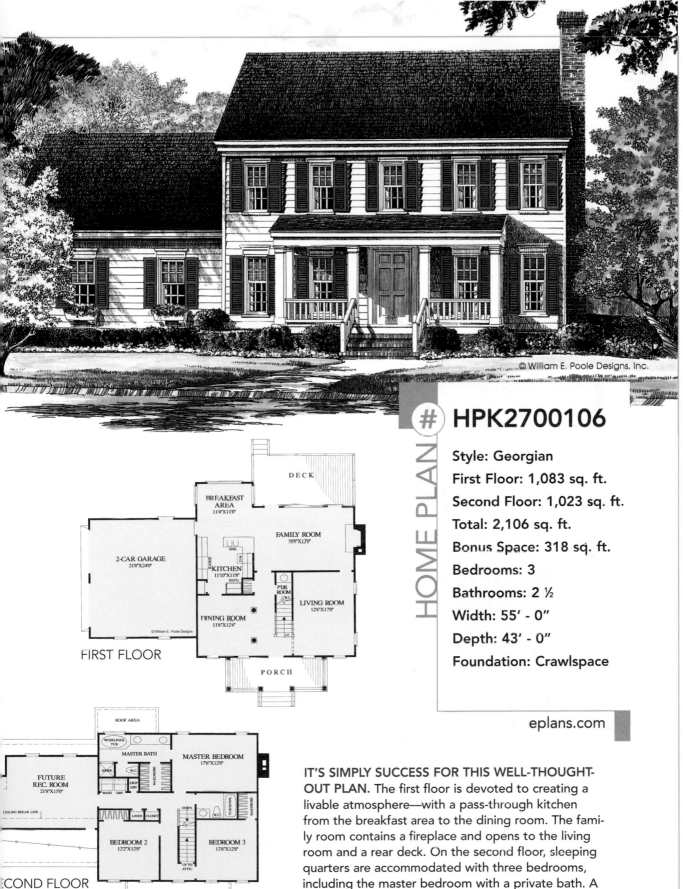

© William E. Poole Designs, Inc.

DECK

BREAKFAST AREA
11'4"X11'0"

FAMILY ROOM
20'8"X13'0"

2-CAR GARAGE
21'8"X24'0"

KITCHEN
11'10"X11'8"

P'DR ROOM

LIVING ROOM
12'6"X17'0"

DINING ROOM
11'6"X12'4"

© William E. Poole Designs

FIRST FLOOR

PORCH

ROOF AREA

WHIRLPOOL TUB

MASTER BATH

MASTER BEDROOM
17'6"X12'0"

FUTURE REC. ROOM
21'8"X15'0"

CEILING BREAK LINE

SHWR   W.C.

WASH DRY

WARDROBE

LINEN CLOSET

DOWN

W.C.

TUB/SHWR

WARDROBE

BEDROOM 2
12'2"X12'0"

BEDROOM 3
12'6"X12'8"

UP TO ATTIC

SECOND FLOOR

ROOF AREA

HPK2700106

Style: Georgian

First Floor: 1,083 sq. ft.

Second Floor: 1,023 sq. ft.

Total: 2,106 sq. ft.

Bonus Space: 318 sq. ft.

Bedrooms: 3

Bathrooms: 2 ½

Width: 55' - 0"

Depth: 43' - 0"

Foundation: Crawlspace

HOME PLAN

eplans.com

IT'S SIMPLY SUCCESS FOR THIS WELL-THOUGHT-OUT PLAN. The first floor is devoted to creating a livable atmosphere—with a pass-through kitchen from the breakfast area to the dining room. The family room contains a fireplace and opens to the living room and a rear deck. On the second floor, sleeping quarters are accommodated with three bedrooms, including the master bedroom with a private bath. A future recreation room may be added above the two-car garage.

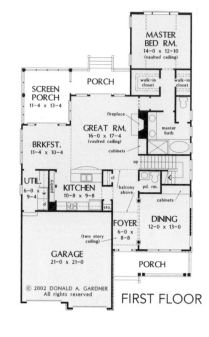

FIRST FLOOR

SECOND FLOOR

HPK2700107

Style: Cottage

First Floor: 1,496 sq. ft.

Second Floor: 615 sq. ft.

Total: 2,111 sq. ft.

Bonus Space: 277 sq. ft.

Bedrooms: 3

Bathrooms: 2 ½

Width: 40' - 4"

Depth: 70' - 0"

eplans.com

STONE, SIDING, AND JACK-ARCH DETAILS CREATE A TRADI-TIONAL CRAFTSMAN PLAN you will love to come home to. Thoughtful details, including built-in cabinets, a fireplace, and a snack bar to the kitchen will make the great room a family favorite. Porches off the great room and breakfast nook, one screened and one open, invite outdoor living. The master suite is located at the rear of the plan for quiet and privacy. Here, His and Hers closets and a lavish bath are sure to delight. Two upstairs bedrooms and a bonus room round out this home.

© 2002 Donald A. Gardner, Inc.

HOME PLAN

HPK2700108

Style: Cottage

First Floor: 1,482 sq. ft.

Second Floor: 631 sq. ft.

Total: 2,113 sq. ft.

Bedrooms: 3

Bathrooms: 2 ½

Width: 41' - 10"

Depth: 56' - 5"

Foundation: Crawlspace, Slab

eplans.com

A CHARMING ELEVATION GIVES THIS HOME ITS CURBSIDE APPEAL. Inside, the two-story foyer opens through archways to the living and dining rooms. Clerestory windows flood the living room with natural light. The kitchen and breakfast room are nearby. An angled sink, with a serving ledge and pass-through, opens the kitchen to the living room beyond. An old-time side porch off the kitchen enhances the look of the home and provides convenient access to the outside. The master bath has all the frills and includes roomy His and Hers walk-in closets. Two bedrooms and a bath are located upstairs. A lovely balcony is located off Bedroom 2. This plan includes a two-car detached garage.

FIRST FLOOR

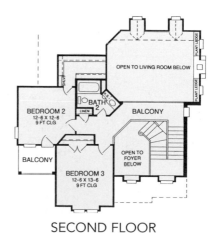

SECOND FLOOR

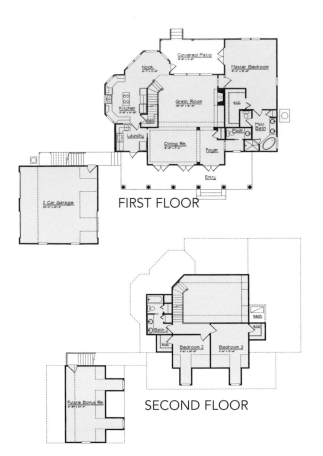

FIRST FLOOR

SECOND FLOOR

THIS ELEGANT HOME HAS MANY TRADITIONAL ARCHITECTURAL FEATURES that make it a classic. Transoms gently light the foyer and dining room. The great room with a fireplace provides convenient access to the rest of the house. A wraparound front porch and covered porch in the back provide areas for quiet relaxation. This home's most unique feature is the drive-through garage, which allows for both a courtyard and side entry. The secluded master suite resides on the first floor, and the two family bedrooms are upstairs. A bonus area above the garage can be used as an apartment for rental income, an in-law suite, teenager's bedroom, detached office/studio, or storage space.

(#) HPK2700109

HOME PLAN

Style: Farmhouse

First Floor: 1,582 sq. ft.

Second Floor: 536 sq. ft.

Total: 2,118 sq. ft.

Bonus Space: 349 sq. ft.

Bedrooms: 3

Bathrooms: 2 ½

Width: 52' - 8"

Depth: 46' - 5"

Foundation: Slab

eplans.com

HPK2700110

Style: Cottage
First Floor: 878 sq. ft.
Second Floor: 1,245 sq. ft.
Total: 2,123 sq. ft.
Bedrooms: 3
Bathrooms: 2 ½
Width: 27' - 6"
Depth: 64' - 0"
Foundation: Crawlspace

eplans.com

[K]EY WEST CONCH STYLE BLENDS OLD WORLD CHARM WITH [N]EW WORLD COMFORT in this picturesque design. A glass-paneled [e]ntry lends a warm welcome and complements a captivating front bal-[c]ony. Two sets of French doors open the great room to wide views and [e]xtend the living areas to the back covered porch. A gourmet kitchen [is] prepared for any occasion with a prep sink, plenty of counter space, [an] ample pantry, and an eating bar. The mid-level landing leads to two [a]dditional bedrooms, a full bath, and a windowed art niche. Double [F]rench doors open the upper-level master suite to a sundeck.

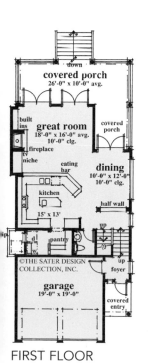

FIRST FLOOR

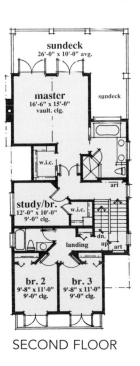

SECOND FLOOR

REAR EXTERIOR

FIRST FLOOR

SECOND FLOOR

A DISTINCTIVE FRONT-GABLE FACADE AND RUSTIC EXTERIOR MATERIALS bring a lot of country charm to this home. The interior provides expansive gathering spaces by only partially separating, by way of a dual-facing fireplace, the great room and dining room. Larger gatherings can incorporate the dine-in kitchen as well as the nook, which opens to the outdoors. The back of the plan holds two bedrooms and a shared bath. The second floor is reserved for the master suite. Lastly, an optional two-car garage can be accessed by way of a rear porch.

HOME PLAN

HPK2700111

Style: Cottage
First Floor: 1,588 sq. ft.
Second Floor: 537 sq. ft.
Total: 2,125 sq. ft.
Bedrooms: 3
Bathrooms: 2 ½
Width: 30' - 8"
Depth: 56' - 2"
Foundation: Crawlspace

eplans.com

ORDER BLUEPRINTS ANYTIME AT EPLANS.COM OR 1-800-521-67

HPK2700112

HOME PLAN

Style: Country

First Floor: 1,694 sq. ft.

Second Floor: 436 sq. ft.

Total: 2,130 sq. ft.

Bonus Space: 345 sq. ft.

Bedrooms: 4

Bathrooms: 3

Width: 54' - 0"

Depth: 53' - 8"

eplans.com

FIRST FLOOR

seat

spa

DECK

walk-in closet

MASTER BED RM.
15-8 x 13-4
(cathedral ceiling)

clerestory above

fireplace

BRKFST.
12-0 x 10-8
(cathedral ceiling)

UTIL.
7-8 x 7-0

GREAT RM.
17-8 x 18-8

KITCHEN
17-0 x 13-0

master bath

bath

cl

up

cl

BED RM./
STUDY
11-0 x 12-6

FOYER
6-4 x 11-6

DINING
12-0 x 13-4
(cathedral ceiling)

GARAGE
21-0 x 22-8

PORCH
19-0 x 7-0

storage

SECOND FLOOR

clerestory window with arched top

attic storage

skylight

great room below

BED RM.
12-0 x 10-4

bath

down

cl

down

attic storage

cl

BED RM.
11-0 x 12-6
(cathedral ceiling)

attic storage

attic storage

BONUS RM.
13-0 x 22-4

skylights

THIS ATTRACTIVE FOUR-BEDROOM HOUSE OFFERS A TOUCH OF COUNTRY with its covered front porch. The foyer, flanked by the dining room and the bedroom/ study, leads to the spacious great room. Here, a fireplace and window wall enhance any gathering. The U-shaped kitchen features a window over the sink and a serving counter to the breakfast room. The dining room and breakfast room have cathedral ceilings with arched windows that fill the house with natural light. The master bedroom boasts a cathedral ceiling and a bath with a whirlpool tub, shower, and double-bowl vanity. Two family bedrooms reside upstairs.

REAR EXTERIOR

FIRST FLOOR

SECOND FLOOR

HPK2700113

Style: Craftsman

First Floor: 1,561 sq. ft.

Second Floor: 578 sq. ft.

Total: 2,139 sq. ft.

Bonus Space: 284 sq. ft.

Bedrooms: 3

Bathrooms: 2 ½

Width: 50' - 0"

Depth: 57' - 0"

Foundation: Crawlspace, Finished Walkout Basement

eplans.com

NOSTALGIC AND EARTHY, this Craftsman design has an attractive floor plan and thoughtful amenities. A column-lined covered porch is the perfect welcome to guests. A large vaulted family room, enhanced by a fireplace, opens to the spacious island kitchen and roomy breakfast area. The private master suite is embellished with a vaulted ceiling, walk-in closet, and vaulted super bath with French-door entry. With family in mind, two secondary bedrooms—each with a walk-in closet—share a computer workstation or loft area. A bonus room can be used as bedroom or home office.

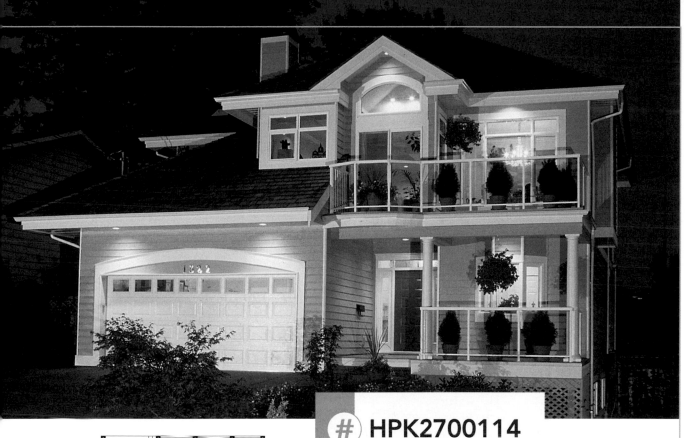

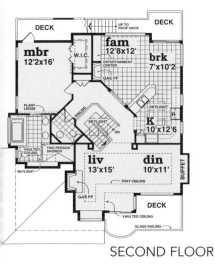

FIRST FLOOR

SECOND FLOOR

HOME PLAN

HPK2700114

Style: Contemporary

First Floor: 832 sq. ft.

Second Floor: 1,331 sq. ft.

Total: 2,163 sq. ft.

Bedrooms: 3

Bathrooms: 2 ½

Width: 37' - 6"

Depth: 48' - 4"

Foundation: Unfinished Basement

eplans.com

THIS HOME OFFERS TWO STORIES, WITH A TWIST!
The living spaces are on the second floor and include a living/dining room combination with a deck and fireplace. The family room also has a fireplace, plus a built-in entertainment center, and is open to the skylit kitchen. The master bedroom is also on this level and features a private bath. Family bedrooms, a full bath, and a cozy den reside on the first level.

FIRST FLOOR

MATCHSTICK TRIM AND ARCH-TOP WINDOWS CREATE PLENTY OF CURB APPEAL with this attractive design. A spacious leisure room with a stepped ceiling highlights the heart of the home. To the left of the plan, a rambling master suite boasts access to a private porch. The formal dining room adjoins the gourmet kitchen, which features a breakfast nook and a walk-in pantry. French doors lead out to the rear porch and an outdoor kitchen. The first-floor master suite features a private bath and walk-in closet.

SECOND FLOOR

HPK2700115

HOME PLAN

Style: Victorian Eclectic
First Floor: 1,493 sq. ft.
Second Floor: 676 sq. ft.
Total: 2,169 sq. ft.
Bedrooms: 3
Bathrooms: 2 ½
Width: 70' - 0"
Depth: 55' - 8"
Foundation: Crawlspace

eplans.com

HOME PLAN

HPK2700116

Style: Craftsman

First Floor: 1,072 sq. ft.

Second Floor: 1,101 sq. ft.

Total: 2,173 sq. ft.

Bedrooms: 4

Bathrooms: 2 ½

Width: 40' - 0"

Depth: 48' - 0"

Foundation: Crawlspace

eplans.com

A COVERED PORCH INTRODUCES THIS TWO-STORY HOME and complements the horizontal wood siding with vertical siding trim. Inside, an open floor plan reigns. The vaulted living room is to the front where double doors open to the porch. Columns separate the living room from the formal dining room and the family room from the main hall. A corner fireplace and built-in shelves adorn the family room. The nook has sliding glass doors to the rear yard and is open to the kitchen. Three family bedrooms, a master suite, and a den are on the second floor. Note the walk-in closet and sumptuous bath in the master suite.

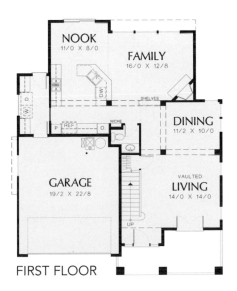

FIRST FLOOR

SECOND FLOOR

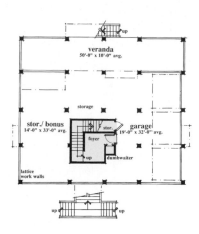

veranda
50'-0" x 10'-0" avg.

storage

stor./ bonus
14'-0" x 33'-0" avg.

foyer

stor.

garage
19'-0" x 32'-0" avg.

up

dumbwaiter

lattice
work walls

up

up

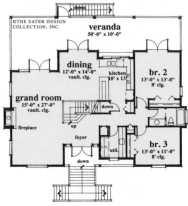

©THE SATER DESIGN
COLLECTION, INC.

down

veranda
50'-0" x 10'-0"

dining
12'-0" x 14'-0"
vault. clg.

kitchen
10' x 13'

br. 2
13'-0" x 13'-8"
8' clg.

grand room
15'-0" x 27'-0"
vault. clg.

down

fireplace

up

foyer

util.

br. 3
13'-0" x 11'-0"
8' clg.

down

FIRST FLOOR

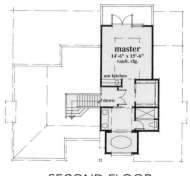

master
14'-6" x 15'-6"
vault. clg.

am kitchen

down

SECOND FLOOR

HOME PLAN

#HPK2700117

Style: Cottage

First Floor: 1,586 sq. ft.

Second Floor: 601 sq. ft.

Total: 2,187 sq. ft.

Bedrooms: 3

Bathrooms: 2

Width: 50' - 0"

Depth: 44' - 0"

Foundation: Pier (same as Piling)

eplans.com

LATTICE WALLS, PICKETS, AND HORIZONTAL SIDING complement a relaxed Key West design that's perfect for waterfront properties. The grand room with a fireplace, the dining room, and Bedroom 2 open through French doors to the veranda. The master suite occupies the entire second floor and features access to a private balcony through double doors. This pampering suite also includes a spacious walk-in closet and a full bath with a whirlpool tub. Enclosed storage/bonus space and a garage are available on the lower level.

REAR EXTERIOR

© William E. Poole Designs, Inc.

HOME PLAN

HPK2700118

THE REBIRTH OF A STYLE—THIS DESIGN SALUTES THE LOOK OF EARLY AMERICA. From the porch, step into the two-story foyer, and either venture to the left towards the living room and dining room, or to the right where the family room sits. A central fireplace in the family room warms the island kitchen. The open design allows unrestricted interaction. Upstairs, the master suite boasts a roomy bath with a dual-sink vanity, a whirlpool tub, a private toilet, a separate shower, and His and Hers walk-in closets. Two additional family bedrooms share a full bath. Future expansion space completes this level.

Style: Georgian
First Floor: 1,209 sq. ft.
Second Floor: 1,005 sq. ft.
Total: 2,214 sq. ft.
Bonus Space: 366 sq. ft.
Bedrooms: 3
Bathrooms: 2 ½
Width: 65' - 4"
Depth: 40' - 4"
Foundation: Crawlspace

eplans.com

FIRST FLOOR

BREAKFAST AREA
10'4"X11'4"
CATHEDRAL CEILING

DINING ROOM
13'0"X11'8"

KITCHEN
12'8"X11'0"

FAMILY ROOM
16'4"X18'0"

2 CAR GARAGE
22'0"X23'4"

LIVING ROOM
13'0"X15'0"

UTILITY
6'6"X8'8"

STORAGE

FOYER
TWO STORY CEILING

PDR. RM.

W.C.

© William E. Poole Designs

PORCH

SECOND FLOOR

ROOF AREA

SEAT

WHIRLPOOL TUB

LINEN

HIS WARDROBE

TUB/SHWR.

W.C.

MASTER BATH

HER WARDROBE

BATH 2

LINEN

BEDROOM 3
12'6"X10'10"

ROOF AREA

CEIL. BREAK LINE

FUTURE REC. ROOM
21'8"X14'0"

CEIL. BREAK LINE

MASTER BEDROOM
13'0"X15'10"

HANDRAIL

OPEN TO BELOW

LIN.

BEDROOM 2
12'10"X12'2"

DOWN

ROOF AREA

FIRST FLOOR

SECOND FLOOR

BASK IN THE GLOW OF THE MOON FROM YOUR PRIVATE DECK in either of two upstairs bedrooms. Indoors, gaze down upon the spacious leisure room while working at your built-in computer desk in the central loft upstairs. The leisure room features a cozy fireplace, a bay-window sitting area and French doors that lead to a rear porch. Space for both formal dining and casual meals flanks the island kitchen. A grand master suite contains a walk-in closet, dual-sink vanity, ba window, whirlpool tub, and oversized shower. Family bedrooms occupy the second floor, on either side of the computer loft.

HOME PLAN

(#) HPK2700119

Style: Farmhouse
First Floor: 1,493 sq. ft.
Second Floor: 723 sq. ft.
Total: 2,216 sq. ft.
Bedrooms: 3
Bathrooms: 2 ½
Width: 70' - 0"
Depth: 55' - 8"
Foundation: Crawlspace

eplans.com

© 2001 Donald A. Gardner, Inc.

HOME PLAN

HPK2700120

Style: Cottage

First Floor: 1,707 sq. ft.

Second Floor: 514 sq. ft.

Total: 2,221 sq. ft.

Bonus Space: 211 sq. ft.

Bedrooms: 4

Bathrooms: 2 ½

Width: 50' - 0"

Depth: 71' - 8"

eplans.com

STONE AND HORIZONTAL SIDING GIVE A DEFINITE COUNTRY FLAVOR to this two-story home. The front study makes an ideal guest room with the adjoining powder room. The formal dining room is accented with decorative columns that define its perimeter. The great room boasts a fireplace, built-ins, and a magnificent view of the backyard beyond one of two rear porches. The master suite boasts two walk-in closets and a private bath. Two bedrooms share a full bath on the second floor.

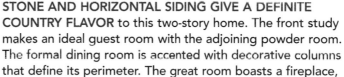

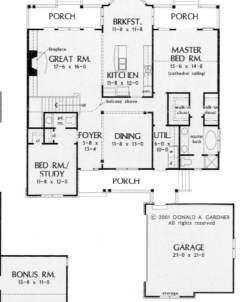

SECOND FLOOR

FIRST FLOOR

A UNIQUE FARMHOUSE DESIGN, ABUNDANT IN OUTDOOR SPACES, provides a grand floor plan comfortable in country or suburban settings. Formal entertaining areas share first-floor space with family gathering rooms and work and service areas. The master suite is also on this floor for convenience and privacy. Upstairs is a guest bedroom, private bath, and loft area that makes a perfect studio. Dormers provide overlooks to the dining and gathering rooms as well as nooks for closets and built-in furniture. Such special features make this a great place to come home to.

FIRST FLOOR

HOME PLAN

HPK2700121

Style: Farmhouse
First Floor: 1,489 sq. ft.
Second Floor: 741 sq. ft.
Total: 2,230 sq. ft.
Bedrooms: 3
Bathrooms: 3
Width: 59' - 0"
Depth: 30' - 0"
Foundation: Slab

eplans.com

SECOND FLOOR

HPK2700122

HOME PLAN

Style: Neoclassical
First Floor: 1,200 sq. ft.
Second Floor: 1,034 sq. ft.
Total: 2,234 sq. ft.
Bonus Space: 231 sq. ft.
Bedrooms: 4
Bathrooms: 3
Width: 53' - 4"
Depth: 39' - 0"
Foundation: Crawlspace, Slab, Unfinished Walkout Basement

eplans.com

LASSIC COLUMNS ACCENTUATE THE STACKED COVERED ORCHES and highlight this Neoclassical design. Flanking the foyer, ne dining and living rooms provide comfort and convenience to uests. At the rear of the floor plan, find casual space that enjoys pen flexibility. A private study—or guest bedroom—is a great place o keep current on business. Upstairs, an enchanting master suite ampers with a tray ceiling, vaulted bath, walk-in closet, dual-sink anities, and separate tub and shower. Two family bedrooms feature alk-in closets. The second-floor laundry is convenient and located ear the bonus space.

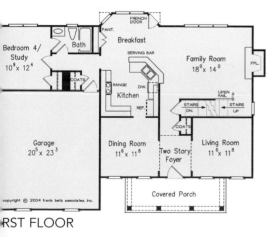

RST FLOOR

SECOND FLOOR

FIRST FLOOR

PATIO

MASTER BED RM.
13-4 x 16-8

FAMILY RM.
18-0 x 16-6
(cathedral ceiling)
fireplace
balcony above

BRKFST.
11-4 x 10-0

UTILITY
8-4 x 6-0
d w
storage

walk-in closet

walk-in closet

pd. rm.

cl

KIT.
11-4 x 12-0

GARAGE
21-0 x 24-0

lin

master bath

LIVING RM./ STUDY
12-0 x 12-0

shelves

FOYER
9-8 x 11-10

DINING
11-4 x 13-0

up

storage

PORCH

© 1998 Donald A Gardner, Inc.

SECOND FLOOR

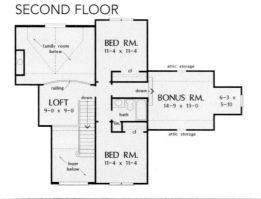

family room below

BED RM.
11-4 x 11-4

cl

attic storage

railing

LOFT
9-0 x 9-0

down

down

BONUS RM.
14-9 x 13-0

6-3 x 5-10

bath

lin

cl

attic storage

foyer below

BED RM.
11-4 x 11-4

COLUMNS, GABLES, MULTIPANE WINDOWS, AND A STONE-AND-STUCCO EXTERIOR give this home its handsome appearance. The interior amenities are just as impressive. The formal rooms are to the right and left of the foyer with a powder room and coat closet down the hall. The family room, with a cathedral ceiling, fireplace, built-ins, and access to the rear patio is open to the breakfast room through a pair of decorative columns. On the opposite side of the plan, the master suite offers two walk-in closets and a compartmented bath. Two family bedrooms on the second floor share a bath and a loft that overlooks the family room.

HPK2700123

Style: French Country
First Floor: 1,701 sq. ft.
Second Floor: 534 sq. ft.
Total: 2,235 sq. ft.
Bonus Space: 274 sq. ft.
Bedrooms: 3
Bathrooms: 2 ½
Width: 65' - 11"
Depth: 43' - 5"

eplans.com

HOME PLAN

© 1998 Donald A. Gardner, Inc.

B·NATHAN

© William E. Poole Designs, Inc.

A CHARMING FACADE AND A FAMILY-FRIENDLY LAYOUT distinguish this home plan. The serviceable island kitchen opens into the cozy breakfast nook and the family room, both with vaulted ceilings. Owners also benefit from the location of the master suite, tucked sensibly away from the high-traffic areas of the home. Additionally, the attending master bath provides the comfort of dual vanities, a large walk-in closet, and a compartmented toilet. Upstairs, two bedrooms share a bath, and a rec room awaits customization.

HOME PLAN

HPK2700124

Style: Cottage

First Floor: 1,634 sq. ft.

Second Floor: 619 sq. ft.

Total: 2,253 sq. ft.

Bonus Space: 229 sq. ft.

Bedrooms: 3

Bathrooms: 2 ½

Width: 46' - 0"

Depth: 54' - 5"

Foundation: Crawlspace, Slab

eplans.com

FIRST FLOOR

SECOND FLOOR

LOFT / DEN
13'10" x 11'2"

Bedroom 2
10'0" x 11'6"

Bath

Bedroom 3
13'0" x 11'6"

SECOND FLO

Master Suite
13'8" x 15'0"

Family Room
13'2" x 22'0"

Covered Patio
10'6" x 10'6"

Dining Room
10'6" x 13'0"

W.I.C.

Master Bath

Utility

Kitchen
10'0" x 17'0"

Foyer

Entry

2 Car Garage
26'0" x 22'2"

Nook
10'7" x 9'2"

FIRST FLOOR

HPK2700125

Style: Mediterranean

First Floor: 1,484 sq. ft.

Second Floor: 770 sq. ft.

Total: 2,254 sq. ft.

Bedrooms: 3

Bathrooms: 2 ½

Width: 45' - 0"

Depth: 58' - 4"

Foundation: Crawlspace, Slab

eplans.com

THIS CONTEMPORARY FLOOR PLAN IS WONDERFULLY CRADLED IN A WARM AND INVITING EXTERIOR, which features a stone and stucco veneer and tasteful bay windows. The gracious foyer opens to the expansive family room with a warming fireplace. Flowing from the family room, the dining area opens to the covered patio—expanding the available living space. The large kitchen is bathed in light through the bayed breakfast nook. Tray ceilings and a well-appointed bath adorn the master suite. The second floor boasts two family bedrooms and a loft—or convert it to another bedroom.

FIRST FLOOR

SECOND FLOOR

HOME PLAN

HPK2700126

Style: Neoclassical

First Floor: 1,168 sq. ft.

Second Floor: 1,100 sq. ft.

Total: 2,268 sq. ft.

Bedrooms: 3

Bathrooms: 2 ½

Width: 69' - 6"

Depth: 31' - 0"

Foundation: Crawlspace, Slab, Unfinished Basement, Block

eplans.com

COVERED PORCHES ACCESSIBLE FROM BOTH FLOORS create a wonderful indoor/outdoor relationship for this Southern Colonial home. The floor plan thoughtfully separates the main living area from the family sleeping quarters, with the great room, kitchen, and dining room downstairs and three bedrooms upstairs. The island kitchen shares a snack bar with the great room, which features a warming fireplace and space to put a small dining table for casual meals. A whirlpool tub, double vanities, and a walk-in closet accent the luxurious master suite, while two additional bedrooms with separate dressing areas share a full bath.

FIRST FLOOR

SECOND FLOOR

WITH THREE DORMERS AND A WELCOMING FRONT DOOR ACCENTED BY SIDELIGHTS AND A SUNBURST, this country cottage is sure to please. The dining room, immediately to the right from the foyer, is defined by decorative columns. In the great room, a volume ceiling heightens the space and showcases a fireplace and built-in bookshelves. The kitchen has plenty of work space and flows into the bayed breakfast nook. A considerate split-bedroom design places the plush master suite to the far left and two family bedrooms to the far right. A fourth bedroom and future space upstairs allow room to grow.

HOME PLAN

HPK2700127

Style: Federal — Adams

First Floor: 1,981 sq. ft.

Second Floor: 291 sq. ft.

Total: 2,272 sq. ft.

Bonus Space: 412 sq. ft.

Bedrooms: 4

Bathrooms: 3 ½

Width: 58' - 0"

Depth: 53' - 0"

Foundation: Crawlspace Basement

eplans.com

© William E. Poole Designs, Inc.

HPK2700128

Style: Country

First Floor: 1,572 sq. ft.

Second Floor: 700 sq. ft.

Total: 2,272 sq. ft.

Bonus Space: 212 sq. ft.

Bedrooms: 4

Bathrooms: 2 ½

Width: 70' - 0"

Depth: 38' - 5"

**Foundation: Slab,
Unfinished Basement**

eplans.com

COUNTRY AND VICTORIAN ELEMENTS give this plan a down-home feel. A charming porch wraps around the front of this farmhouse, whose entry opens to a formal dining room. The island kitchen and sun-filled breakfast area are located nearby. The family room is warmed by a fireplace flanked by windows. Located for privacy, the first-floor master bedroom features its own covered patio and a private bath designed for relaxation. The second floor contains three family bedrooms—each with walk-in closets—a full bath, and a future bonus room.

FIRST FLOOR

SECOND FLOOR

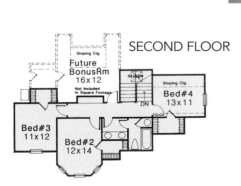

FIRST FLOOR

Breakfast

Kitchen
DW.

RANGE ISLAND

REF. PANTRY

Dining Room
13⁰ x 11²

Laund.

DECORATIVE
COLUMNS

Living Room
13⁰ x 12³

STAIRS
UP

STAIRS
DN.

OPEN
RAIL

Two Story
Foyer

FRENCH
DOOR

FPL.

Two Story
Family Room
14⁰ x 18⁰

Bedroom 4
11² x 12⁰

COATS

Bath

Garage
20⁰ x 20⁶

COVERED ENTRY

copyright © 1996 frank betz associates, inc.

SECOND FLOOR

PLANT
SHELF
ABOVE

RAD.
WDW.

SEAT

SHWR.

LINEN

W.i.c.

Vaulted
M.Bath

K.S.

FRENCH
DOOR

LINEN

Master Suite
13⁰ x 17⁰

TRAY CEILING

STAIRS
DN.
OPEN
RAIL

Foyer
Below

W.i.c.

Family Room
Below

OVERLOOK

OPEN RAIL

Bedroom 3
11² x 11⁰

Bath

Bedroom 2
11⁰ x 12⁷

Opt. Bonus
Room
11⁶ x 11⁰

HOME PLAN # HPK2700129

Style: New American

First Floor: 1,290 sq. ft.

Second Floor: 985 sq. ft.

Total: 2,275 sq. ft.

Bonus Space: 186 sq. ft.

Bedrooms: 4

Bathrooms: 3

Width: 45' - 0"

Depth: 43' - 4"

Foundation: Crawlspace, Slab, Unfinished Walkout Basement

eplans.com

THIS CASUALLY ELEGANT NEW AMERICAN HOME offers more than just a slice of everything you've always wanted: it is designed with room to grow. Formal living and dining rooms are defined by decorative columns and open from a two-story foyer, which leads to open family space. A two-story family room offers a fireplace and shares a French door to the rear property with the breakfast room. A gallery hall with a balcony overlook connects two sleeping wings upstairs. The master suite boasts a vaulted bath, and the family hall leads to bonus space.

HOME PLAN

HPK2700130

Style: Farmhouse

First Floor: 1,371 sq. ft.

Second Floor: 916 sq. ft.

Total: 2,287 sq. ft.

Bedrooms: 3

Bathrooms: 2 ½

Width: 43' - 0"

Depth: 69' - 0"

Foundation: Crawlspace

eplans.com

FIRST FLOOR

SECOND FLOOR

THE DECORATIVE PILLARS AND THE WRAPAROUND PORCH are just the beginning of this comfortable home. Inside, an angled, U-shaped stairway leads to the second-floor sleeping zone. On the first floor, French doors lead to a bay-windowed den that shares a see-through fireplace with the two-story family room. The large island kitchen includes a writing desk, a corner sink, a breakfast nook, and access to the laundry room, the powder room, and the two-car garage. Upstairs, the master suite is a real treat with its French-door access, vaulted ceiling, and luxurious bath. Two other bedrooms and a full bath complete the second floor.

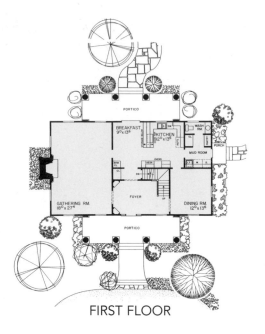

FIRST FLOOR

SECOND FLOOR

REMINISCENT OF THE PAST, THIS HOME REFLECTS THE GREEK REVIVAL HERITAGE so prevalent in the southern United States. This is demonstrated in its front and rear porticos which have graceful columns. While the exterior comes from yesteryear, the floor plan is designed to serve today's active family. Imagine the activities that can be enjoyed in the huge gathering room. It stretches from the front to the rear of the house. Three bedrooms are on the second floor, including master bedroom with dressing room and full bath. You won't be disappointed.

HOME PLAN

HPK2700131

Style: Greek Revival

First Floor: 1,344 sq. ft.

Second Floor: 947 sq. ft.

Total: 2,291 sq. ft.

Bedrooms: 3

Bathrooms: 2 ½

Width: 48' - 0"

Depth: 51' - 4"

Foundation: Unfinished Basement

eplans.com

HPK2700132

HOME PLAN

Style: French Country

First Floor: 1,542 sq. ft.

Second Floor: 752 sq. ft.

Total: 2,294 sq. ft.

Bonus Space: 370 sq. ft.

Bedrooms: 3

Bathrooms: 2 ½

Width: 44' - 4"

Depth: 54' - 0"

eplans.com

FIRST FLOOR

MASTER BED RM. 16-0 x 13-0

walk-in closet | walk-in closet

master bath

SUN RM. 15-0 x 13-0

PORCH

KITCHEN 15-0 x 8-0

DINING 12-0 x 15-4

UTIL 6-0 x 6-0 | pd. rm. | sto.

balcony above

fireplace

GREAT RM. 16-6 x 15-0

shelves

up

GARAGE 21-0 x 21-0

FOYER 7-8 x 4-4

PORCH

PORCH

SECOND FLOOR

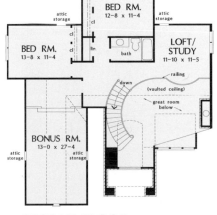

7-0 x 3-0

BED RM. 12-8 x 11-4

attic storage | attic storage

BED RM. 13-8 x 11-4

cl | cl | lin | bath

LOFT/ STUDY 11-10 x 11-5

railing

down | (vaulted ceiling)

great room below

BONUS RM. 13-0 x 27-4

attic storage | attic storage

A UNIQUE MIXTURE OF STONE, SIDING, AND WINDOWS creates character in this French Country design. Columns, decorative railing and a metal roof add architectural interest to an intimate front porch, while a rock entryway frames a French door flanked by sidelights and crowned with a transom. An elegant, curved staircase highlights the grand two-story foyer and great room. A clerestory floods both the great room and second-floor loft with light. A delightful sunroom can be accessed from the dining room and is open to the kitchen. Upstairs, closets act as noise barriers between two bedrooms, and the bonus room can be used as a home theatre or recreation room.

THIS HOME IS PERFECT FOR ENTERTAINING ON A GRAND SCALE. As you enter the home, before you lies a large family room with a direct view to the covered patio beyond. Turn to the right to see the dining room with bay window. Beyond is a large family kitchen with plenty of counter and cabinet space. Enjoy your morning coffee in the breakfast nook while taking in the views of the backyard. The master bedroom shares the same view of the property from the other side of the house and features a large walk-in closet. Enjoy the master bath with a double vanity, separate shower and tub, and private toilet chamber. Upstairs, the children have their own area for work and play.

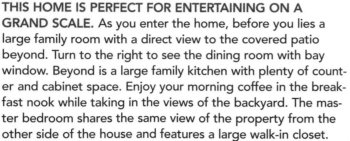

FIRST FLOOR

SECOND FLOOR

HPK2700133

Style: Country

First Floor: 1,530 sq. ft.

Second Floor: 777 sq. ft.

Total: 2,307 sq. ft.

Bonus Space: 361 sq. ft.

Bedrooms: 3

Bathrooms: 3 ½

Width: 61' - 4"

Depth: 78' - 0"

Foundation: Slab

eplans.com

FOR A BIG FAMILY THAT LIKES TO SOCIALIZE, this delightful two-story home can't be beat. Four bedrooms, including a deluxe master suite on the main level, offer ample family sleeping space. Formal living and dining rooms toward the front will give hours of congenial get-togethers with friends. The kitchen is very special, enjoying a built-in oven and microwave, as well as a walk-in pantry. It adjoins a breakfast nook and a cozy family room, which both open to a rear patio. A handy utility room is near the stairway to the second floor.

HOME PLAN

HPK2700134

Style: New American

First Floor: 1,649 sq. ft.

Second Floor: 660 sq. ft.

Total: 2,309 sq. ft.

Bedrooms: 4

Bathrooms: 2 ½

Width: 55' - 0"

Depth: 54' - 4"

Foundation: Crawlspace, Finished Basement, Slab

eplans.com

FIRST FLOOR

SECOND FLOOR

FIRST FLOOR

SECOND FLOOR

HPK2700135

Style: Craftsman

First Floor: 1,387 sq. ft.

Second Floor: 929 sq. ft.

Total: 2,316 sq. ft.

Bedrooms: 4

Bathrooms: 3

Width: 30' - 0"

Depth: 51' - 8"

Foundation: Crawlspace

eplans.com

PERFECT FOR A NARROW LOT,

this shingle-and-stone Nantucket Cape home caters to the casual lifestyle. The side entrance gives direct access to the wonderfully open living areas: gathering room with fireplace and an abundance of windows; island kitchen with angled, pass-through snack bar; and dining area with sliding glass doors to a covered eating area. Note also the large deck that further extends the living potential. Also on this floor is the large master suite with a compartmented bath, private dressing room, and walk-in closet. Upstairs, you'll find the three family bedrooms. Of the two bedrooms that share a bath, one features a private balcony.

FIRST FLOOR

SECOND FLOOR

HOME PLAN

HPK2700136

Style: Country

First Floor: 1,260 sq. ft.

Second Floor: 1,057 sq. ft.

Total: 2,317 sq. ft.

Bedrooms: 5

Bathrooms: 2 ½

Width: 35' - 0"

Depth: 56' - 0"

Foundation: Slab

eplans.com

AT HOME IN THE CITY, this narrow-lot design takes advantage of street views. A rear-loading, two-car garage is accessed via a rear porch and breakfast room. The adjoining C-shaped kitchen is only steps from the formal dining room. A warming fireplace can be enjoyed in the great room (and even from the dining room). A first-floor master suite provides convenience and comfort. Two walk-in closets, dual-sink vanity, soaking tub, and enclosed shower pamper and dissolve stress. The second floor is home to four bedrooms—or three bedrooms and a loft. A roomy laundry area is located on the second floor.

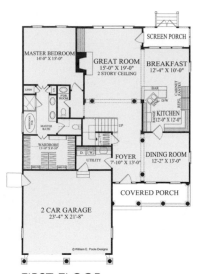

FIRST FLOOR

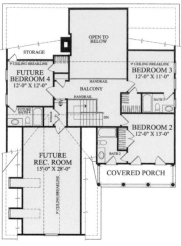

SECOND FLOOR

THIS SOUTHERN COLONIAL BEAUTY FEATURES THREE PORCHES: one welcomes visitors to the first floor, the second offers a pleasant retreat from a bedroom upstairs, and the third, a screened porch, sits at the rear of the house, accessed from the great room. A centrally located fireplace in the great room warms the entire area, including the kitchen and the breakfast room. The spacious kitchen is a family favorite with a snack bar and a scenic view of the backyard. The left side of the plan is dominated by the master suite. The master bath boasts a dual sink vanity, a whirlpool tub, a separate shower, a compartmented toilet, and His and Hers walk-in closets. Upstairs, there are two additional family bedrooms, each with a full bath. Future space on the second floor invites the possibility of a fourth bedroom and a recreation room. A two-car garage completes the plan.

HOME PLAN

HPK2700137

Style: Colonial
First Floor: 1,688 sq. ft.
Second Floor: 630 sq. ft.
Total: 2,318 sq. ft.
Bonus Space: 506 sq. ft.
Bedrooms: 3
Bathrooms: 3 ½
Width: 44' - 4"
Depth: 62' - 4"
Foundation: Crawlspace

eplans.com

© William E. Poole Designs, Inc.

A COVERED PORCH, MULTIPANE WINDOWS, AND SHINGLE-WITH-STONE SIDING combine to give this bungalow plenty of curb appeal. Inside, the foyer is flanked by the formal living room and an angled staircase. The formal dining room adjoins the living room, and the kitchen is accessible through double doors. A large family room is graced by a fireplace and opens off a cozy eating nook. The second level presents many attractive angles. The master suite has a spacious walk-in closet and a sumptuous bath complete with a garden tub and separate shower. Three family bedrooms share a full hall bath.

HOME PLAN

HPK2700138

Style: Craftsman
First Floor: 1,205 sq. ft.
Second Floor: 1,123 sq. ft.
Total: 2,328 sq. ft.
Bedrooms: 4
Bathrooms: 2 ½
Width: 57' - 2"
Depth: 58' - 7"
Foundation: Crawlspace

eplans.com

FIRST FLOOR

SECOND FLOOR

FIRST FLOOR

HERE'S A NEW AMERICAN FARMHOUSE THAT'S JUST RIGHT FOR ANY NEIGHBORHOOD—in town or far away. A perfect interior starts with an open foyer and interior vistas through a fabulous great room. A fireplace anchors the living space while a beamed, vaulted ceiling adds volume. Decorative columns open the central interior to the gourmet kitchen and breakfast area, which boasts a bay window. The master wing includes a study that easily converts to a home office. Upstairs, the secondary bedrooms feature built-in desks and walk-in closets.

HOME PLAN

HPK2700139

Style: Farmhouse

First Floor: 1,710 sq. ft.

Second Floor: 618 sq. ft.

Total: 2,328 sq. ft.

Bedrooms: 3

Bathrooms: 3

Width: 47' - 0"

Depth: 50' - 0"

Foundation: Crawlspace

eplans.com

SECOND FLOOR

HPK2700140

Style: Victorian Eclectic

First Floor: 1,710 sq. ft.

Second Floor: 618 sq. ft.

Total: 2,328 sq. ft.

Bedrooms: 3

Bathrooms: 3

Width: 47' - 0"

Depth: 50' - 0"

Foundation: Crawlspace

eplans.com

FIRST FLOOR

Master Suite
15'-0" x 13'-8"
Stepped Clg.

© THE SATER DESIGN COLLECTION, INC.

built-in

WIC

WIC

M. Bath
L.

CL.

L.

Bath 2

Study/Office
13'-0" x 11'-6"
Coffered Clg.

Porch
16'-0" x 8'-0"

Great Room
15'-10" x 15'-4"
Vaulted Clg.

fireplace

Foyer

Up

Dining
11'-0" x 13'-10"
Tray Clg.

Breakfast
12'-0" x 9'-10"

9'-4" Flat Clg.

Kitchen
12'-6" x 11'-8"

L.

Utility
5'-6"x9'-4"

Porch
31'-0" x 6'-0"

DECORATIVE DETAILS COMPLEMENT THIS HOME'S COUNTRY FACADE, and pedimented arches and a covered porch add sophistication. The foyer leads to the vaulted great room where a fireplace awaits. Both the magnificent master suite and the great room showcase French doors to the rear vaulted porch. The breakfast bay sheds sunlight onto the spacious kitchen. An elegant coffered ceiling and three-window bay dress up the front study (or make it into an office). Two bedrooms, both with walk-in closets, share the second level with a bath and an equipment room.

Bedroom 1
11'-0" x 13'-0"
8'-0" Flat Clg.

Bath 3

open to below

WIC

desk

desk

Dn.

Dn.

WIC

L.

open to below

Bedroom 2
11'-0" x 13'-6"
8'-0" Flat Clg.

Equip.

plant shelf

SECOND FLOOR

FIRST FLOOR

Porch
16'-0" x 8'-0"
Vaulted Clg.

Master Suite
15'-0" x 13'-8"
Stepped Clg.

© THE SATER DESIGN COLLECTION, INC.

Breakfast
12'-0" x 9'-10"
9'-4" Flat Clg.

built-in

Great Room
15'-10" x 15'-4"
Vaulted Clg.

WIC

WIC

fireplace

Kitchen
12'-6" x 11'-8"

M. Bath

CL.

Utility
5'-6"x9'-4"

Bath 2

Foyer

Dining
11'-8" x 13'-10"
Tray Clg.

bench   Up

Study/Office
13'-0" x 11'-6"
Coffered Clg.

Porch
31'-0" x 6'-0"
9'-4" Flat Clg.

SECOND FLOOR

Bedroom 1
11'-0' x 13'-0"
8'-0' Flat Clg.

Bath 3

open to below

WIC

desk

Dn.   Dn.

desk

open to
below

Bedroom 2
11'-0' x 13'-6"
8'-0' Flat Clg.

WIC

L.

Equip.

plant
shelf

plant
shelf

THIS COUNTRY FARMHOUSE ENJOYS SPECIAL FEATURES such as gables, dormers, plenty of windows, and a covered front porch. Columns adorn the home throughout for an extra touch of elegance. The formal dining room enjoys a tray ceiling and is open to the kitchen, which enjoys access to either a utility room or the breakfast nook with a bay window. The massive great room enjoys a vaulted ceiling, a cozy fireplace, and built-ins—French doors tie this room to a vaulted rear porch. On the left of this home is a study/office along with the sumptuous master suite. The second floor holds two family bedrooms—both with walk-in closets and built-in desks—sharing a full bath.

HOME PLAN

HPK2700141

Style: Farmhouse

First Floor: 1,716 sq. ft.

Second Floor: 618 sq. ft.

Total: 2,334 sq. ft.

Bedrooms: 3

Bathrooms: 3

Width: 47' - 0"

Depth: 50' - 0"

Foundation: Crawlspace

eplans.com

© HOME DESIGN SERVICES, INC.

COLUMNS ADD THE FINISHING TOUCHES TO THIS HOME WITH A CHOICE OF FACADES. The double-door entry opens to the foyer with a front-to-back view. The adjacent vaulted living room has sliding glass doors to the covered patio. The kitchen is open to both the family room and the sunny breakfast room. Interesting angles and a volume ceiling add appeal to the formal dining room. The first-floor master bedroom features twin vanities, a separate tub and shower and a large walk-in closet. A study or bedroom completes this level. Upstairs, three additional bedrooms share a full bath that includes a dual vanity. The plan includes both elevations.

HOME PLAN

HPK2700142

Style: Mediterranean
First Floor: 1,657 sq. ft.
Second Floor: 678 sq. ft.
Total: 2,335 sq. ft.
Bedrooms: 4
Bathrooms: 2 ½
Width: 58' - 8"
Depth: 56' - 0"
Foundation: Slab

eplans.com

FIRST FLOOR

SECOND FLOOR

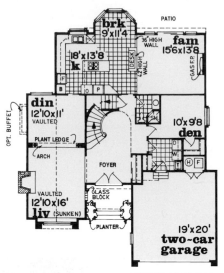

FIRST FLOOR

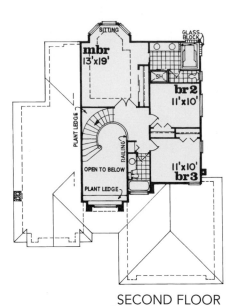

SECOND FLOOR

HPK2700143

Style: New American

First Floor: 1,463 sq. ft.

Second Floor: 872 sq. ft.

Total: 2,335 sq. ft.

Bedrooms: 3

Bathrooms: 3

Width: 44' - 0"

Depth: 58' - 10"

Foundation: Crawlspace, Unfinished Basement

eplans.com

TWO DIFFERENT FACADES ARE AVAILABLE FOR THIS HOME: a California stucco or a traditional brick-and-siding version. The interior plan begins with a vaulted foyer hosting a sweeping curved staircase spilling into a sunken living room with a masonry fireplace and vaulted ceiling. The kitchen features a pantry, center cooking island, built-in desk, and sunny breakfast bay. A den with a walk-in closet and nearby bath can easily double as a guest room. The master suite on the second floor boasts a drop ceiling, bayed sitting area, and lavish bath. The family bedrooms share a full bath.

HERE'S A GREAT FARMHOUSE ADAPTATION with all the most up-to-date features. A welcoming front porch encourages relaxation and also leads friends and family into an efficient layout. The quiet corner living room opens to the sizable dining room, which includes a bay window. The kitchen features many built-ins and a pass-through to the beam-ceilinged breakfast room. Sliding glass doors to the terrace are found in both the family room and the breakfast room. Four bedrooms and two baths are located on the second floor.

HOME PLAN

HPK2700144

Style: Farmhouse

First Floor: 1,370 sq. ft.

Second Floor: 969 sq. ft.

Total: 2,339 sq. ft.

Bedrooms: 4

Bathrooms: 2 ½

Width: 59' - 8"

Depth: 44' - 0"

Foundation: Unfinished Basement

eplans.com

FIRST FLOOR

SECOND FLOOR

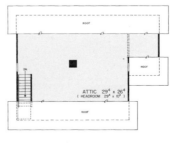

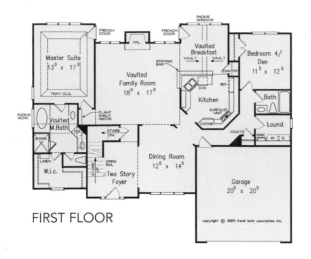

FIRST FLOOR

SECOND FLOOR

DECORATIVE ARCHES AND QUOINS GIVE THIS HOME WONDERFUL CURB APPEAL that matches its comfortable interior. The two-story foyer is bathed in natural light as it leads to the formal dining room and beyond to the counter-filled kitchen and the vaulted breakfast nook. A den, or possible fourth bedroom, is tucked away at the rear for privacy and includes a full bath. A spacious master suite with a luxurious private bath is located on the first floor. Two family bedrooms and a full bath reside on the second floor, as well as a balcony that looks down to the family room and the foyer. An optional bonus room is available for expanding at a later date.

HOME PLAN

HPK2700145

Style: New American

First Floor: 1,761 sq. ft.

Second Floor: 580 sq. ft.

Total: 2,341 sq. ft.

Bonus Space: 276 sq. ft.

Bedrooms: 4

Bathrooms: 3

Width: 56' - 0"

Depth: 47' - 6"

Foundation: Crawlspace, Slab, Unfinished Walkout Basement

eplans.com

HOME PLAN

HPK2700146

Style: New American

First Floor: 1,617 sq. ft.

Second Floor: 725 sq. ft.

Total: 2,342 sq. ft.

Bedrooms: 4

Bathrooms: 2 ½

Width: 62' - 0"

Depth: 41' - 0"

Foundation: Unfinished Basement

eplans.com

WITH TWO END GABLES AND FIVE FRONT GABLES, this design becomes an updated "house of the seven gables." Meanwhile, brick veneer, the use of horizontal siding, radial head windows, and interesting roof planes add an extra measure of charm. The attached side-loading, two-car garage is a delightfully integral part of the appealing exterior. Designed for a growing family with a modest building budget, the floor plan incorporates four bedrooms and both formal and informal living areas. The central foyer, with its open staircase to the second floor, draws eyes up toward the balcony. The spacious family room offers a high ceiling and a dramatic view of the rear terrace.

In the U-shaped kitchen, a snack bar caters to on-the-run meals.

FIRST FLOOR

SECOND FLOOR

Lower Porch
30'-0" x 7'-2"

Storage/Bonus

Garage
24'-0" x 25'-6"

UP

Storage

FIRST FLOOR

Porch
30'-10" x 12'-8"
10 Clg.

Dining
12'-0" x 11'-4"
10'-0" Clg.

Great Room
16'-4" x 18'-0"
19'-4" - 20'-0" Clg.
Fireplace

Kitchen
12'-2" x 13'-4"
10'-0" Clg.

Master Suite
13'-0" x 16'-0"
9'-0" - 10'-0" Clg.

Entertainment Center

Niche

Master Bath
10'-0" Clg.

Powder
10'-0" Clg.

WIC

Whirlpool

Foyer
9'-10" clg.

Utility

Porch
12'-0" clg.

SECOND FLOOR

Open Deck
30'-10" x 12'-8"

Porch
8' Clg

Bedroom 3
12'-0" x 15'-0"
8'-0" - 9'-4" Clg.

Porch
8' Clg

Open to Below

Bedroom 2
13'-2" x 12'-0"
8'-0" - 9'-4" clg.

Bath 3
10'-0" Clg

WIC

Loft
10'-4" x 11'-4"
8' Clg

Down

Open to Below

Bath 2
10'-0" Clg

Window Seat

THIS LOVELY PIER HOME IS THE PICTURE OF ISLAND LIVING.
Space on the lower level is devoted to the garage, but allows for a storage area if needed. The first floor holds the great room, with access to a rear porch. The dining room and kitchen are nearby for easy access. The master suite is also on this floor and features porch access and a stunning bath. Two family bedrooms with private baths and a loft area are found on the second floor. A porch can be accessed from each of the bedrooms.

HPK2700147

HOME PLAN

Style: Italianate

First Floor: 1,510 sq. ft.

Second Floor: 864 sq. ft.

Total: 2,374 sq. ft.

Bedrooms: 3

Bathrooms: 3 ½

Width: 44' - 0"

Depth: 48' - 0"

Foundation: Island Basement

eplans.com

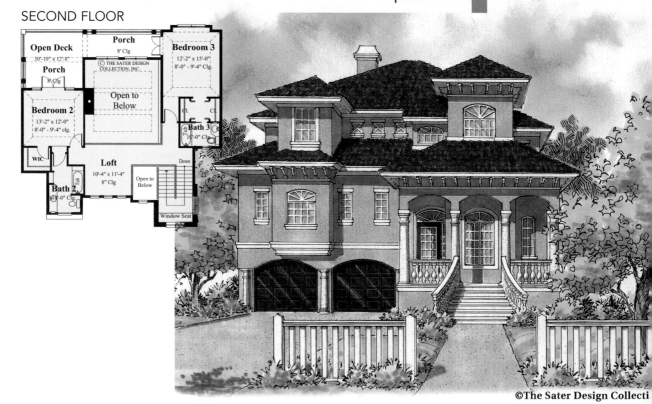

©The Sater Design Collecti

FIRST FLOOR

ⓒ THE SATER DESIGN COLLECTION, INC.

Porch
10'-0" Clg.

Dining
12'-0" X 11'-4"
10'-0" Clg.

Great Room
16'-4" x 18'-0"
Open to Above
Fireplace

Master Suite
13'-0" x 16'-0"
9'-0" to 10'-0"
Stepped Clg.

Kitchen
12'-2" x 13'-4"
10'-0" Clg.

Entertainment Center

Niche

Master Bath
10'-0" Clg.
Whirlpool

W.I.C.

Powder

Foyer

UP

Down

UP

Closet

Utility
10'-0" Clg.

Porch
12'-0" Clg.

UP

ski/sports equip. storage

storage/ bonus
29'-6" x 39'-0"

garage
24'-0" x 25'-6"

mud room

HPK2700148

Style: New American
First Floor: 1,492 sq. ft.
Second Floor: 854 sq. ft.
Total: 2,346 sq. ft.
Bonus Space: 810 sq. ft.
Bedrooms: 3
Bathrooms: 3 ½
Width: 44' - 0"
Depth: 48' - 0"
Foundation: Unfinished Walkout Basement

eplans.com

SECOND FLOOR

open deck
30'-10" x 12'-8"

porch
8' clg.

porch
8' clg.

bedroom
12'-2" x 14'-0"
tray

bedroom
13'-2" x 12'-0"
tray

open

bath

w.i.c.

bath

loft
10'-4" x 11'-4"
8' clg.

open

VICTORIAN DETAILING IN THE GABLES, TRANSOM WINDOWS, AND HEAVY COLUMNS at the front porch add a touch of country elegance to this beautiful home. Inside, a two-story great room at the center of the plan adds air and space. Tray ceilings adorn all the bedrooms, which also have their own baths, walk-in closets, and porch access. The owners suite, with a private location on the first floor, has access to the rear porch, a luxurious garden tub, and extra-large shower. A loft on the second floor provides a great location for quiet contemplation. The basement has a two-car garage conveniently tucked under the house, as well as plenty of additional space for storage and a bonus room.

HPK2700149

Style: New American

First Floor: 1,537 sq. ft.

Second Floor: 812 sq. ft.

Total: 2,349 sq. ft.

Bonus Space: 869 sq. ft.

Bedrooms: 3

Bathrooms: 2 ½

Width: 45' - 4"

Depth: 50' - 0"

Foundation: Island Basement

eplans.com

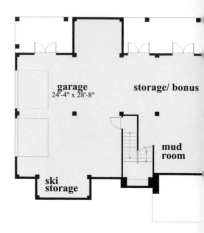

FIRST FLOOR

SECOND FLOOR

DRAMATIC ROOFLINES COMPLEMENT A STRIKING ARCHED-PEDIMENT ENTRY and a variety of windows on this refined facade. The entry porch leads to a landing that rises to the main-level living area—an arrangement well suited for unpredictable climates. A fireplace warms the great room, which sports a tray ceiling and opens to the rear porch through lovely French doors. The gourmet kitchen serves a stunning formal dining room, which offers wide views through a wall of windows. Separate sets of French doors let in natural light and fresh air and permit access to both of the rear porches.

© William E. Poole Designs, Inc.

HOME PLAN

HPK2700150

Style: Federal — Adams

First Floor: 1,305 sq. ft.

Second Floor: 1,052 sq. ft.

Total: 2,357 sq. ft.

Bonus Space: 430 sq. ft.

Bedrooms: 3

Bathrooms: 2 ½

Width: 69' - 4"

Depth: 35' - 10"

Foundation: Crawlspace, Unfinished Basement

eplans.com

FIRST FLOOR

SECOND FLOOR

WITH A HIPPED ROOFLINE, WHITEWASHED BRICK, AND ATTRACTIVE SHUTTERS, this fine Colonial will dress up any neighborhood. Inside, the foyer introduces the formal living room to the right, which is separated from the formal dining room by graceful columns—a perfect layout for dinner parties. The spacious family room offers a warming fireplace, built-ins, and backyard access. Designed with an efficient island, the kitchen easily serves the formal dining room as well as the sunny breakfast area. Upstairs, two family bedrooms share a hall bath, and the master suite provides privacy with a lavish bath and His and Hers walk-in closets. Don't miss the future recreation room, perfect as a home office, gym, or playroom.

FIRST FLOOR

SECOND FLOOR

HPK2700151

Style: New American

First Floor: 1,289 sq. ft.

Second Floor: 1,069 sq. ft.

Total: 2,358 sq. ft.

Bonus Space: 168 sq. ft.

Bedrooms: 4

Bathrooms: 3

Width: 54' - 4"

Depth: 37' - 6"

Foundation: Crawlspace, Slab, Unfinished Walkout Basement

eplans.com

TRADITIONAL STYLINGS—PILASTER AND SIDELIGHT ACCENTS AT THE FRONT ENTRY AND KEYSTONE JACK-ARCHED WINDOWS WITH SHUTTERS—present a home with class and appeal. The two-story foyer is flanked by the formal dining room and the living room. Beyond the enclosed staircase, the family room, warmed with a fireplace, offers a cozy environment for intimate gatherings. The angled kitchen enjoys a serving bar and is situated between the dining room and breakfast area for convenience. Note the home office/bedroom, tucked away on the left, with its private entrance to the full bath. The lavish master suite resides on the second floor along with two additional bedrooms, a full bath, laundry, and bonus room.

©1998 Donald A. Gardner, Inc.

FIRST FLOOR

SECOND FLOOR

HOME PLAN

HPK2700152

Style: Shingle

First Floor: 1,650 sq. ft.

Second Floor: 712 sq. ft.

Total: 2,362 sq. ft.

Bedrooms: 3

Bathrooms: 2 ½

Width: 58' - 10"

Depth: 47' - 4"

eplans.com

CEDAR SHAKES AND STRIKING GABLES WITH DECORATIVE SCALLOPED INSETS adorn the exterior of this lovely coastal home. The generous great room is expanded by a rear wall of windows, with additional light from transom windows above the front door and a rear clerestory dormer. The kitchen features a pass-through to the great room. The dining room, great room, and study all access an inviting back porch. The master bedroom is a treat with a private balcony, His and Hers walk-in closets, and an impeccable bath. Upstairs, a room-sized loft with an arched opening overlooks the great room below. Two more bedrooms, one with its own private balcony, share a hall bath.

storage/ bonus
29'-6" x 39'-0"

garage
24'-0" x 25'-6"

THE STAIRCASE LEADING TO A COLUMNED FRONT PORCH lends a touch of grandeur to this coastal residence. The great room is inviting, with a fireplace and twin sets of double doors opening to a wraparound porch that's also accessed by the master suite. This spacious suite features luxurious extras like His and Hers sinks, a separate garden tub and shower, and a huge walk-in closet. The kitchen provides plenty of counter space and overlooks the formal dining room. Upstairs, two additional bedrooms open up to a second-floor porch and have their own private baths and walk-in closets.

FIRST FLOOR

SECOND FLOOR

HPK2700153

Style: Mediterranean

First Floor: 1,510 sq. ft.

Second Floor: 864 sq. ft.

Total: 2,374 sq. ft.

Bedrooms: 3

Bathrooms: 3 ½

Width: 44' - 0"

Depth: 49' - 0"

Foundation: Unfinished Basement

HOME PLAN

eplans.com

©The Sater Design Collection, Inc.

REAR EXTERIOR

HOME PLAN

HPK2700154

Style: Cottage

First Floor: 1,736 sq. ft.

Second Floor: 640 sq. ft.

Total: 2,376 sq. ft.

Bonus Space: 840 sq. ft.

Bedrooms: 3

Bathrooms: 2

Width: 54' - 0"

Depth: 44' - 0"

Foundation: Slab, Basement

eplans.com

ATTICE DOOR PANELS, SHUTTERS, A BALUSTRADE, AND A ETAL ROOF add character to this delightful coastal home. Double oors flanking a fireplace open to the side sundeck from the spacious reat room. Access to the rear veranda is also provided from this om. An adjacent dining room provides views of the rear grounds nd space for formal and informal entertaining. The glassed-in nook ares space with the L-shaped kitchen containing a center work land. Bedrooms 2 and 3, a full bath, and a utility room complete this oor. Upstairs, a sumptuous master suite awaits. Double doors extend a private deck from the master bedroom. His and Hers walk-in osets lead the way to a grand bath featuring an arched whirlpool b, a double-bowl vanity, and a separate shower.

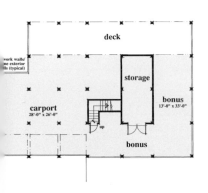

FIRST FLOOR

SECOND FLOOR

FIRST FLOOR

SECOND FLOOR

HPK2700155

Style: Federal - Adams

First Floor: 1,291 sq. ft.

Second Floor: 1,087 sq. ft.

Total: 2,378 sq. ft.

Bonus Space: 366 sq. ft.

Bedrooms: 3

Bathrooms: 2 ½

Width: 65' - 4"

Depth: 40' - 0"

Foundation: Crawlspace

eplans.com

THIS HOME EXUDES EARLY AMERICAN ELEGANCE.

Inside, a central fireplace in the family room conveniently warms the adjacent island kitchen and cathedral-ceilinged breakfast area. A built-in entertainment center is an added bonus to this area. Upstairs, the master suite features a sitting area, a dual-sink vanity, a private toilet, whirlpool tub, separate shower, and His and Hers walk-in closets. Two additional family bedrooms share a full hall bath.

© William E. Poole Designs, Inc.

HOME PLAN

HPK2700156

Style: Country

First Floor: 1,200 sq. ft.

Second Floor: 1,168 sq. ft.

Total: 2,368 sq. ft.

Bedrooms: 4

Bathrooms: 2 ½

Width: 56' - 0"

Depth: 39' - 0"

Foundation: Crawlspace, Slab, Unfinished Walkout Basement

eplans.com

THIS TWO-STORY TRADITIONAL HOME IS IDEAL FOR THE HOMEOWNER THAT TRULY ENJOYS ENTERTAINING. A Palladian window spills sunlight into the two-story foyer that is flanked by a formal dining room and the living room. The dining room is easily accessed by the island kitchen where a sunny breakfast area offers casual dining. The heart of this home is the two-story family room that delights with a fireplace flanked by windows, built-in shelves and a serving bar opening to the kitchen. Upstairs, the master suite reigns supreme with its tray ceiling, lavish bath and optional sitting room. Three additional bedrooms share a full bath.

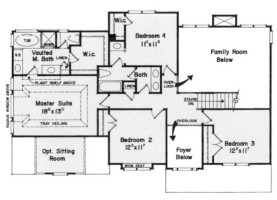

SECOND FLOOR

FIRST FLOOR

FIRST FLOOR

CLASSIC CLAPBOARD SIDING WITH BRICK ACCENTS THAT ADD SPLASH complement asymmetrical gables and a quaint covered porch on this 21st-Century traditional design. A cultivated interior starts with a two-story foyer that leads to a vaulted family room with an extended-hearth fireplace. The kitchen boasts a serving bar and ample pantry, and serves an elegant dining room with transom windows. An elegant master suite enjoys a private wing of the home and offers a vaulted bath with a whirlpool spa tub and a generous walk-in closet. Upstairs, three family bedrooms share a full bath and a hall with a balcony overlook.

SECOND FLOOR

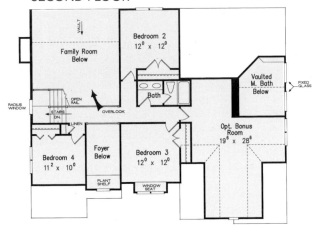

HOME PLAN

HPK2700157

Style: New American

First Floor: 1,687 sq. ft.

Second Floor: 694 sq. ft.

Total: 2,381 sq. ft.

Bonus Space: 407 sq. ft.

Bedrooms: 5

Bathrooms: 3

Width: 55' - 10"

Depth: 44' - 6"

Foundation: Crawlspace, Unfinished Walkout Basement

eplans.com

GRACED BY A WRAPAROUND VERANDA, MULTIPANED SHUTTERS, AND DECORATIVE WOOD TRIM, this four-bedroom design is as attractive as it is comfortable. Large bay windows and high ceilings throughout the first level further enhance the charm. The living room, with a masonry fireplace, extends to the bayed dining area. Eating or serving bars on the counter and center preparation island make easy work of mealtimes. Upstairs are the bayed master suite and three additional family bedrooms.

HOME PLAN

HPK2700158

Style: Farmhouse

First Floor: 1,193 sq. ft.

Second Floor: 1,188 sq. ft.

Total: 2,381 sq. ft.

Bedrooms: 4

Bathrooms: 2 ½

Width: 62' - 0"

Depth: 47' - 0"

Foundation: Crawlspace, Unfinished Basement

eplans.com

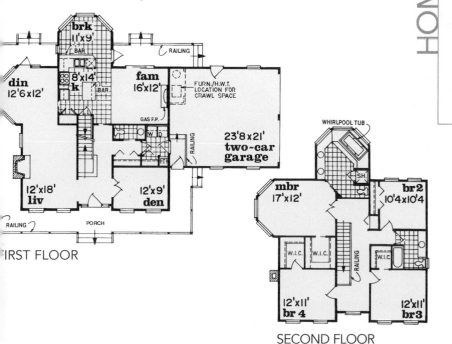

FIRST FLOOR

SECOND FLOOR

FIRST FLOOR

SECOND FLOOR

MULTIPLE GABLES AND A BRICK-AND-STONE FACADE create a home that is equally as decorative inside. The foyer introduces a beautiful great room with built-in cabinets, a gas fireplace, a 12-foot ceiling, and an arched-top window. Multiple windows allow lots of light to warm the great room and dining area. French doors at the rear are an invitation to the delightful screened porch. The spacious kitchen and breakfast area boast a work-top island, large pantry, and nine-foot ceiling. The master suite enjoys a whirlpool tub, shower enclosure, and private commode room. Access to the laundry room from the master bath is convenient. Split stairs lead to a second floor where a private computer area and two additional bedrooms complete this wonderful home.

HPK2700159

HOME PLAN

Style: French Country

First Floor: 1,795 sq. ft.

Second Floor: 591 sq. ft.

Total: 2,386 sq. ft.

Bonus Space: 298 sq. ft.

Bedrooms: 3

Bathrooms: 2 ½

Width: 62' - 0"

Depth: 55' - 4"

Foundation: Unfinished Basement

eplans.com

HOME PLAN #

HPK2700160

Style: Country

First Floor: 1,223 sq. ft.

Second Floor: 1,163 sq. ft.

Total: 2,386 sq. ft.

Bonus Space: 204 sq. ft.

Bedrooms: 4

Bathrooms: 2 ½

Width: 50' - 0"

Depth: 48' - 0"

Foundation: Crawlspace, Unfinished Walkout Basement

eplans.com

CLASSIC CAPSTONES AND ARCHED WINDOWS complement rectangular shutters and pillars on this traditional facade. The family room offsets a formal dining room and shares a see-through fireplace with the keeping room. The gourmet kitchen boasts a food-preparation island with a serving bar, a generous pantry, and French-door access to the rear property. Upstairs, a sensational master suite—with a tray ceiling and a vaulted bath with a plant shelf, whirlpool spa, and walk-in closet—opens from a gallery hall with a balcony overlook. Bonus space offers the possibility of an adjoining sitting room. Three additional bedrooms share a full bath.

FIRST FLOOR

SECOND FLOOR

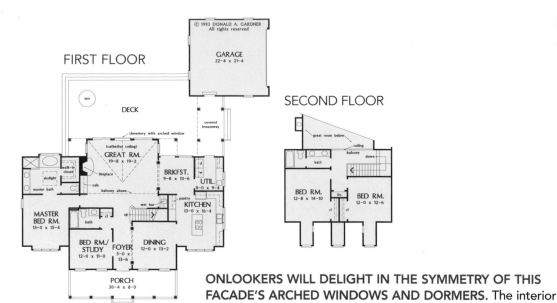

FIRST FLOOR

GARAGE
22-4 x 21-4

SECOND FLOOR

DECK

covered
breezeway

clerestory with arched window

(cathedral ceiling)
GREAT RM.
19-8 x 19-2

BRKFST.
9-8 x 10-6

UTIL.
8-0 x 9-4

KITCHEN
13-0 x 16-4

spa

walk-in
closet

skylight

fireplace

master bath

cab.

balcony above

MASTER
BED RM.
13-0 x 15-4

bath

wet bar

pantry

up

BED RM./
STUDY
12-0 x 11-0

FOYER
5-0 x
13-6

DINING
12-0 x 13-2

PORCH
30-4 x 8-0

great room below

railing

balcony

down

bath

BED RM.
12-8 x 14-10

lin.

cl   cl

BED RM.
12-0 x 12-6

ONLOOKERS WILL DELIGHT IN THE SYMMETRY OF THIS FACADE'S ARCHED WINDOWS AND DORMERS. The interior offers a great room with a cathedral ceiling. This open plan is also packed with the latest design features, including a kitchen with a large island, a wet bar in the great room, a bedroom/ study combination on the first floor, and a gorgeous master suite with a spa-style bath. Upstairs, two family bedrooms share a compartmented hall bath. An expansive rear deck and generous covered front porch offer maximum outdoor livability.

HOME PLAN

HPK2700161

Style: Country

First Floor: 1,783 sq. ft.

Second Floor: 611 sq. ft.

Total: 2,394 sq. ft.

Bedrooms: 4

Bathrooms: 3

Width: 70' - 0"

Depth: 79' - 2"

eplans.com

REAR EXTERIOR

B. NATHAN

THE STUNNING EXTERIOR OF THIS HOME ENJOYS AN ATTRACTIVE FRONT with two columns and two bay windows with copper hoods. The island kitchen c onveniently accesses the bay-window family dining area, a breakfast area, utility room, powder room, and the spacious family room with built-ins. Wood-burning fireplaces are enjoyed in the family room, living room, and master bedroom. The master bedroom also enjoys a private deck with a spiral staircase leading down to the patio and a luxurious private bath with skylights and a sloped ceiling. Three additional bedrooms also enjoy sloped ceilings and share a full bath that includes dual vanities.

HOME PLAN

 # HPK2700162

Style: New American
First Floor: 1,342 sq. ft.
Second Floor: 1,057 sq. ft.
Total: 2,399 sq. ft.
Bedrooms: 4
Bathrooms: 2 ½
Width: 65' - 0"
Depth: 41' - 10"
Foundation: Crawlspace, Slab, Unfinished Basement

eplans.com

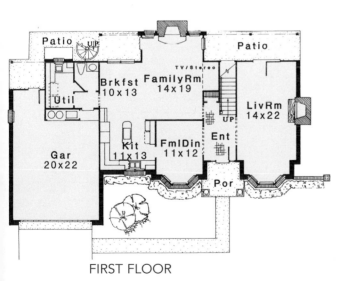

FIRST FLOOR

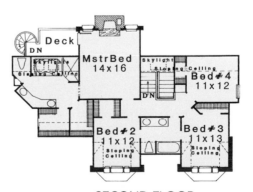

SECOND FLOOR

FIRST FLOOR

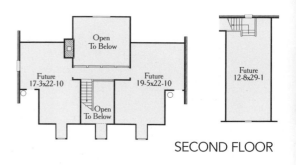

SECOND FLOOR

IF YOU ARE SEARCHING FOR A BEAUTIFUL SOUTHERN COLONIAL HOME with the details you've come to expect from our top designers, you've found it. Outside, Palladian style accents a brick-and-stucco facade for a truly breathtaking impression. Inside, a cathedral ceiling soars in the living room, adding height and grandeur. An extended-hearth fireplace warms, and rear-porch access invites outdoor living. The unique shape of the kitchen provides expansive workspace and uninhibited access to the dining area. A sloped ceiling in the breakfast room adds architectural interest. Two family bedrooms share a full bath to the far left. In the luxurious master suite, a sloped ceiling and pampering bath with a Roman tub will complement your lifestyle. Future space upstairs has room for bedrooms, a study, whatever you desire.

HOME PLAN

HPK2700163

Style: Colonial Revival

First Floor: 2,335 sq. ft.

Second Floor: 65 sq. ft.

Total: 2,400 sq. ft.

Bedrooms: 3

Bathrooms: 2 ½

Width: 77' - 0"

Depth: 64' - 2"

Foundation: Crawlspace, Slab, Unfinished Basement

eplans.com

© William E. Poole Designs, Inc

HOME PLAN

HPK2700164

Style: Farmhouse

First Floor: 1,776 sq. ft.

Second Floor: 643 sq. ft.

Total: 2,419 sq. ft.

Bonus Space: 367 sq. ft.

Bedrooms: 4

Bathrooms: 3

Width: 61' - 8"

Depth: 74' - 4"

Foundation: Crawlspace, Unfinished Basement

eplans.com

FIRST FLOOR   SECOND FLOOR

© William E. Poole Designs

A COVERED PORCH THAT STRETCHES THE ENTIRE WIDTH OF THE HOUSE welcomes friends and family to this fine four-bedroom home. Inside, the foyer is flanked by the staircase to the right and an arched opening into the formal dining room to the left. The great room, with a two-story ceiling, fireplace, and wall of windows, has easy access to the bayed breakfast area and the efficient kitchen. Two bedrooms occupy this level—one a lavish master suite complete with a walk-in closet and pampering bath, the other a family bedroom with easy access to a full bath. Upstairs, two more bedrooms share a hall bath and a balcony overlooking the great room.

FIRST FLOOR

SECOND FLOOR

HPK2700165

Style: Country

First Floor: 1,353 sq. ft.

Second Floor: 1,072 sq. ft.

Total: 2,425 sq. ft.

Bonus Space: 322 sq. ft.

Bedrooms: 4

Bathrooms: 3

Width: 54' - 4"

Depth: 45' - 6"

Foundation: Crawlspace, Unfinished Walkout Basement

eplans.com

HOME PLAN

THE TWO-STORY DESIGN CREATES BROAD AREAS FOR CASUAL AND FORMAL GATHERINGS on the first floor and reserves the second floor for quiet enjoyment. At the rear of the plan, the vaulted keeping room, breakfast nook, and family room enjoy great flow-through layout and receive plenty of natural light. A gourmet's kitchen at the center makes entertaining easier. Upstairs, the master suite is the star of the show and features a tray ceiling, vaulted bath, corner whirlpool, dual vanities, compartmented toilet, and oversized walk-in closet. An optional bonus room leaves room for growth and customization.

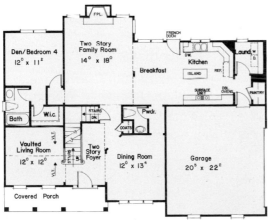

FIRST FLOOR

HPK2700166

HOME PLAN #

Style: Country

First Floor: 1,415 sq. ft.

Second Floor: 1,015 sq. ft.

Total: 2,430 sq. ft.

Bonus Space: 169 sq. ft.

Bedrooms: 4

Bathrooms: 3 ½

Width: 54' - 0"

Depth: 43' - 4"

Foundation: Crawlspace, Unfinished Walkout Basement

eplans.com

THIS STRIKING DESIGN IS REMINISCENT OF THE GRAND HOMES OF THE PAST CENTURY. Its wood siding and covered porch are complemented by shuttered windows and a glass-paneled entry. Historic design is updated in the floor plan to include a vaulted living room, a two-story family room, and a den that doubles as a guest suite on the first floor. Second-floor bedrooms feature a master suite with tray ceiling and vaulted bath. An optional loft on the second floor may be finished as a study area.

SECOND FLOOR

FIRST FLOOR

SECOND FLOOR

EXPERIENCE OUTDOOR LIVING AT ITS BEST in this cute country cottage. If engaging in neighborly chat sounds appealing, you can set out on the front porch in the evenings. If hiding out with a book is more your style, head to the screened porch, where a vaulted ceiling helps keep the space cool on muggy afternoons. Not to be overlooked, the spacious deck will hold a host of holiday barbecues. In chillier weather, the windows lining the rear wall allow the outdoor-lover to enjoy the scenery from the comfort of the cozy family living areas.

HOME PLAN

HPK2700167

Style: Craftsman

First Floor: 1,616 sq. ft.

Second Floor: 815 sq. ft.

Total: 2,431 sq. ft.

Bonus Space: 263 sq. ft.

Bedrooms: 3

Bathrooms: 3 ½

Width: 55' - 0"

Depth: 49' - 0"

Foundation: Crawlspace, Slab, Unfinished Walkout Basement

eplans.com

HOME PLAN # HPK2700168

Style: French Country
First Floor: 1,226 sq. ft.
Second Floor: 1,215 sq. ft.
Total: 2,441 sq. ft.
Bedrooms: 4
Bathrooms: 2 ½
Width: 47' - 0"
Depth: 60' - 8"
Foundation: Slab

eplans.com

STONE ACCENTS, COPPER ROOFS, AND A BALCONY make this quaint two-story home hard to resist. The entry welcomes you to the foyer, which has a stone floor and gently curving staircase. The formal living room adjoins the dining room through an arch framed by columns. A country kitchen with a work island and bay window opens to the covered patio. The master suite dominates the second floor, with a balcony overlooking the front entry, a fireplace, a media wall, a private bath, and a walk-in closet.

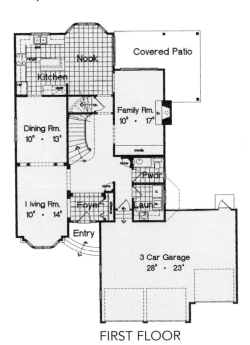

FIRST FLOOR

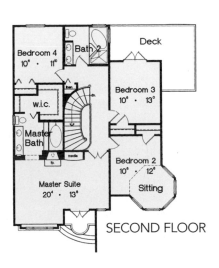

SECOND FLOOR

FIRST FLOOR

SECOND FLOOR

#HPK2700169

Style: New American

First Floor: 1,673 sq. ft.

Second Floor: 772 sq. ft.

Total: 2,445 sq. ft.

Bonus Space: 208 sq. ft.

Bedrooms: 4

Bathrooms: 2 ½

Width: 54' - 0"

Depth: 47' - 0"

Foundation: Crawlspace, Unfinished Walkout Basement

eplans.com

ASYMMETRICAL GABLES SET OFF A FRESH BLEND OF SHINGLES AND SIDING on this historical adaptation. An up-to-date interior looks established but takes on 21st-Century characteristics with amenities that draw on the future, starting with a balcony bridge that overlooks both the foyer and the family room. A first-floor gallery hall leads to casual living space and views to the outdoors, set off by a centered fireplace. A luxuriant master bedroom opens to a bayed sitting area with French door access to the rear property. Upstairs, three family bedrooms share a full bath and a hall that leads to an optional bonus room.

HPK2700170

Style: Farmhouse

First Floor: 1,261 sq. ft.

Second Floor: 1,185 sq. ft.

Total: 2,446 sq. ft.

Bedrooms: 4

Bathrooms: 2 ½

Width: 60' - 0"

Depth: 44' - 0"

Foundation: Crawlspace, Unfinished Basement

eplans.com

COVERED PORCHES AT THE FRONT AND REAR MAKE THIS A VERY COMFORTABLE FARMHOUSE. Double doors open to the foyer, flanked by the formal dining room and sunken living room. A butler's pantry, complete with a wet bar, separates the dining room and L-shaped island kitchen. A sunny breakfast room adjoins the kitchen on one side and the family room with a fireplace on the other. Double doors open to the rear porch. The master suite on the second level offers a walk-in closet and full bath with a corner whirlpool tub, separate shower, and double vanity. Three family bedrooms share a full bath that includes a dressing room with a vanity. The two-car garage connects to the main house via a service area/laundry room.

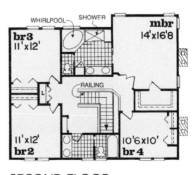

SECOND FLOOR

FIRST FLOOR

FIRST FLOOR

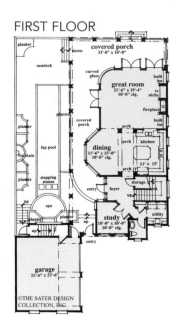

©THE SATER DESIGN COLLECTION, INC.

SECOND FLOOR

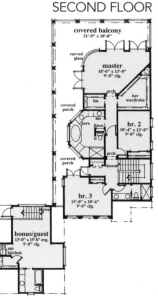

LOUVERED SHUTTERS, CIRCLE-HEAD WINDOWS, AND A COURTYARD are images from the Charleston Row past brought up-to-date in a floor plan for today's lifestyles. From the great room, three sets of French doors open to the covered porch and sundeck. The U-shaped kitchen includes a central island and adjoins the dining bay. The second floor includes two family bedrooms, a master suite, and a bonus room with a private bath, walk-in closet, and morning kitchen. A covered balcony is accessible from the master suite and Bedroom 3.

REAR EXTERIOR

©The Sater Design Collection, Inc.

HPK2700172

Style: Mediterranean

First Floor: 1,840 sq. ft.

Second Floor: 608 sq. ft.

Total: 2,448 sq. ft.

Bedrooms: 3

Bathrooms: 2 ½

Width: 65' - 0"

Depth: 55' - 0"

Foundation: Slab

HOME PLAN

eplans.com

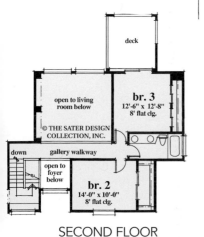

FIRST FLOOR

nook
11'-0" x 8'-4"
14' flat clg.

lanai
53'-0" x 12'-4" avg.

leisure
16'-0" x 14'-10" avg.
14' flat clg.

fireplace

kitchen

desk

living
15'-6" x 14'-10"
17'-4" flat clg.

master
suite
13'-0" x 18'-6"
8' flat clg.

1/2 wall

dining
12'-0" x 12'-8"
14' flat clg.

up

foyer

entry

utility

workshop

garage
20'-8" x 22'-8"

©The Sater Group, Inc.

SECOND FLOOR

deck

open to living
room below

© THE SATER DESIGN
COLLECTION, INC.

br. 3
12'-6" x 12'-8"
8' flat clg.

down

gallery walkway

open to
foyer
below

br. 2
14'-0" x 10'-0"
8' flat clg.

THIS STYLISH STUCCO HOME CATERS TO EVEN THE MOST DIS-CRIMINATING TASTES. The informal living area makes the most of the lanai. Other areas with access to the lanai include the spacious leisure room with its welcoming fireplace, the bay-windowed nook overlooking the rear grounds and the open kitchen complete with a walk-in pantry and a planning desk. The formal dining room is separated from the kitchen by a half-wall, thus making entertaining easy. The secluded master suite opens to the lanai also and features a huge walk-in closet and a master bath with a raised corner tub, a separate shower and dual vanities. The second floor contains two secondary bedrooms, a full bath and a rear deck.

THIS HOME IS UNIQUE BECAUSE OF ITS FARMHOUSE STYLING AND THE MULTITUDE OF WINDOWS—Palladian, decorative, and sunburst—that grace the exterior of the plan. A large front porch and flower box add even more charm. A rounded formal dining room looks out through windows to the front porch. The kitchen, with an island, leads to the dining area, which offers access to the patio. Upstairs, the master bedroom boasts a vaulted ceiling and a private sitting area, as well as a full bath and walk-in closet. Bedrooms 2 and 3 share a full bath.

HOME PLAN

HPK2700173

Style: New American

First Floor: 1,447 sq. ft.

Second Floor: 1,008 sq. ft.

Total: 2,455 sq. ft.

Bonus Space: 352 sq. ft.

Bedrooms: 3

Bathrooms: 2 ½

Width: 65' - 0"

Depth: 37' - 11"

Foundation: Crawlspace, Slab, Unfinished Basement

eplans.com

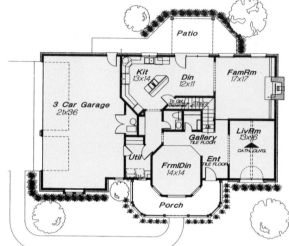

FIRST FLOOR

SECOND FLOOR

© William E. Poole Designs, Inc.

HOME PLAN

HPK2700174

Style: Cottage

First Floor: 1,819 sq. ft.

Second Floor: 638 sq. ft.

Total: 2,457 sq. ft.

Bonus Space: 385 sq. ft.

Bedrooms: 3

Bathrooms: 2 ½

Width: 47' - 4"

Depth: 82' - 8"

Foundation: Crawlspace, Unfinished Basement

eplans.com

GRACEFUL DORMERS TOP A WELCOMING COVERED PORCH that is enhanced by Victorian details on this fine three-bedroom home. Inside, the foyer leads past the formal dining room back to the spacious two-story great room. Here, a fireplace, built-ins, and outdoor access make any gathering special. The nearby kitchen features a work island, a pantry, a serving bar, and an adjacent bayed breakfast area. Located on the first floor for privacy, the master suite is designed to pamper. Upstairs, two family bedrooms share a hall bath. Note the bonus space above the two-car garage.

FIRST FLOOR

SECOND FLOOR

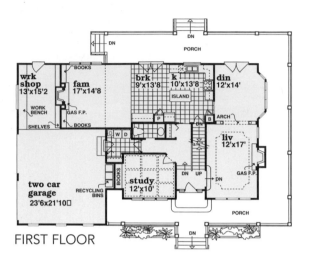

FIRST FLOOR

SECOND FLOOR

A LARGE WRAPAROUND PORCH GRACES THE EXTERIOR OF THIS HOME and gives it great outdoor livability. The raised foyer spills into a hearth-warmed living room and to the bay-windowed dining room beyond. French doors open from the breakfast and dining rooms to the spacious porch. Built-ins surround another hearth in the family room. The front study is adorned by a beamed ceiling and also features built-ins. Three bedrooms and a master suite are found on the second floor. The master suite features a walk-in closet and a private bath. Don't miss the workshop area in the garage.

HPK2700175

HOME PLAN

Style: Farmhouse

First Floor: 1,333 sq. ft.

Second Floor: 1,129 sq. ft.

Total: 2,462 sq. ft.

Bedrooms: 4

Bathrooms: 2 ½

Width: 69' - 8"

Depth: 49' - 0"

Foundation: Crawlspace, Unfinished Basement

eplans.com

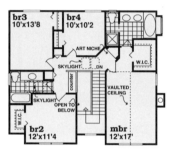

HOME PLAN

HPK2700176

Style: New American

First Floor: 1,815 sq. ft.

Second Floor: 650 sq. ft.

Total: 2,465 sq. ft.

Bonus Space: 124 sq. ft.

Bedrooms: 4

Bathrooms: 2 ½

Width: 55' - 0"

Depth: 55' - 7"

Foundation: Slab

eplans.com

FIRST FLOOR

SECOND FLOOR

TOWERING BRICK GABLES, ARCH-TOP WINDOWS AND WOODEN SHUTTERS create excellent curb appeal in this traditional two-story design. A high-ceilinged entry reveals cedar posts around an inviting formal dining room and a long gallery paved with brick. Opposite is a comfortable study with full-wall bookshelves flanking an arch-top window. A wall of windows frames the spacious living room. A short hall leads to the even larger family room with a vaulted ceiling and brick fireplace. Secluded at the rear of the house, the master suite provides a high sloped ceiling and atrium doors that open to a private patio. Upstairs, three additional bedrooms with a full bath complete this marvelous home.

A TRADITIONAL DESIGN WITH NONTRADITIONAL AMENITIES, this mid-size home is sure to please. The front-facing den, enhanced by French doors, is bathed in natural light. The great room sits at the heart of the home with an optional media center in the corner and a central fireplace along the right wall. The open design leads nicely into the adjoining dining room and kitchen. An island cooktop/serving bar conveniently serves the area. A future deck is accessible from the breakfast nook. Upstairs, the spacious master suite boasts a dual-sink vanity, a spa tub, a separate shower, a compartmented toilet, and an enormous walk-in closet. Two additional family bedrooms share a full bath. A bonus room and a practical second-floor laundry room complete this level.

FIRST FLOOR

HOME PLAN

HPK2700177

Style: Cottage

First Floor: 1,204 sq. ft.

Second Floor: 1,264 sq. ft.

Total: 2,468 sq. ft.

Bonus Space: 213 sq. ft.

Bedrooms: 3

Bathrooms: 2 ½

Width: 35' - 0"

Depth: 63' - 0"

Foundation: Crawlspace

eplans.com

SECOND FLOOR

© 2001 Donald A. Gardner, Inc.

HOME PLAN

(#) HPK2700178

Style: Country

First Floor: 1,667 sq. ft.

Second Floor: 803 sq. ft.

Total: 2,470 sq. ft.

Bonus Space: 318 sq. ft.

Bedrooms: 4

Bathrooms: 2 ½

Width: 52' - 4"

Depth: 57' - 0"

eplans.com

COUNTRY ACCENTS AND FARMHOUSE STYLE enhance the facade of this lovely two-story home. The first floor provides a formal dining room and great room warmed by a fireplace. The kitchen connects to a breakfast bay—perfect for casual morning meals. The first-floor master suite includes two walk-in closets and a private bath. Upstairs, a loft overlooks the two-story great room. Three second-floor bedrooms share a hall bath. The bonus room above the garage is great for a home office or guest suite.

FIRST FLOOR

SECOND FLOOR

FIRST FLOOR

SECOND FLOOR

A TASTE OF EUROPE IS REFLECTED IN ARCHED WINDOWS topped off by keystones in this traditional design. Formal rooms flank the foyer, which leads to a two-story family room with a focal-point fireplace. The sunny breakfast nook opens to a private covered porch through a French door. A spacious, well-organized kitchen features angled, wrapping counters, double ovens, and a walk-in pantry. The garage offers a service entrance to the utility area and pantry. An angled staircase leads from the two-story foyer to the sleeping quarters upstairs. Here, a gallery hall with a balcony overlooks the foyer and family room and connects the family bedrooms. A private hall leads to the master suite. It boasts a well-lit sitting area, a walk-in closet with linen storage, and a lavish bath with a vaulted ceiling and plant shelves.

HOME PLAN

HPK2700179

Style: French Country

First Floor: 1,205 sq. ft.

Second Floor: 1,277 sq. ft.

Total: 2,482 sq. ft.

Bedrooms: 4

Bathrooms: 2 ½

Width: 53' - 6"

Depth: 39' - 4"

Foundation: Crawlspace, Slab, Unfinished Walkout Basement

eplans.com

THIS TWO-STORY TRADITIONAL HOME OFFERS SPACE FOR EVERYONE. A handsome brick exterior, keystone arches, and an attractive shed dormer provide tons of curb appeal. The foyer is flanked by a study and the dining room. To the rear are the more casual spaces. The grand room features two-story ceilings, a fireplace, and is within steps of the island kitchen and breakfast room. The first-floor master suite is convenient as well as secluded, and offers walk-in closets, a full bath, and tray ceiling. Upstairs, three roomy secondary bedrooms—two with walk-in closets—share a full bath.

HOME PLAN

HPK2700180

Style: Country

First Floor: 1,773 sq. ft.

Second Floor: 709 sq. ft.

Total: 2,482 sq. ft.

Bedrooms: 4

Bathrooms: 2 ½

Width: 54' - 0"

Depth: 47' - 6"

Foundation: Slab, Unfinished Walkout Basement

eplans.com

FIRST FLOOR

SECOND FLOOR

PORCH

BRKFST.
13-4 x 10-0

UTILITY
11-0 x
5-8   d w

storage

fireplace

GREAT RM.
19-8 x 15-4

KITCHEN
13-4 x 11-8

GARAGE
21-4 x 21-4

shelves

walk-in
closet

bath

BUTLER'S
PANTRY

© 2002 DONALD A. GARDNER
All rights reserved

BED RM./
STUDY
13-4 x 12-0

balcony
above

DINING
13-4 x 12-0

FOYER
6-0 x
11-8

FIRST FLOOR

PORCH

MASTER
BED RM.
13-4 x 17-4

walk-in
closet

walk-in
closet

seat

master
bath

attic
storage

BONUS RM.
21-4 x 15-4

walk-in
closet

bath

down

railing

linen

walk-in
closet

attic
storage

BED RM.
13-4 x 12-0

railing

foyer
below

BED RM.
13-4 x 12-0

SECOND FLOOR

HPK2700181

Style: Farmhouse

First Floor: 1,420 sq. ft.

Second Floor: 1,065 sq. ft.

Total: 2,485 sq. ft.

Bonus Space: 411 sq. ft.

Bedrooms: 4

Bathrooms: 3

Width: 57' - 8"

Depth: 49' - 0"

LOOKING EVERY BIT LIKE THE BIG COUNTRY HOMES OF YESTERYEAR, this plan's traditional facade belies the up-to-date floor plan inside. The two-story foyer—lit by a glorious Palladian window on top—opens to flex space on the left. This room can be a bedroom or a study, depending on your needs. On the other side of the foyer lies the dining room, which accesses the kitchen through a convenient butler's pantry. The roomy island kitchen flows into a sunny breakfast room, which in turn accesses the hearth-warmed great room. The rear porch can be accessed by the great room and the breakfast room. Upstairs, two family bedrooms share a hall bath and the deluxe master suite boasts two walk-in closets and a twin-vanity bath with a garden tub. To the right is bonus space, which can convert to a number of uses.

eplans.com

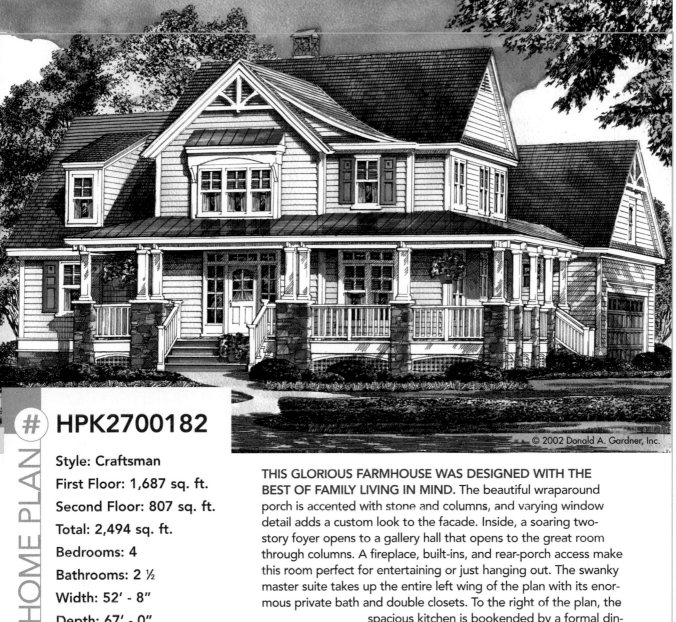

HOME PLAN

HPK2700182

Style: Craftsman

First Floor: 1,687 sq. ft.

Second Floor: 807 sq. ft.

Total: 2,494 sq. ft.

Bedrooms: 4

Bathrooms: 2 ½

Width: 52' - 8"

Depth: 67' - 0"

eplans.com

THIS GLORIOUS FARMHOUSE WAS DESIGNED WITH THE BEST OF FAMILY LIVING IN MIND. The beautiful wraparound porch is accented with stone and columns, and varying window detail adds a custom look to the facade. Inside, a soaring two-story foyer opens to a gallery hall that opens to the great room through columns. A fireplace, built-ins, and rear-porch access make this room perfect for entertaining or just hanging out. The swanky master suite takes up the entire left wing of the plan with its enormous private bath and double closets. To the right of the plan, the spacious kitchen is bookended by a formal dining room at the front and a cozy breakfast nook to the rear. A utility room opens to the garage. Upstairs, three bedrooms share a bath as well as attic storage. A balcony looks down into the foyer and great room.

FIRST FLOOR

SECOND FLOOR

EYE-CATCHING TWIN CHIMNEYS DOMINATE THE EXTERIOR OF THIS GRAND DESIGN, but on closer approach you will delight in the covered porch with decorated pediment and the tall windows across the front of the house. A long hallway separates the family room, with a fireplace, from the rest of the house. A large U-shaped kitchen features an island work center and direct access to the sunny breakfast room and the formal dining room. A study/living room (with an optional second fireplace) completes the first floor. Upstairs, you'll find a well-appointed master suite, two family bedrooms, and a bonus room over the garage.

FIRST FLOOR

SECOND FLOOR

© 1996 Donald A. Gardner Architects, Inc.

HOME PLAN

HPK2700183

Style: Country

First Floor: 1,428 sq. ft.

Second Floor: 1,067 sq. ft.

Total: 2,495 sq. ft.

Bonus Space: 342 sq. ft.

Bedrooms: 3

Bathrooms: 2 ½

Width: 74' - 0"

Depth: 64' - 8"

eplans.com

© 1996 Donald A. Gardner Architects, Inc.

THE TIMELESS INFLUENCE OF THE FRENCH QUARTER is exemplified in this home designed for riverfront living. The double French-door entry opens into a large living room/dining room area separated by a double archway. A railed balcony with a loft on the second floor overlooks the living room. A pass-through between the kitchen and dining room also provides seating at a bar for informal dining. The spacious master bedroom at the rear includes a sitting area and a roomy bath with a large walk-in closet. Two additional bedrooms, a bath, and a bonus area for an office or game room are located upstairs.

HOME PLAN # HPK2700184

Style: Neoclassical

First Floor: 1,530 sq. ft.

Second Floor: 968 sq. ft.

Total: 2,498 sq. ft.

Bonus Space: 326 sq. ft.

Bedrooms: 3

Bathrooms: 2 ½

Width: 40' - 0"

Depth: 66' - 4"

Foundation: Crawlspace, Slab, Unfinished Basement

eplans.com

FIRST FLOOR

SECOND FLOOR

All in the Family—
Something for Everyone

These spacious designs are made for homeowners who want a little bit of everything: an open layout, formal rooms, casual gathering places, and enough space to accommodate family and friends alike. A home found here would work well for the growing family or for empty-nesters who want to reserve a room for visiting family and friends.

Family is an important consideration for plans of this size. Homeowners can choose a plan with a first-floor master suite, secluded from household goings-on, or one on the second floor near the family brood. In this suite, parents can pamper themselves with sought-after bathroom amenities, such as steam showers and spa tubs. Additionally, guest rooms on the first floor offer space for aging visitors or live-in parents. Separate family or recreation rooms and living rooms appear in these designs, often near the kitchen or on the second floor, maintaining a division from the formal living room near the foyer. The open kitchen remains the heart of the home, using island snack bars for quick meals and nooks for sit-down family time. This area continues to be an open space that keeps conversation flowing from room to room. For more formal occasions, a dining room is usually at the front of the home near the entrance and foyer, with separation from the kitchen.

Having ample storage is a consideration for every family. Most plans come with multibay garages, which offer room for seasonal equipment and workshops as well as the family fleet. A bonus room provides flexibility: use it for storage, as a guest room, or a home office. If this is still not enough, flip through our plans of detached sheds and garages.

Even with so much square footage within, these designs don't forget the all-important outdoor spaces. Find sunrooms and porches to decks and balconies off the kitchens, nooks, great rooms, and master suites, there are numerous ways the houses take advantage of spending time outside and even further extending living space.

AS SQUARE FOOTAGE INCREASES, so does the lavishness of the master bath.

ROOMS provide a
th transition from indoor
tdoor spaces, not to
ion a pleasant area to
morning coffee.

FIRST FLOOR

PORCH

FAMILY RM
17'-6"x13'-4"

DINETTE
10'-0"x13'-4"

KITCHEN
9'-0"x13'-4"

STORAGE

LIVING RM
13'-4"x13'-4"

FOYER

DINING RM
11'-4"x13'-4"

GARAGE
23'-8"x21'-8"

SECOND FLOOR

BEDRM 4
12'-8"x10'-4"

BEDRM 3
10'-4"x12'-4"

MSTR SUITE
15'-4"x13'-4"

BEDRM 2
11'-4"x14'-0"

THREE DORMERS ON A SIDE-GABLE ROOF AND CLASSIC FENESTRATION ESTABLISH A PLEASING COLONIAL STYLE to this home's facade. The attention to the entryway and second-floor balcony are finer touches owners will appreciate. The interior offers an uncomplicated layout—gathering spaces on the lower floor and sleeping quarters above. The family room enjoys a majestic fireplace and incredible views through the intimate bay window. The family room, dinette, and kitchen form one large area, with direct access from kitchen to formal dining room. A handy large closet and laundry are also accessible from the kitchen.

HOME PLAN

HPK2700185

Style: Colonial Revival

First Floor: 1,368 sq. ft.

Second Floor: 1,140 sq. ft.

Total: 2,508 sq. ft.

Bedrooms: 4

Bathrooms: 2 ½

Width: 62' - 0"

Depth: 48' - 0"

Foundation: Unfinished Basement

eplans.com

AN OVERSIZED DORMER ABOVE THE ENTRYWAY AND A STEEP, SIDE-GABLED ROOF bring an interesting front perspective to this Craftsman-style vacation home. Inside, a wood-burning fireplace warms the family room, overlooked by the second-floor walkway. To the left, the master suite is attended by a large walk-in closet and double vanities in the bathroom. Owners will also appreciate the private access to the deck. The full-sized garage at the right of the plan features a bonus room on the upper floor.

FIRST FLOOR

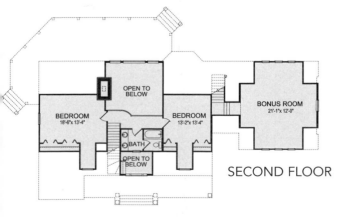

SECOND FLOOR

HOME PLAN

HPK2700186

Style: Craftsman

First Floor: 1,799 sq. ft.

Second Floor: 709 sq. ft.

Total: 2,508 sq. ft.

Bonus Space: 384 sq. ft.

Bedrooms: 3

Bathrooms: 2 ½

Width: 77' - 4"

Depth: 41' - 4"

Foundation: Unfinished Walkout Basement

eplans.com

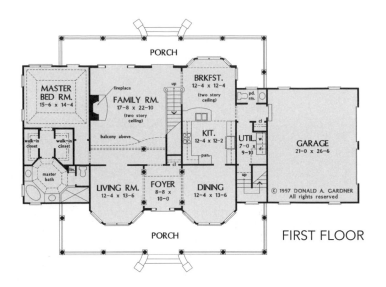

FIRST FLOOR

SECOND FLOOR

FILLED WITH THE CHARM OF FARM-HOUSE DETAILS, SUCH AS TWIN DORMERS AND BAY WINDOWS, this design begins with a classic covered porch. The entry leads to a foyer flanked by columns that separate it from the formal dining and living rooms. The U-shaped kitchen separates the dining room from the bayed breakfast room. The first-floor master suite features a bedroom with a tray ceiling and a luxurious private bath.

HOME PLAN

HPK2700187

Style: Farmhouse

First Floor: 1,914 sq. ft.

Second Floor: 597 sq. ft.

Total: 2,511 sq. ft.

Bonus Space: 487 sq. ft.

Bedrooms: 3

Bathrooms: 2 ½

Width: 79' - 2"

Depth: 51' - 6"

eplans.com

1997 Donald A. Gardner, Inc.

THREE BEDROOMS, SPACIOUS FAMILY LIVING AREAS, and plenty of amenities make this Craftsman design a pleasure to come home to. Vaulted ceilings enhance the den and living room, and built-in bookshelves, a media center, and a fireplace highlight the family room. The kitchen, with a built-in desk and island cooktop, serves the breakfast nook and dining room with ease. Sleeping quarters—the vaulted master suite and two family bedrooms—are upstairs, along with a bonus room and the utility area.

 # HPK2700188

Style: Craftsman

First Floor: 1,360 sq. ft.

Second Floor: 1,154 sq. ft.

Total: 2,514 sq. ft.

Bonus Space: 202 sq. ft.

Bedrooms: 3

Bathrooms: 2 ½

Width: 52' - 0"

Depth: 45' - 6"

Foundation: Crawlspace

eplans.com

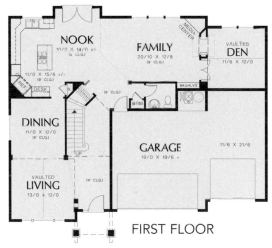

FIRST FLOOR

SECOND FLOOR

FIRST FLOOR

MASTER BATH
GREAT ROOM
20-6 X 16-0
PORCH
BREAKFAST
13-8 X 10-0
MASTER SUITE
16-0 X 18-0
KITCHEN
12-6 X 12-8
PWDR
DINING ROOM
11-6 X 12-6
ENTRY
PAN
STORAGE
5-6 X 12-0
UTILITY
10-4 X 5-6
PORCH
© Larry E. Belk Designs
GARAGE
21-4 X 21-4
FALSE PORCH

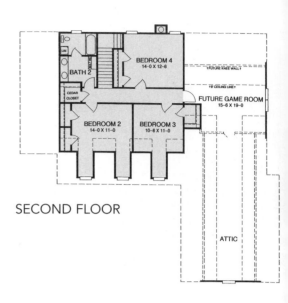

SECOND FLOOR

BEDROOM 4
14-0 X 12-6
BATH 2
FUTURE KNEE WALL
1/2 CEILING LINE
CEDAR
CLOSET
FUTURE GAME ROOM
15-6 X 19-0
BEDROOM 2
14-0 X 11-0
BEDROOM 3
10-8 X 11-0
ATTIC

HPK2700189

Style: Country

First Floor: 1,638 sq. ft.

Second Floor: 877 sq. ft.

Total: 2,515 sq. ft.

Bonus Space: 277 sq. ft.

Bedrooms: 4

Bathrooms: 2 ½

Width: 60' - 10"

Depth: 61' - 4"

Foundation: Crawlspace, Slab

eplans.com

A CHARMING EXTERIOR WELCOMES VISITORS TO THIS COMPACT FOUR-BEDROOM HOME. A roomy front porch provides a great place for relaxing during hot summer evenings. The small porch off the garage is added for decoration and is a good site for displaying hanging baskets full of blooming flowers. Inside, the entry leads to an oversized great room and a formal dining room with an entrance flanked by square columns. The kitchen features a large breakfast room. The master suite is located downstairs and includes a private bath with a corner whirlpool. Upstairs, Bedrooms 2 and 3 are located at the front of the house; Bedroom 4 and a compartmented bath are located at the rear. A future game room is shown with access to attic space for later expansion.

© 2002 Donald A. Gardner, Inc.

FIRST FLOOR

SECOND FLOOR

THIS RUSTIC FRENCH COUNTRY EXTERIOR OPENS UP TO A PLAN FULL OF MODERN AMENITIES. The foyer, preceded by a petite porch, leads into a gallery hall that opens to a sunny, vaulted great room. With its fireplace and porch access, this will be the most popular room in the house. As an added convenience, the great room flows into the breakfast room, with its box-bay window and built-ins. The island kitchen features a pantry and plenty of counter space. A formal dining room is adjacent. The deluxe master suite awaits on the left of the plan, enjoying a pampering bath and double walk-in closets.

Upstairs, two bedrooms boast ample closet space and a private bath. Bonus space awaits expansion over the garage.

HPK2700190

HOME PLAN

Style: French Country

First Floor: 1,834 sq. ft.

Second Floor: 681 sq. ft.

Total: 2,515 sq. ft.

Bonus Space: 365 sq. ft.

Bedrooms: 3

Bathrooms: 3 ½

Width: 50' - 8"

Depth: 66' - 8"

eplans.com

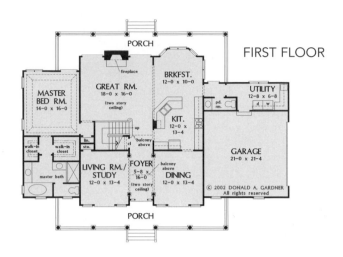

FIRST FLOOR

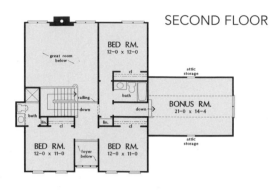

SECOND FLOOR

WITH SPACIOUS FRONT AND REAR PORCHES, TWIN GABLES, AND AN ARCHED ENTRANCE, this home has charm and curb appeal. Columns make a grand impression both inside and outside, and transoms above French doors brighten both the front and rear of the floor plan. An angled counter separates the kitchen from the great room and breakfast area, and the mudroom/utility area is complete with a sink. A tray ceiling tops the master bedroom, and the formal living room/study and bonus room are flexible spaces, tailoring to family needs. A balcony overlooks the foyer and great room; an additional upstairs bedroom has its own bath and can be used as a guest suite.

HPK2700191

Style: Farmhouse
First Floor: 1,798 sq. ft.
Second Floor: 723 sq. ft.
Total: 2,521 sq. ft.
Bonus Space: 349 sq. ft.
Bedrooms: 4
Bathrooms: 3 ½
Width: 66' - 8"
Depth: 49' - 8"

HOME PLAN

eplans.com

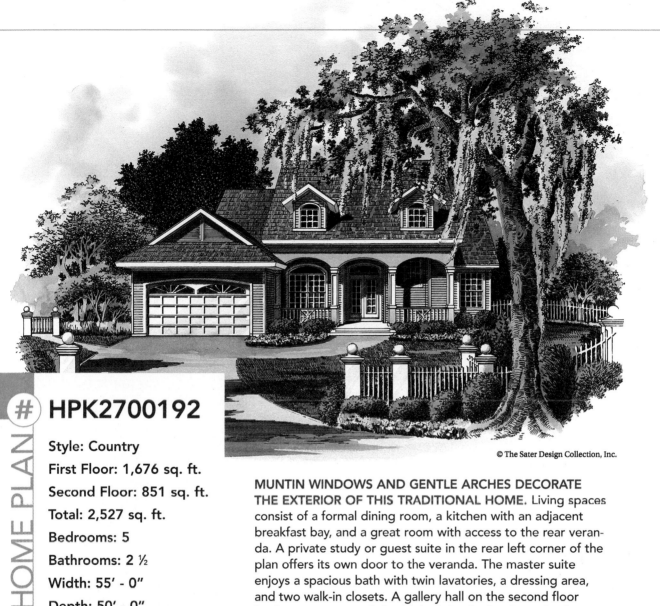

© The Sater Design Collection, Inc.

HOME PLAN

HPK2700192

Style: Country

First Floor: 1,676 sq. ft.

Second Floor: 851 sq. ft.

Total: 2,527 sq. ft.

Bedrooms: 5

Bathrooms: 2 ½

Width: 55' - 0"

Depth: 50' - 0"

Foundation: Slab

eplans.com

MUNTIN WINDOWS AND GENTLE ARCHES DECORATE THE EXTERIOR OF THIS TRADITIONAL HOME. Living spaces consist of a formal dining room, a kitchen with an adjacent breakfast bay, and a great room with access to the rear veranda. A private study or guest suite in the rear left corner of the plan offers its own door to the veranda. The master suite enjoys a spacious bath with twin lavatories, a dressing area, and two walk-in closets. A gallery hall on the second floor leads to a computer loft with built-ins for books and software.

SECOND FLOOR

FIRST FLOOR

FIRST FLOOR

SECOND FLOOR

HPK2700193

Style: New American

First Floor: 1,799 sq. ft.

Second Floor: 730 sq. ft.

Total: 2,529 sq. ft.

Bonus Space: 328 sq. ft.

Bedrooms: 4

Bathrooms: 2 ½

Width: 55' - 4"

Depth: 61' - 4"

eplans.com

HOME PLAN

A MULTIPANE DORMER, SHUTTERS, AND A COVERED FRONT PORCH invite you to call this house a home. Inside, to the left of the foyer is a room that could function as either a formal living room or an elegant study. To the right, through a pair of columns, a formal dining room has direct access to the U-shaped kitchen. For informal meals, a breakfast room is just off the kitchen via a snack bar. With a cathedral ceiling and a warming fireplace, the family room is sure to please. The first-floor master suite is full of pleasing details, including a large walk-in closet, a garden tub, and a separate shower. Upstairs, three family bedrooms share a full hall bath with dual vanities.

FIRST FLOOR

SECOND FLOOR

THIS GRACIOUS, FOUR-BEDROOM, FRENCH COUNTRY home has an appealing stone-and-brick and rough-hewn cedar exterior. A curving stairway in the entry leads to the family or guest bedrooms on the second floor. Downstairs, both the great room with a fireplace and built-in entertainment center and the master bedroom with a private bath and fitted walk-in closet face the large covered patio that extends across the back of the house. The formal dining room at the front is just a few steps from the island kitchen, with sloped ceilings and a bright breakfast area. A powder room and utility room are off the hall that leads to the two-car garage.

HOME PLAN

HPK2700194

Style: French Country
First Floor: 1,719 sq. ft.
Second Floor: 819 sq. ft.
Total: 2,538 sq. ft.
Bedrooms: 4
Bathrooms: 3 ½
Width: 56' - 0"
Depth: 51' - 8"
Foundation: Slab

eplans.com

HPK2700195

Style: Floridian

First Floor: 1,383 sq. ft.

Second Floor: 1,156 sq. ft.

Total: 2,539 sq. ft.

Bedrooms: 4

Bathrooms: 3

Width: 40' - 0"

Depth: 59' - 0"

Foundation: Crawlspace, Unfinished Basement

eplans.com

THIS WELL-PLANNED STUCCO HOME IS SUITED FOR A NARROW LOT. Its interior begins with a two-story foyer that displays a sweeping, curved staircase, an art niche, and a plant ledge. The vaulted ceiling in the living room is enhanced by a full-height window and a fireplace. Columns separate the living and dining rooms; the dining room has a tray ceiling. The step-saving kitchen is adjacent to a carousel breakfast room with a French door to the rear yard. A gas fireplace warms the family room, which features a room-divider display counter and sliding glass doors. A den with a tray ceiling rounds out the first floor. The master suite boasts a tray ceiling, window seat, raised whirlpool tub, and separate shower. Three family bedrooms share a full bath.

FIRST FLOOR

brk
11'x10'6
BREAKFAST COUNTER

fam
16'x13'

k
10'x10'8

DISPLAY COUNTER

GAS F.P.

TRAY CEILING
din
12'x11

den
11'4"x11'
TRAY CEILING

ART NICHE

DECORATIVE COLUMNS

FOYER

VAULTED
12'x15'
liv

GLASS BLOCK

19'x 20'
two-car garage

SECOND FLOOR

WHIRLPOOL TUB

SITTING

STEP

mbr
13'8"x15'6

SH.

WALK IN CLOSET

TRAY CEILING

RAILING

br4
10'x11'

br2
10'6"x11'

PLANT LEDGE

PLANT LEDGE
OPEN TO LIVING ROOM BELOW

PLANT LEDGE

OPEN TO FOYER

15'x10'
br3

HPK2700196

HOME PLAN

Style: New American

First Floor: 1,904 sq. ft.

Second Floor: 645 sq. ft.

Total: 2,549 sq. ft.

Bonus Space: 434 sq. ft.

Bedrooms: 3

Bathrooms: 2 ½

Width: 71' - 2"

Depth: 45' - 8"

eplans.com

FIRST FLOOR

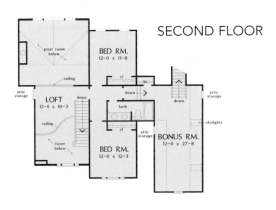

SECOND FLOOR

THIS STUCCO HOME CONTRASTS GENTLY CURVED ARCHES WITH GABLES and uses large multipane windows to flood the interior with natural light. Square pillars form an impressive entry, leading to a two-story foyer. The living room is set apart from the informal area of the house and could serve as a cozy study instead. The back patio can be reached from both the breakfast nook and the family room, which features a cathedral ceiling and a fireplace. The master suite offers two walk-in closets and a bath with twin vanities, a garden tub, and separate shower.

FIRST FLOOR

SECOND FLOOR

A BEAUTIFUL ONE-STORY TURRET is accompanied by arched windows and a stucco facade. A terrific casual combination of kitchen, breakfast area, and a vaulted keeping room provide space for family gatherings. Both the keeping room and great room sport cheery fireplaces. The master suite is secluded on the first floor. This relaxing retreat offers a sitting room, His and Hers walk-in closets, dual vanities, and compartmented toilet. Two family bedrooms share a full bath on the second floor. An optional bonus room can be used as a game room or home office.

HOME PLAN

HPK2700197

Style: New American

First Floor: 1,972 sq. ft.

Second Floor: 579 sq. ft.

Total: 2,551 sq. ft.

Bonus Space: 256 sq. ft.

Bedrooms: 3

Bathrooms: 2 ½

Width: 57' - 4"

Depth: 51' - 2"

Foundation: Crawlspace, Slab, Unfinished Walkout Basement

eplans.com

ORDER BLUEPRINTS ANYTIME AT EPLANS.COM OR 1-800-521-6797

HOME PLAN

HPK2700198

Style: Country

First Floor: 1,784 sq. ft.

Second Floor: 777 sq. ft.

Total: 2,561 sq. ft.

Bonus Space: 232 sq. ft.

Bedrooms: 4

Bathrooms: 2 ½

Width: 60' - 0"

Depth: 51' - 0"

Foundation: Crawlspace

eplans.com

THIS TRADITIONAL COUNTRY HOME IS A PERFECT SEMBLANCE OF OLD-FASHIONED STYLE AND MODERN FEATURES. Triple dormers and a front covered porch add country accents to the facade. A dining room and study flank the foyer. Vaulted ceilings enhance the great room and breakfast nook. The first-floor master bedroom is complete with two closets and a private bath. Three additional bedrooms and a bonus room reside upstairs.

THIS STATELY BRICK COTTAGE PERFECTLY BLENDS THE AMENITIES OF A LARGER HOME with the coziness of a Colonial cottage. The living and dining rooms open off the foyer, each detailed with a corner fireplace and multi-pane windows. Casual living areas, to the rear of the plan, include a large eat-in country kitchen with a snack bar, planning desk, and breakfast nook. A media room features a full-wall entertainment center. Upstairs, the master bedroom is highlighted with an expansive walk-in closet with a dressing room and a bath with twin vanities. A second bedroom suite has a fireplace and private access to a large compartmented bath. A smaller bedroom next to the master suite would make a perfect study or nursery.

FIRST FLOOR

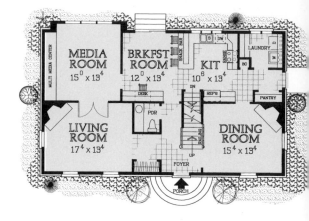

HOME PLAN

HPK2700199

Style: Cape Cod

First Floor: 1,396 sq. ft.

Second Floor: 1,169 sq. ft.

Total: 2,565 sq. ft.

Bedrooms: 3

Bathrooms: 2 ½

Width: 48' - 0"

Depth: 28' - 8"

Foundation: Unfinished Basement

eplans.com

SECOND FLOOR

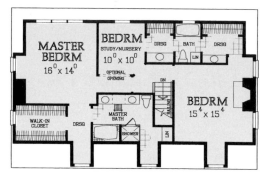

FIRST FLOOR

MASTER BEDRM
13-4 X 16-4
10 FT TRAY CLG

BRKFST ROOM
11-4 X 13-0
10 FT TRAY CLG

PORCH

KITCHEN
18-6 X 13-4
9 FT CLG

MASTER
BATH

GREAT ROOM
17-0 X 20-6
10 FT TRAY CLG

STORAGE

UTIL
11-4 X 8-0
9 FT CLG

PAN

BATH 2

ARCH

GARAGE

DINING ROOM
12-6 X 13-4
10 FT CLG

FOYER
2 STORY CLG

BEDROOM 2
12-6 X 13-6
9 FT CLG

PORCH

© Larry E. Belk Designs

SECOND FLOOR

ATTIC

EXPANDABLE AREA
17-4 X 18-0

BEDROOM 4
13-4 X 10-4

BATH 3

OPEN TO
FOYER BELOW

BEDROOM 3
13-0 X 11-6

PLANT LEDGE

HOME PLAN

HPK2700200

Style: Country

First Floor: 2,028 sq. ft.

Second Floor: 558 sq. ft.

Total: 2,586 sq. ft.

Bonus Space: 272 sq. ft.

Bedrooms: 4

Bathrooms: 3

Width: 64' - 10"

Depth: 61' - 0"

Foundation: Crawlspace, Slab, Unfinished Basement

eplans.com

DOUBLE COLUMNS AND AN ARCH-TOP CLERESTORY WINDOW create an inviting entry to this fresh interpretation of traditional style. ecorative columns and arches open to the formal dining room and to the octagonal great room, which has a 10-foot tray ceiling. The U-shaped kitchen looks over an angled counter to a breakfast bay that brings in the outdoors and shares a through-fireplace with the great room. A sitting area and a lavish bath set off the secluded master suite. A nearby secondary bedroom with its own bath could be used as a guest suite. Upstairs, two family bedrooms share a full bath and a hall that leads to an expandable area.

FIRST FLOOR

SECOND FLOOR

HPK2700201

Style: New American

First Floor: 1,152 sq. ft.

Second Floor: 1,434 sq. ft.

Total: 2,586 sq. ft.

Bedrooms: 4

Bathrooms: 3

Width: 44' - 0"

Depth: 44' - 0"

Foundation: Unfinished Basement

HOME PLAN

eplans.com

TALL, ROBUST COLUMNS FLANK THE IMPRESSIVE TWO-STORY ENTRY OF THIS EUROPEAN-STYLE HOME. Views can be had in the living room—in the turret—and with the open dining area just steps away, entertaining will be a splendid affair. The kitchen features a breakfast bar and adjoining sun room. Upstairs, the master suite is enhanced by a large sitting area, bumped-out bay window, and a relaxing bath. Three family bedrooms and a full bath complete this level.

HOME PLAN

HPK2700202

Style: Farmhouse

First Floor: 1,809 sq. ft.

Second Floor: 777 sq. ft.

Total: 2,586 sq. ft.

Bonus Space: 264 sq. ft.

Bedrooms: 4

Bathrooms: 3 ½

Width: 70' - 7"

Depth: 48' - 4"

eplans.com

WRAPPING TRADITIONAL BRICK WITH TWO COUNTRY PORCHES creates a modern exterior that ís big on southern charm. Bold columns and a metal roof welcome guests inside to an equally impressive interior. Both the foyer and family room have two-story ceilings. The family room includes such amenities as a fireplace, built-in shelves, and access to the rear porch. A bay window expands the breakfast nook, located adjacent to the U-shaped kitchen. The living room/study and bonus room add flexibility for changing needs. The master suite, conveniently located on the first level, is complete with linen shelves, two walk-in closets, and a master bath featuring a double vanity, garden tub, separate shower, and private privy. The second level holds three more bedrooms, two bathrooms, bonus space, and an overlook to the family room.

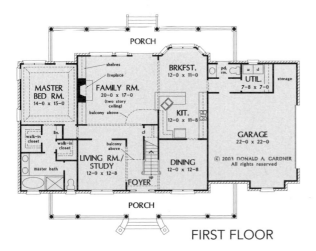

FIRST FLOOR

SECOND FLOOR

FIRST FLOOR

SECOND FLOOR

© 1998 DONALD A. GARDNER
All rights reserved

STORAGE
12-0 x 8-10

GARAGE
22-0 x 22-0

storage

UTILITY

DECK

BRKFST.
9-8 x 13-0

KITCHEN
11-0 x 13-2

pan.

storage

STUDY
11-0 x 13-0

master
bath

walk-in
closet

DINING
11-0 x 17-4

(cathedral ceiling)

GREAT RM.
22-0 x 18-0

(cathedral ceiling)

fireplace

MASTER
BED RM.
15-0 x 17-10

PORCH

attic storage

STORAGE
11-4 x 15-8

attic storage

BED RM.
11-4 x 12-8

attic storage

BED RM.
13-0 x 13-0

bath

skylight

up

up
down

LOFT/
STUDY
12-0 x 13-0

attic storage

dining room
below

great room
below

THIS FINE THREE-BEDROOM HOME IS FULL OF AMENITIES AND WILL SURELY BE A FAMILY FAVORITE! A covered porch leads into the great room/dining room. Here, a fireplace reigns at one end, casting its glow throughout the room. A private study is tucked away, perfect for a home office or computer study. The master bedroom suite offers a bayed sitting area, large walk-in closet, and pampering bath. With plenty of counter and cabinet space and an adjacent breakfast area, the kitchen will be a favorite gathering place for casual mealtimes. The family sleeping zone is upstairs and includes two bedrooms, a full bath, a loft/study area, and a huge storage room.

HOME PLAN

 # HPK2700203

Style: Country
First Floor: 1,896 sq. ft.
Second Floor: 692 sq. ft.
Total: 2,588 sq. ft.
Bedrooms: 3
Bathrooms: 2 ½
Width: 60' - 0"
Depth: 84' - 10"

eplans.com

THIS MODERN TAKE ON THE ITALIAN

villa boasts plenty of indoor/outdoor flow. Four sets of double
doors wrap around the great room and dining area and open to the stunning veranda.
The great room is enhanced by a coffered ceiling and built-in cabinetry, and the entire first floor is bathed in
sunlight from a wall of glass doors overlooking the veranda. The dining room connects to a gourmet island
kitchen. Upstairs, a beautiful deck wraps gracefully around the family bedrooms. The master suite is a skylit
haven enhanced by a sitting bay, which features a vaulted octagonal ceiling and a cozy two-sided fireplace.
Private double doors access the sundeck from the master suite,
the secondary bedrooms, and the study.

HOME PLAN

HPK2700204

Style: Italianate

First Floor: 1,266 sq. ft.

Second Floor: 1,324 sq. ft.

Total: 2,590 sq. ft.

Bedrooms: 3

Bathrooms: 2 ½

Width: 34' - 0"

Depth: 63' - 2"

Foundation: Slab

eplans.com

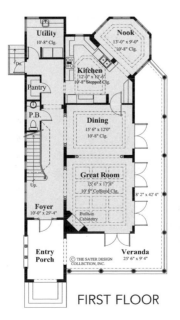

FIRST FLOOR

SECOND FLOOR

FIRST FLOOR

SECOND FLOOR

HOME PLAN

HPK2700205

Style: Colonial Revival

First Floor: 1,809 sq. ft.

Second Floor: 785 sq. ft.

Total: 2,594 sq. ft.

Bonus Space: 353 sq. ft.

Bedrooms: 5

Bathrooms: 4

Width: 72' - 7"

Depth: 51' - 5"

Foundation: Crawlspace, Slab, Unfinished Walkout Basement

eplans.com

WITH ELEMENTS OF COUNTRY STYLE, THIS UNIQUE COLONIAL-INSPIRED HOME presents a rustic attitude blended with the delicate features that make this design one of a kind. Upon entry, a second-story arched window lights the foyer. Straight ahead, the family room soars with a two-story vault balanced by a cozy fireplace. A pass-through from the island kitchen keeps conversation going as the family chef whips up delectable feasts for the formal dining room or bayed breakfast nook. A bedroom at the rear provides plenty of privacy for guests, or as a home office. The master suite takes up the entire right wing, hosting a bayed sitting area and marvelous vaulted bath. Upstairs, three bedrooms access a versatile bonus room, limited only by your imagination.

HOME PLAN

HPK2700206

Style: Tudor

First Floor: 2,050 sq. ft.

Second Floor: 561 sq. ft.

Total: 2,611 sq. ft.

Bonus Space: 272 sq. ft.

Bedrooms: 4

Bathrooms: 3

Width: 64' - 10"

Depth: 64' - 0"

Foundation: Crawlspace, Slab, Unfinished Basement

eplans.com

OLD WORLD AMBIANCE CHARACTERIZES THIS EUROPEAN-STYLE HOME. The elegant stone entrance opens to the two-story foyer. A well-proportioned dining room is viewed through an arch flanked by columns. The oversized great room features a coffered ceiling and a see-through fireplace that can be viewed from the kitchen, breakfast room, and great room. The master suite includes a luxury bath and a cozy sitting area off the bedroom. A second bedroom on this floor acts as a nursery, guest room, or study. Upstairs, two bedrooms share a bath, and an expandable area is available for future use.

FIRST FLOOR

SECOND FLOOR

BREAKFAST AREA 12'-1" X 9'-10"

PORCH

STORAGE

UTILITY

SINK

KITCHEN 12'-6" X 11'-0"

BAR

FAMILY ROOM 20'-0" X 15'-4"

CHINA

OVENS

PANTRY

P'DR ROOM

GARAGE 21'-0" X 22'-0"

DINING ROOM 12'-6" X 12'-0"

UP

LIVING ROOM 13'-0" X 12'-0"

© William E. Poole Designs

FIRST FLOOR

PORCH

PORCH

ROOF AREA

MASTER BEDROOM 17'-0" X 15'-4"

WHIRLPOOL TUB

MASTER BATH

LINEN

BEDROOM 4 15'-6" X 15'-0"

BATH 3

WARDROBE 15'-6" X 6'-0"

DOWN

WOOD RAIL

WALK-IN CLOSET

8' CEILING BREAK LINE

LINEN

BEDROOM 2 12'-6" X 12'-0"

BATH 2

BEDROOM 3 12'-0" X 12'-0"

ROOF AREA

SECOND FLOOR

PORCH

THIS TWO-STORY HOME SUITS THE NEEDS OF EACH HOUSEHOLD MEMBER. Family gatherings won't be crowded in the spacious family room, which is adjacent to the kitchen and the breakfast area. Just beyond the foyer, the dining and living rooms view the front yard. The master suite features its own full bath with dual vanities, a whirlpool tub, and separate shower. Three family bedrooms—one with a walk-in closet—and two full hall baths are available upstairs. Extra storage space is found in the two-car garage

HPK2700207

HOME PLAN

Style: Neoclassical

First Floor: 1,273 sq. ft.

Second Floor: 1,358 sq. ft.

Total: 2,631 sq. ft.

Bedrooms: 4

Bathrooms: 3 ½

Width: 54' - 10"

Depth: 48' - 6"

Foundation: Crawlspace

eplans.com

© William E. Poole Designs, Inc.

HOME PLAN

HPK2700208

Style: Queen Anne

First Floor: 1,362 sq. ft.

Second Floor: 1,270 sq. ft.

Total: 2,632 sq. ft.

Bedrooms: 4

Bathrooms: 2 ½

Width: 79' - 0"

Depth: 44' - 0"

Foundation: Crawlspace, Unfinished Basement

eplans.com

RICH WITH VICTORIAN DETAILS—SCALLOPED SHINGLES, a wraparound veranda, and turrets—this beautiful facade conceals a modern floor plan. Archways announce a distinctive tray-ceilinged living room and help define the dining room. An octagonal den across from the foyer provides a private spot for reading or studying. The U-shaped island kitchen holds an octagonal breakfast bay and a pass-through breakfast bar to the family room. Upstairs, three family bedrooms share a hall bath—one bedroom is within a turret. The master suite is complete with a sitting room with a bay window, along with a fancy bath set in another of the turrets.

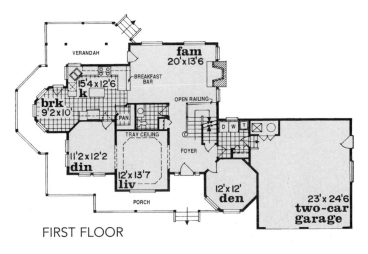

FIRST FLOOR

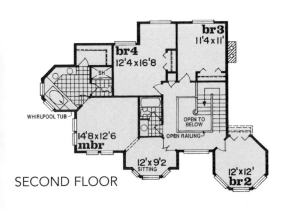

SECOND FLOOR

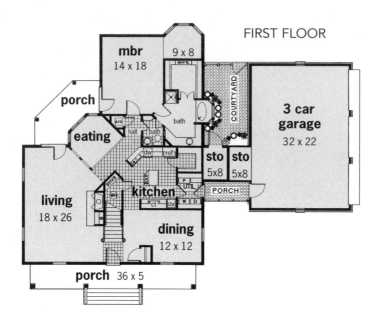

FIRST FLOOR

SECOND FLOOR

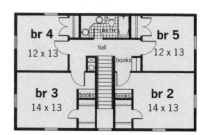

BEAUTIFUL BY THE SEA OR OUT IN THE COUNTRY, this wonderful home is designed for outdoor living. Three porches and a brick-paved courtyard are easily accessible for year-round relaxation and endless entertaining possibilities. Enter the home and turn to the left for an ample living room, warmed by a fireplace. Just ahead, the tiled kitchen offers a brilliant layout and an island serving bar, easily hosting the eating nook and dining room. At the rear, the master suite offers a bayed sitting area and a lavish bath with a spa tub. Upstairs, four generous bedrooms share a dual-vanity bath. The home is completed by a three-car garage and plenty of extra storage.

HOME PLAN

HPK2700209

Style: Tidewater

First Floor: 1,671 sq. ft.

Second Floor: 980 sq. ft.

Total: 2,651 sq. ft.

Bedrooms: 5

Bathrooms: 2

Width: 72' - 0"

Depth: 58' - 0"

Foundation: Crawlspace, Slab, Unfinished Basement

eplans.com

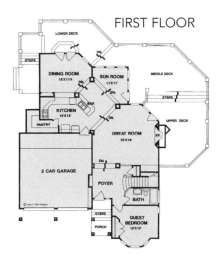

REAR EXTERIOR

CLEAN, CONTEMPORARY LINES, A UNIQUE FLOOR PLAN, and a metal roof with a cupola set this plan apart. Remote-control transoms in the cupola open to create an airy and decidedly unique foyer. The great room, sunroom, dining room, and kitchen flow from one to another for casual entertaining with flair. The rear of the home is fashioned with plenty of windows overlooking the multilevel deck. A front bedroom and bath would make a comfortable guest suite. The master bedroom and bath upstairs are bridged by a pipe-rail balcony that also gives access to a rear deck. An additional bedroom, home office, and bath complete this very special plan.

HOME PLAN

HPK2700210

Style: New American

First Floor: 1,309 sq. ft.

Second Floor: 1,343 sq. ft.

Total: 2,652 sq. ft.

Bedrooms: 3

Bathrooms: 3

Width: 44' - 4"

Depth: 58' - 2"

Foundation: Crawlspace

eplans.com

FIRST FLOOR   SECOND FLOOR

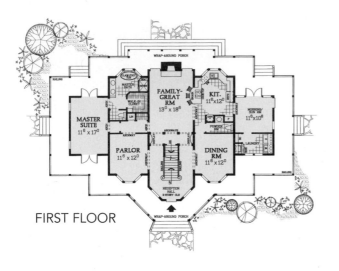

FIRST FLOOR

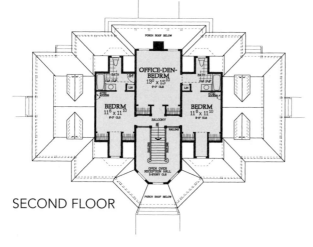

SECOND FLOOR

DELIGHTFULLY PROPORTIONED AND SUPERBLY SYMMETRICAL, this Victorian farmhouse has lots of curb appeal. The wraparound porch offers rustic columns and railings, and broad steps present easy access to the front, rear, and side yards. Archways, display niches, and columns help define the great room, which offers a fireplace framed by views to the rear property. A formal parlor and a dining room flank the reception hall, and each offers a bay window. The master suite boasts two sets of French doors to the wraparound porch and a private bath with a clawfoot tub, twin lavatories, a walk-in closet, and a stall shower. Upstairs, a spacious office/den adjoins two family bedrooms, each with a private bath.

HPK2700211

Style: Victorian Eclectic

First Floor: 1,752 sq. ft.

Second Floor: 906 sq. ft.

Total: 2,658 sq. ft.

Bedrooms: 4

Bathrooms: 3 ½

Width: 74' - 0"

Depth: 51' - 7"

Foundation: Unfinished Basement

HOME PLAN

eplans.com

A SWEEPING FRONT PORCH AND A REAR COVERED PATIO

that leads to an inviting swimming pool mark this outstanding plan as the right home for an active, outward-looking family. An impressive entrance brings you to a spacious gallery that opens to a study, the formal dining room, and to a living room designed for gracious entertaining. The kitchen boasts an island counter that will put most tasks within an arm's reach. An absolutely lavish master suite is also found on the main floor, and two other bedrooms, a full bath, and lots of room for expansion are located upstairs. The house comes with a three-car garage.

HOME PLAN

HPK2700212

Style: Farmhouse

First Floor: 2,074 sq. ft.

Second Floor: 600 sq. ft.

Total: 2,674 sq. ft.

Bonus Space: 520 sq. ft.

Bedrooms: 4

Bathrooms: 3

Width: 88' - 0"

Depth: 36' - 10"

Foundation: Slab

eplans.com

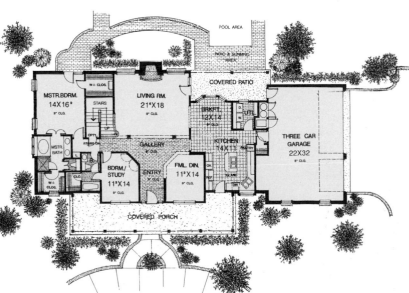

FIRST FLOOR

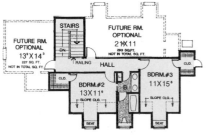

SECOND FLOOR

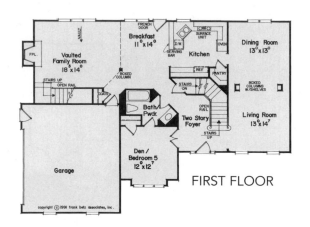

FIRST FLOOR

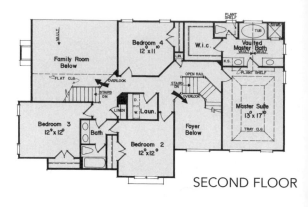

SECOND FLOOR

HOME PLAN #

HPK2700213

Style: New American

First Floor: 1,424 sq. ft.

Second Floor: 1,256 sq. ft.

Total: 2,680 sq. ft.

Bedrooms: 5

Bathrooms: 3

Width: 57' - 0"

Depth: 41' - 0"

Foundation: Crawlspace, Slab, Unfinished Walkout Basement

eplans.com

A GRAND TWO-STORY FOYER TAKES ITS CHARM FROM A BRIGHT CLERESTORY WINDOW. Just off the foyer lies the formal living area, where the living room joins the dining room with twin boxed columns that are personalized with shelves. The kitchen is placed to easily serve the dining room, yet it remains open to the breakfast area and vaulted family room. Upstairs, the master suite and bath are nicely balanced with three family bedrooms, a full hall bath, and convenient laundry room.

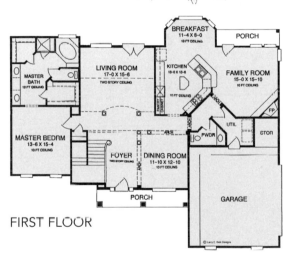

FIRST FLOOR

SECOND FLOOR

 # HPK2700214

HOME PLAN

Style: New American
First Floor: 1,844 sq. ft.
Second Floor: 841 sq. ft.
Total: 2,685 sq. ft.
Bonus Space: 455 sq. ft.
Bedrooms: 4
Bathrooms: 2 ½
Width: 62' - 6"
Depth: 52' - 10"
Foundation: Slab

eplans.com

TWO SHED DORMERS AND A FRONT PORCH THAT'S PERFECT FOR EVENING RELAXATION
evoke the charm of the country farmhouse in a home designed for the constraints of a suburban lot. Inside, impact is created at the front door with a dining room defined by columns and connecting arched openings. The conveniently designed kitchen features a work island and an eating bar. The family room, with its corner fireplace, accesses a rear covered porch. Three bedrooms and a bath are located on the second floor. A large area for a future game room or craft room is located over the garage and makes this plan a great choice for the growing family.

FIRST FLOOR

SECOND FLOOR

A GRAND FACADE IS A PERFECT INTRODUCTION to this stately two-story home that's designed for both formal and casual family living. A two-story foyer that leads to the vaulted living room is punctuated by a dramatic arch with a plant shelf above. Formal entertaining areas are nicely balanced with the vaulted family room and the gourmet kitchen and breakfast nook. The first-floor master suite is designed for luxury and privacy. Upstairs are three family bedrooms—each has a walk-in closet and private bath access.

HOME PLAN

HPK2700215

Style: New American

First Floor: 1,883 sq. ft.

Second Floor: 803 sq. ft.

Total: 2,686 sq. ft.

Bedrooms: 4

Bathrooms: 3 ½

Width: 58' - 6"

Depth: 59' - 4"

Foundation: Crawlspace, Unfinished Walkout Basement

eplans.com

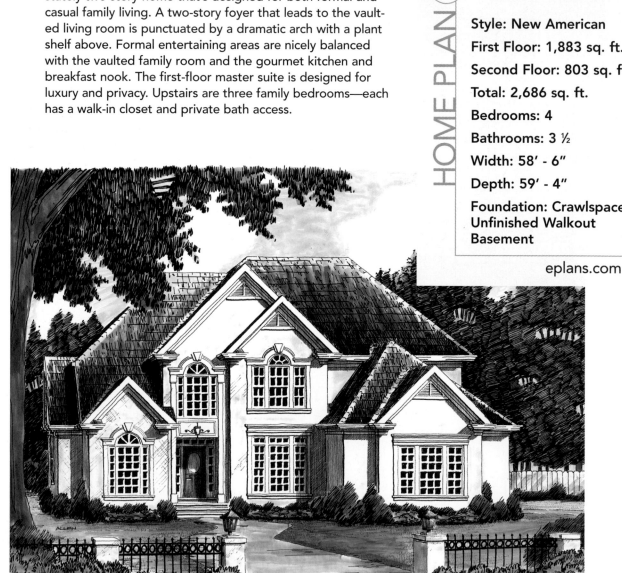

HOME PLAN

HPK2700216

Design: HPK2700216

Style: Farmhouse

First Floor: 1,883 sq. ft.

Second Floor: 803 sq. ft.

Total: 2,686 sq. ft.

Bonus Space: 489 sq. ft.

Bedrooms: 3

Bathrooms: 3 ½

Width: 63' - 0"

Depth: 81' - 10"

Foundation: Crawlspace

eplans.com

WHERE CREEKS CONVERGE AND MARSH GRASSES SWAY in gentle breezes, this is a classical low-country home. Steep rooflines, high ceilings, front and back porches, plus long and low windows are typical details of these charming planter's cottages. The foyer is flanked by the formal dining room and the living room, which opens to the family room. Here, several windows look out to the terrace and a fireplace removes the chill on a winter's night. The sunny breakfast room, which adjoins the kitchen, offers a wonderful space for casual dining. Two bedrooms, the lavish master suite, and the two-car garage complete the floor plan.

FIRST FLOOR

SECOND FLOOR

FIRST FLOOR

SECOND FLOOR

HPK2700217

Style: Farmhouse

First Floor: 1,297 sq. ft.

Second Floor: 1,390 sq. ft.

Total: 2,687 sq. ft.

Bonus Space: 229 sq. ft.

Bedrooms: 3

Bathrooms: 2 ½

Width: 60' - 0"

Depth: 44' - 0"

Foundation: Unfinished Basement

eplans.com

A TRULY LAVISH MASTER SUITE RESIDES ON THE SECOND FLOOR OF THIS COMPLEX TWO-STORY FARMHOUSE. The recessed entry opens to the dining room and kitchen with the family room on the right. The massive wraparound porch can be accessed from the family room, living room, and the sunny breakfast bay. The island kitchen is conveniently placed between the dining room and the well-equipped utility room. On the second floor, the master suite enjoys a fireplace, a pampering bath, and access to the second-floor deck.

© 2003 Donald A. Gardner, Inc.

THIS FARMHOUSE HAS A TOUCH OF LOW-COUNTRY FLAIR. Columns and dormers accent a deep porch, and gables and half-circle transoms add angles and soft curves for architectural interest. Floor space is expanded by bay windows, which usher light into the home. Convenient features such as a central kitchen island, large utility room/mudroom, and two built-in desks in the secondary bedrooms make living easier for active families. The master suite includes a tray ceiling, dual walk-ins, and a private bath. A versatile study/bedroom and bonus room adapt as your family grows.

HOME PLAN

HPK2700218

Style: Tidewater

First Floor: 1,972 sq. ft.

Second Floor: 721 sq. ft.

Total: 2,693 sq. ft.

Bonus Space: 377 sq. ft.

Bedrooms: 4

Bathrooms: 3

Width: 77' - 4"

Depth: 50' - 8"

eplans.com

FIRST FLOOR

SECOND FLOOR

FIRST FLOOR

SECOND FLOOR

HPK2700219

Style: French Country

First Floor: 1,904 sq. ft.

Second Floor: 792 sq. ft.

Total: 2,696 sq. ft.

Bedrooms: 4

Bathrooms: 3

Width: 67' - 8"

Depth: 64' - 10"

Foundation: Crawlspace, Slab, Unfinished Basement

eplans.com

THIS CHARMING COTTAGE HAS ALL THE ACCOUTREMENTS OF A FRENCH COUNTRY HOME. Inside, the angled foyer directs the eye to the arched entrances of the formal dining room and the great room with its fireplace and patio access. The master bedroom and a guest bedroom (or possible study) are located at the opposite end of the house for privacy. Two additional bedrooms, a full bath, a game room and an upper deck are located on the second floor.

Photo Courtesy of: Karen Stuthard. This home, as shown in photographs, may differ from the actual blueprints. For more detailed information, please check the floor plans carefully.

THIS RUSTIC STONE-AND-SIDING EXTERIOR with Craftsman influences includes a multitude of windows flooding the interior with natural light. The foyer opens to the great room, which is complete with three sets of French doors and a two-sided fireplace. The master suite offers an expansive private bath, two large walk-in closets, a bay window, and a tray ceiling. The dining room, kitchen, and utility room make an efficient trio.

 HOME PLAN

HPK2700220

Style: Farmhouse

First Floor: 1,798 sq. ft.

Second Floor: 900 sq. ft.

Total: 2,698 sq. ft.

Bedrooms: 3

Bathrooms: 3 ½

Width: 54' - 0"

Depth: 57' - 0"

Foundation: Crawlspace

eplans.com

FIRST FLOOR

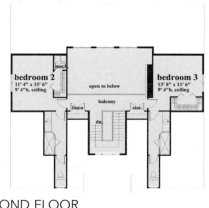

SECOND FLOOR

A FRENCH COUNTRY DESIGN WITH A TASTE FOR FORMAL LIVING, this plan provides good separation between the kitchen and dining room. The study at the left of the home, featuring a tray ceiling, is similarly suited for quiet use. The first-floor master suite provides a full set of amenities, including direct access to the porch. The two-story great room brings light and air to the center of the plan. Head upstairs for the home's remaining bedrooms, which find privacy at opposite ends of the plan. No sharing of bathrooms is necessary in this family-minded design.

FIRST FLOOR

HOME PLAN

HPK2700221

Style: French Country

First Floor: 1,931 sq. ft.

Second Floor: 768 sq. ft.

Total: 2,699 sq. ft.

Bonus Space: 220 sq. ft.

Bedrooms: 4

Bathrooms: 3 ½

Width: 56' - 0"

Depth: 56' - 7"

Foundation: Slab

eplans.com

SECOND FLOOR

THIS GORGEOUS FARMHOUSE COMES WITH THREE DORMERS, A COVERED PORCH, and a facade of stone, shingles, and siding. A side-facing garage helps create an appealing neighborhood design. An open dining room sits off the foyer, and features decorative columns and window alcove. The two-story grand room shows off its two-way fireplace, and views to the rear yard. The kitchen will be the hub of activity with an island workspace, breakfast area, adjoining keeping room with fireplace, and built-ins. The first-floor master suite is the picture of indulgence, offering a coffered ceiling, see-through fireplace, His and Hers walk-in closets, and sumptuous bath. Upstairs, three family bedrooms—one with its own bath—can share a bonus room and plenty of closet space.

HPK2700222

Style: Country

First Floor: 1,878 sq. ft.

Second Floor: 826 sq. ft.

Total: 2,704 sq. ft.

Bonus Space: 299 sq. ft.

Bedrooms: 4

Bathrooms: 3 ½

Width: 54' - 0"

Depth: 64' - 0"

Foundation: Slab, Unfinished Walkout Basement

eplans.com

FIRST FLOOR

SECOND FLOOR

FIRST FLOOR

SECOND FLOOR

HPK2700223

Style: New American

First Floor: 1,930 sq. ft.

Second Floor: 791 sq. ft.

Total: 2,721 sq. ft.

Bedrooms: 4

Bathrooms: 3

Width: 64' - 4"

Depth: 62' - 0"

Foundation: Crawlspace, Slab, Unfinished Basement

eplans.com

A DELIGHTFUL FACADE WITH A FLARED ROOF CAPTURES THE EYE and provides just the right touch for this inviting home. Inside, an angled foyer with a volume ceiling directs attention to the enormous great room. The detailed dining room includes massive round columns connected by arches and shares a through-fireplace with the great room. The master suite includes an upscale bath and access to a private covered porch. Nearby, Bedroom 2 is perfect for a nursery or home office/study. The kitchen features a large cooktop island and walk-in pantry. The second floor is dominated by an oversized game room. Two family bedrooms, a bath, and a linen closet complete the upstairs.

THE COLUMNED FOYER OF THIS HOME WEL-COMES YOU into a series of spaces that reach out in all directions. The living room has a spectacular view of the huge covered patio area that's perfect for summer entertaining. The dining room features a tray ceiling and French doors that lead to a covered porch. A secluded master suite affords great views through French doors and also has a tray ceiling. The family wing combines an island kitchen, nook, and family gathering space, with the built in media/fireplace wall the center of attention. Two secondary bedrooms share a bath. A staircase overlooking the family room takes you up to the sunroom complete with a full bath.

HPK2700224

Style: Mediterranean

First Floor: 2,365 sq. ft.

Second Floor: 364 sq. ft.

Total: 2,729 sq. ft.

Bedrooms: 3

Bathrooms: 3

Width: 69' - 0"

Depth: 70' - 0"

Foundation: Slab

HOME PLAN

eplans.com

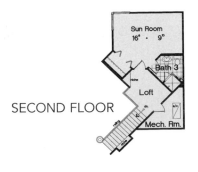

FIRST FLOOR

SECOND FLOOR

FIRST FLOOR

SECOND FLOOR

STONE AND SIDING, GABLES AND RAFTER TAILS, WINDOW DETAIL, and a wonderful floor plan—all elements of a fantastic Craftsman home. This two-story four-bedroom home is designed for today's active family. The foyer is flanked by a spacious living room with a fireplace to the right and a cozy den entered through double doors to the left. At the rear of the home, a large family room offers a corner fireplace and a wall of windows. A huge kitchen is enhanced by plenty of counter and cabinet space, a large cooktop work island, a corner sink, and an adjacent sunny nook with access to the rear yard. Upstairs, three family bedrooms share a full hall bath, while the master bedroom is filled with amenities.

HOME PLAN

HPK2700225

Style: Craftsman

First Floor: 1,578 sq. ft.

Second Floor: 1,159 sq. ft.

Total: 2,737 sq. ft.

Bedrooms: 4

Bathrooms: 3

Width: 63' - 0"

Depth: 53' - 0"

Foundation: Crawlspace

eplans.com

MULTIPANE GLASS WINDOWS, FRENCH DOORS, and an arched pediment with columns create a spectacular exterior with this blue-ribbon design. A two-story foyer opens to formal areas and, through French doors, to a secluded den with built-in cabinetry and a coat closet. The gourmet kitchen enjoys a morning nook. Second-floor sleeping quarters include a master bedroom with a tile-rimmed spa tub, twin vanities, and a walk-in closet. This plan offers the option of replacing the family room's vaulted ceiling with a fifth bedroom above.

HOME PLAN

HPK2700226

Style: New American

First Floor: 1,470 sq. ft.

Second Floor: 1,269 sq. ft.

Total: 2,739 sq. ft.

Bedrooms: 4

Bathrooms: 2 ½

Width: 70' - 0"

Depth: 47' - 0"

Foundation: Crawlspace

eplans.com

FIRST FLOOR

SECOND FLOOR

THE ARCHED COURTYARD ENTRANCE IS A PERFECT INTRODUCTION to this plan's wonderful livability—indoors and out. Open spaces and interesting angles greet you at the foyer, which is elegantly intersected with a curved stairway. The formal dining room opens to the large covered patio, perfect for entertaining and outdoor meals. The living room enjoys a dramatic corner fireplace with a raised hearth and is open to the oversized kitchen through a snack bar. A built-in breakfast booth joins the kitchen to the casual family room. The master suite is a welcome retreat thanks to a raised-hearth fireplace, patio door, and lavish bath. Up the grand stairway, a lovely window bench frames the hallway leading to two family bedrooms, which share a compartmented bath, and to the guest suite with a private bath.

FIRST FLOOR

HPK2700227

Style: Pueblo

First Floor: 1,911 sq. ft.

Second Floor: 828 sq. ft.

Total: 2,739 sq. ft.

Bedrooms: 4

Bathrooms: 3 ½

Width: 87' - 10"

Depth: 60' - 8"

Foundation: Slab

HOME PLAN

SECOND FLOOR

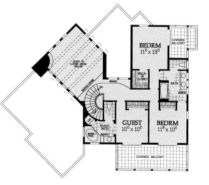

eplans.com

A TOUCH OF VICTORIANA ENHANCES THE FACADE of this home: a turret roof over a wraparound porch with turned wood spindles. Special attractions on the first floor include a tray ceiling in the octagonal living room, fireplaces in the country kitchen and the living room, a coffered ceiling in the family room, and double-door access to the cozy den. The master suite, set in the upper level of the turret, boasts a coffered ceiling, walk-in closet, and whirlpool tub. Three family bedrooms and a full hall bath join the master suite on the second floor.

HOME PLAN

HPK2700228

Style: Queen Anne

First Floor: 1,462 sq. ft.

Second Floor: 1,288 sq. ft.

Total: 2,750 sq. ft.

Bedrooms: 4

Bathrooms: 2 ½

Width: 70' - 8"

Depth: 54' - 0"

Foundation: Crawlspace, Unfinished Basement

eplans.com

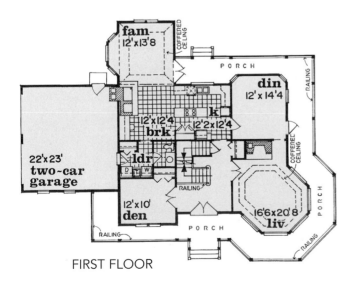

FIRST FLOOR

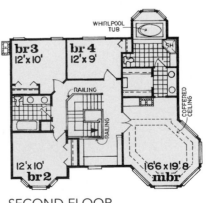

SECOND FLOOR

FIRST FLOOR

SECOND FLOOR

THIS CHARMING TWO-STORY TRADITIONAL HOME WELCOMES IN ABUNDANT NATURAL LIGHT with its multitude of windows. The two-story foyer with its grand staircase is flanked by the dining room to the left and the living room to the right. The vaulted family room to the rear delights with picturesque views and a warming fireplace. The angled kitchen will easily serve the dining room, breakfast area, and family room. A study/bedroom is tucked away to the left, and the master suite finds privacy to the right. Two additional bedrooms and optional space for a third are located on the second floor along with two full baths.

HOME PLAN

HPK2700229

Style: New American

First Floor: 2,026 sq. ft.

Second Floor: 726 sq. ft.

Total: 2,752 sq. ft.

Bonus Space: 277 sq. ft.

Bedrooms: 4

Bathrooms: 4 ½

Width: 61' - 6"

Depth: 56' - 0"

Foundation: Crawlspace, Slab, Unfinished Walkout Basement

eplans.com

HOME PLAN

HPK2700230

Style: French Country

First Floor: 2,084 sq. ft.

Second Floor: 671 sq. ft.

Total: 2,755 sq. ft.

Bedrooms: 4

Bathrooms: 3

Width: 57' - 4"

Depth: 55' - 10"

Foundation: Crawlspace, Slab

eplans.com

A CREATIVE BLEND OF EXTERIOR MATERIALS GIVES THIS HOME A STUNNING FACADE. The generous great room will provide the perfect setting for family gatherings. Preparing and serving meals will be a breeze in this kitchen with adjoining breakfast and dining rooms. A spacious grilling porch also lends outdoor options. The master suite is nestled in the rear of this home on the main level. A trip to the upper floor offers beautiful balcony views of the great room and the foyer, as well as two more bedrooms and a media room option.

FIRST FLOOR

SECOND FLOOR

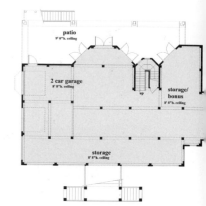

FIRST FLOOR

SECOND FLOOR

THIS SOUTHERN TIDEWATER COTTAGE IS THE PERFECT VACATION HIDEAWAY. An octagonal great room with a multifaceted vaulted ceiling illuminates the interior. The island kitchen is brightened by a bumped-out window and a pass-through to the lanai. Two walk-in closets and a whirlpool bath await to indulge the homeowner in the master suite. A set of double doors opens to the vaulted master lanai for quiet comfort. The U-shaped staircase leads to a loft, which overlooks the great room and the foyer. Two additional family bedrooms offer private baths. A computer center and a morning kitchen complete the upper level.

HOME PLAN # HPK2700231

Style: Plantation

First Floor: 1,855 sq. ft.

Second Floor: 901 sq. ft.

Total: 2,756 sq. ft.

Bedrooms: 3

Bathrooms: 3 ½

Width: 66' - 0"

Depth: 50' - 0"

Foundation: Island Basement

eplans.com

© William E. Poole Designs, Inc.

HOME PLAN

HPK2700232

Style: French Country

First Floor: 1,805 sq. ft.

Second Floor: 952 sq. ft.

Total: 2,757 sq. ft.

Bonus Space: 475 sq. ft.

Bedrooms: 4

Bathrooms: 3 ½

Width: 48' - 10"

Depth: 64' - 10"

Foundation: Crawlspace, Unfinished Basement

eplans.com

FIRST FLOOR

© William E. Poole Designs

SECOND FLOOR

THE EUROPEAN ALLURE OF THIS STUNNING TWO-STORY HOME WILL BE THE DELIGHT OF THE NEIGHBORHOOD. With the living room to the right, the foyer leads to the family room with a magnificent view of the outdoors. The island kitchen is thoughtfully situated between the sunny breakfast area and the formal dining room, which opens to the side terrace. The master suite finds privacy on the first floor; the three family bedrooms share two full baths on the second floor.

HOME PLAN

HPK2700233

Style: Colonial Revival

First Floor: 1,364 sq. ft.

Second Floor: 1,398 sq. ft.

Total: 2,762 sq. ft.

Bedrooms: 5

Bathrooms: 4

Width: 51' - 0"

Depth: 45' - 4"

Foundation: Crawlspace, Unfinished Walkout Basement

eplans.com

THIS STURDY SOUTHERN COLONIAL HOME is perfect for a large family that likes to stretch out—and it's great for entertaining, too. Upstairs, four bedrooms, including a ravishing master suite, provide ample sleeping quarters. A laundry is conveniently located on this level. Downstairs, a den that could serve as a guest bedroom enjoys hall access to a full bath. Nearby is a study. The two-story family room opens one way to the formal dining area, and the other way to the casual eating area and kitchen, outfitted with a time-saving island counter.

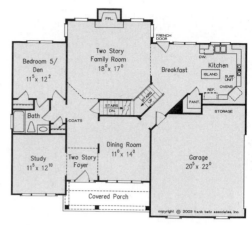

FIRST FLOOR

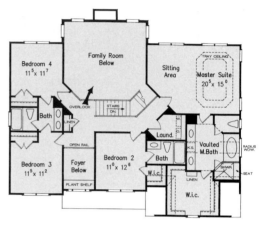

SECOND FLOOR

THE EXTERIOR OF THIS HOME IS STRIKING WITH ITS BRICK FACADE, quoins, sunburst window above the doorway, French-style shutters, and cut-brick jack arches above the windows. The two-story entry leads to a family dining room on the left and a living room with a fireplace on the right. It leads further through a gallery to the family room. The kitchen flows into a charming breakfast area that accesses a large patio, perfect for barbecues and small outdoor get-togethers. The master suite is located downstairs, allowing for privacy, while Bedrooms 2, 3 and 4 reside upstairs, where they share a balcony that overlooks the family room below.

HOME PLAN

HPK2700234

Style: New American

First Floor: 1,896 sq. ft.

Second Floor: 872 sq. ft.

Total: 2,768 sq. ft.

Bedrooms: 4

Bathrooms: 3 ½

Width: 61' - 0"

Depth: 57' - 0"

Foundation: Slab, Unfinished Basement

eplans.com

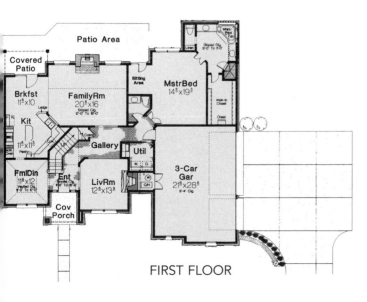

FIRST FLOOR

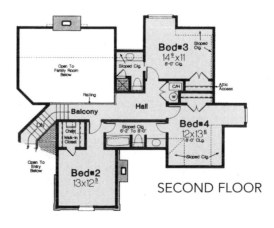

SECOND FLOOR

A WRAPAROUND PORCH MAKES THIS UNIQUE VICTORIAN FARMHOUSE stand out with style and grace, as does the lovely detailing of this plan. This design is versatile enough to accommodate either a small or large family. The entry is flanked on the left side by a large kitchen/breakfast area with an island, and on the right side by a parlor/music room. The family room is enhanced with a bar ledge, fireplace, and built-in entertainment center. The master suite has access to a covered deck. The upstairs level is shared by three bedrooms, two full baths, and a bonus room. A 448-square-foot apartment is located over the garage.

SECOND FLOOR

HOME PLAN # HPK2700235

Style: Gothic Revival

First Floor: 2,023 sq. ft.

Second Floor: 749 sq. ft.

Total: 2,772 sq. ft.

Bonus Space: 242 sq. ft.

Bedrooms: 5

Bathrooms: 4 ½

Width: 77' - 2"

Depth: 57' - 11"

Foundation: Slab, Unfinished Basement

eplans.com

FIRST FLOOR

A FRONT PORCH AND

A WRAPAROUND SIDE PORCH provide plenty of outdoor living space for this lovely colonial home. The great room is warmed by a cozy fireplace and provides dual access to the wraparound porch. The U-shaped kitchen shares space with a breakfast nook-perfect for informal meals. The other end of the kitchen adjoins the bay-windowed dining room. The second floor contains the master suite, two secondary bedrooms, and a full bath. The spacious master bedroom furnishes angled entry to a luxurious bath with a corner whirlpool tub, a separate shower, and a huge walk-in closet. This home is designed with a basement foundation.

 # HPK2700236

Style: Federal - Adams

First Floor: 1,440 sq. ft.

Second Floor: 1,339 sq. ft.

Total: 2,779 sq. ft.

Bedrooms: 3

Bathrooms: 2 ½

Width: 47' - 6"

Depth: 75' - 3"

Foundation: Finished Walkout Basement

eplans.com

FIRST FLOOR

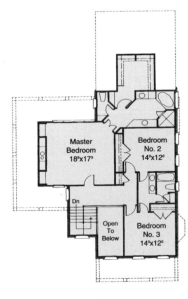

SECOND FLOOR

HPK2700237

Style: Georgian

First Floor: 1,587 sq. ft.

Second Floor: 1,191 sq. ft.

Total: 2,778 sq. ft.

Bedrooms: 3

Bathrooms: 2 ½

Width: 29' - 6"

Depth: 93' - 8"

Foundation: Slab

eplans.com

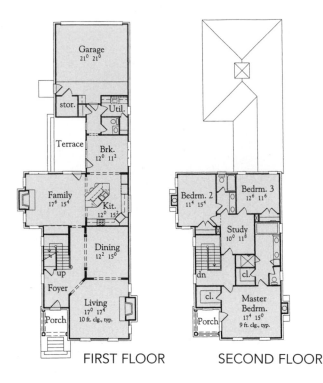

FIRST FLOOR   SECOND FLOOR

BOX-PANELED SHUTTERS ADD A TOUCH OF CLASS TO THIS TOWN DESIGN—A HOME that is simply the ultimate in comfort and style. A winding staircase highlights a refined foyer that sets the pace for the entire home. Fireplaces warm the formal and casual rooms, which can accommodate all occasions. The well-organized kitchen provides a snack bar for easy meals and serves the formal dining room with ease. Upstairs, two secondary bedrooms share a full bath and a study that could be used as a computer room. The master suite boasts two walk-in closets, an indulgent bath, and a private porch.

HPK2700238

Style: Greek Revival

First Floor: 1,332 sq. ft.

Second Floor: 1,457 sq. ft.

Total: 2,789 sq. ft.

Bedrooms: 4

Bathrooms: 2 ½

Width: 58' - 0"

Depth: 46' - 6"

Foundation: Crawlspace, Unfinished Walkout Basement

eplans.com

THIS DREAM HOME FEATURES DORMERS, MULTI-PANE WINDOWS, and a pediment supported by columns at the entry to accent its brick-and-siding facade. To the right of the entry the dining room accesses both the covered front porch and the angled kitchen. The adjoining breakfast nook offers expansive views to the rear while the spacious family room to the left creates a friendly atmosphere with a warming fireplace. For more formal entertaining, the living room resides to the left of the foyer. Upstairs, three bedrooms share a full bath. The extravagant master suite enjoys a sunny sitting area and an enormous walk-in closet.

FIRST FLOOR

SECOND FLOOR

FIRST FLOOR

SECOND FLOOR

THIS CHARMING SOUTHERN PLANTATION HOME packs quite a punch in 2,800 square feet! The elegant foyer is flanked by the formal dining room and the living room. To the rear, the family room enjoys a fireplace and expansive view of the outdoors. An archway leads to the breakfast area and on to the island kitchen. The luxurious master suite is tucked away for privacy behind the two-car garage. Three additional bedrooms rest on the second floor where they share two full baths. Space above the garage is available for future development.

HPK2700239

HOME PLAN

Style: Federal - Adams

First Floor: 1,927 sq. ft.

Second Floor: 879 sq. ft.

Total: 2,806 sq. ft.

Bonus Space: 459 sq. ft.

Bedrooms: 4

Bathrooms: 3 ½

Width: 71' - 0"

Depth: 53' - 0"

Foundation: Crawlspace

eplans.com

© William E. Poole Designs, Inc.

HOME PLAN #

HPK2700240

Style: Queen Anne

First Floor: 1,632 sq. ft.

Second Floor: 1,188 sq. ft.

Total: 2,820 sq. ft.

Bedrooms: 3

Bathrooms: 2 ½

Width: 61' - 3"

Depth: 68' - 6"

Foundation: Slab

eplans.com

THIS VICTORIAN FARMHOUSE IS DISTINCT BECAUSE OF ITS ORNATE DETAILING, including the decorative pinnacle, covered porch, and front-facing chimney. The living room is graced with a fireplace, wet bar, and tray ceiling. The family room also includes some appreciated amenities: an entertainment center, built-in bookshelves, and access to the covered patio. Upstairs, both the master suite and Bedroom 2 easily access a deck, and all bed rooms sport spacious walk-in closets. Ample attic space is also available for storage.

FIRST FLOOR

SECOND FLOOR

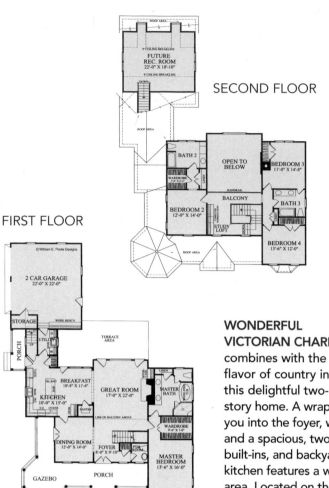

SECOND FLOOR

FIRST FLOOR

HPK2700241

Style: Farmhouse

First Floor: 1,734 sq. ft.

Second Floor: 1,091 sq. ft.

Total: 2,825 sq. ft.

Bonus Space: 488 sq. ft.

Bedrooms: 4

Bathrooms: 3 ½

Width: 57' - 6"

Depth: 80' - 11"

Foundation: Crawlspace, Unfinished Basement

eplans.com

WONDERFUL VICTORIAN CHARM

combines with the flavor of country in this delightful two-story home. A wraparound porch with a gazebo corner welcomes you into the foyer, where the formal dining room waits to the left and a spacious, two-story great room is just ahead. Here, a fireplace, built-ins, and backyard access add to the charm. The L-shaped kitchen features a work-top island, walk-in pantry, and breakfast area. Located on the first floor for privacy, the master suite offers a large walk-in closet and a pampering bath. Upstairs, three bedrooms—one with a private bath—share access to a study loft.

© William E. Poole Designs, Inc.

MASSIVE STONE QUOINS OUT-LINE THE VERTICAL DIMENSIONS of this imposing two-story Georgian design. A recessed entryway looks through the large family room with a fireplace to the covered rear porch. Formal living and dining rooms flank the two-story foyer, and stairs lead up to three bedrooms and two full baths. The first-floor master suite features a large walk-in closet and a full bath. The kitchen opens to a corner breakfast room. The utility room sits just off the kitchen and opens to a hall that leads from the house to the two-car garage.

HOME PLAN

HPK2700242

Style: Georgian

First Floor: 1,904 sq. ft.

Second Floor: 922 sq. ft.

Total: 2,826 sq. ft.

Bedrooms: 4

Bathrooms: 3 ½

Width: 60' - 6"

Depth: 74' - 0"

Foundation: Crawlspace, Slab

eplans.com

FIRST FLOOR

Two-car Garage
21'4" x 25'8"

Utility

Covered Porch
22'6" x 10'

Kitchen

Family Room
22'2" x 17'

Bath

Breakfast Room
12'8" x 10'

12'8" x 17'

Master Bedroom
12'8" x 16'

Dining Room
11'4" x 14'

Foyer

Living Room
11'4" x 10'6"

Porch

SECOND FLOOR

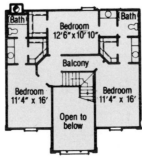

Bath

Bedroom
12'6" x 10'10"

Bath

Balcony

Bedroom
11'4" x 16'

Bedroom
11'4" x 16'

Open to below

FIRST FLOOR

SECOND FLOOR

HOME PLAN

HPK2700243

Style: Contemporary

First Floor: 1,466 sq. ft.

Second Floor: 1,369 sq. ft.

Total: 2,835 sq. ft.

Bedrooms: 4

Bathrooms: 2 ½

Width: 50' - 0"

Depth: 60' - 6"

Foundation: Crawlspace

eplans.com

HERE'S A CONTEMPORARY HOME WITH A SPIRIT!

Comfortably elegant formal rooms reside to the front of the plan, with a focal-point fireplace, a bay window, and decorative columns to help define the space. A central hall leads to the family area, which includes a gourmet kitchen with an island cooktop counter, a bayed breakfast nook, and a vaulted family room with an inglenook. Upstairs, a lavish master suite opens through French doors to a private deck, and a spacious bath boasts a windowed, tile-rimmed spa tub, twin vanities, and a generous walk-in closet. Three family bedrooms cluster around a central hall, which opens to a quiet den and enjoys a balcony overlook.

THIS ELEGANT TWO-STORY BRICK HOME, WITH ITS CORNER QUOINS, VARIED ROOFLINES, AND MULTIPANE WINDOWS, has so many amenities to offer! Enter the two-story foyer graced by an elegant, curved staircase. The formal dining room, defined by columns, is nearby and has double-door access to the efficient island kitchen. The large great room is enhanced by a warming fireplace and direct access to the rear patio. The first-floor master bedroom suite is nicely secluded for privacy and pampers with its own covered porch, His and Hers walk-in closets, and a lavish bath. Upstairs, all three family bedrooms have walk-in closets and share a full hall bath.

FIRST FLOOR

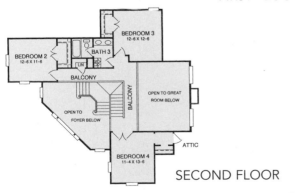

SECOND FLOOR

HPK2700244

HOME PLAN

Style: New American

First Floor: 1,966 sq. ft.

Second Floor: 872 sq. ft.

Total: 2,838 sq. ft.

Bedrooms: 5

Bathrooms: 3

Width: 79' - 10"

Depth: 63' - 10"

Foundation: Crawlspace, Slab, Unfinished Basement

eplans.com

FIRST FLOOR

SECOND FLOOR

HOME PLAN

HPK2700245

Style: Bungalow

First Floor: 2,270 sq. ft.

Second Floor: 461 sq. ft.

Total: 2,731 sq. ft.

Bedrooms: 3

Bathrooms: 3

Width: 70' - 0"

Depth: 73' - 8"

Foundation: Slab

eplans.com

THE WARMTH OF A WRAPAROUND PORCH AND THE TASTEFUL USE OF STACKED FIELDSTONE are what sets this home apart. Upon entry, the relationship between the conversational area and the formal dining room brings a new twist in a traditional layout, by introducing both spaces at an angle. The master suite enjoys living "on the water" with the pool up close. Generous His and Her walk-in closets cap the well-appointed bath. Note the added sink in the toilet chamber! No home built today would be complete without a home office, and this home has one with French doors and a porch. Both secondary bedrooms include private baths.

A LARGE ARCHED WINDOW, TWIN DORMERS, AND AN ENTRY ACCENTED BY A SWOOP ROOF add charm to this inviting two-story home. A rand entry opens to the formal dining room and great room with a fireplace. The roomy kitchen has a large pantry, cooktop island, and snack bar area. Natural sunlight streams in from the bay window in the breakfast area. The master bedroom provides access to a covered patio offering a quiet outdoor retreat. The master bath enjoys a private bath with a large walk-in closet. An adjacent secondary bedroom and full bath is easily a nursery or study. The second floor contains two family bedrooms, a full bath, game room, loft, and deck.

HOME PLAN

HPK2700246

Style: New American

First Floor: 2,012 sq. ft.

Second Floor: 832 sq. ft.

Total: 2,844 sq. ft.

Bedrooms: 4

Bathrooms: 3

Width: 67' - 8"

Depth: 73' - 0"

Foundation: Crawlspace, Slab

eplans.com

FIRST FLOOR

SECOND FLOOR

FIRST FLOOR

SECOND FLOOR

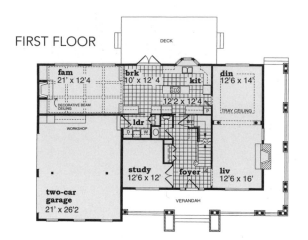

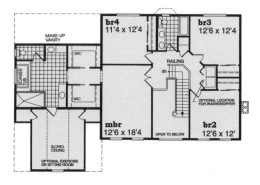

CHOOSE FROM ONE OF TWO EXTERIORS FOR THIS GRAND DESIGN—A LOVELY WOOD-SIDED farmhouse or a stately brick traditional. Plans include details for both facades. Special moldings and trim add interest to the nine-foot ceilings on the first floor. The dining room features a tray ceiling and is separated from the hearth-warmed living room by decorative columns. A study is secluded behind double doors just off the entry. The centrally located kitchen features a large cooking island, pantry, telephone desk, and ample cupboard and counter space. The family room has a decorative beam ceiling and fireplace. The private master bedroom has a most exquisite bath with His and Hers walk-in closets, a soaking tub, separate shower, and make-up vanity. An optional exercise/sitting room adds 241 square feet to the total. Family bedrooms share a full bath.

HPK2700247

Style: Country
First Floor: 1,439 sq. ft.
Second Floor: 1,419 sq. ft.
Total: 2,858 sq. ft.
Bonus Space: 241 sq. ft.
Bedrooms: 4
Bathrooms: 2 ½
Width: 63' - 10"
Depth: 40' - 4"
Foundation: Crawlspace, Unfinished Basement

eplans.com

WONDERFUL WINDOWS
SHOWCASE THIS FABULOUS FOUR-BEDROOM HOME.

Sunburst transoms, French doors, dormers, and Palladian windows flood the interior with light. Entertain elegantly in the dining and living rooms set around the foyer and defined by graceful columns. Relax in the two-story family room or utilize one of two double French doors to the rear covered porch. The master suite and one family bedroom occupy the left side of the plan. Preparing meals will be a breeze in this U-shaped kitchen with its island work space and serving bar to the breakfast room. Upstairs, dormer windows adorn Bedrooms 3 and 4.

HPK2700248

Style: Mediterranean

First Floor: 2,152 sq. ft.

Second Floor: 717 sq. ft.

Total: 2,869 sq. ft.

Bedrooms: 4

Bathrooms: 3

Width: 62' - 4"

Depth: 53' - 0"

Foundation: Crawlspace, Slab

eplans.com

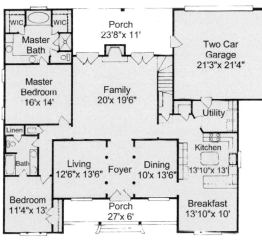

FIRST FLOOR

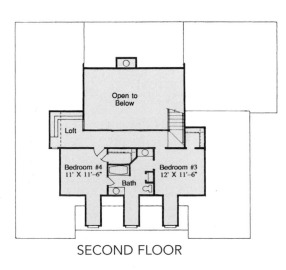

SECOND FLOOR

AN IMPRESSIVE TWO-STORY ENTRANCE WELCOMES YOU TO THIS STATELY HOME. Massive chimneys and pillars and varying rooflines add interest to the stucco exterior. The foyer, lighted by a clerestory window, opens to the formal living and dining rooms. The living room—which could also serve as a study—features a fireplace, as does the family room. Both rooms access the patio. The L-shaped island kitchen opens to a bay-windowed breakfast nook, which is echoed by the sitting area in the master suite. A room next to the kitchen could serve as a bedroom or a home office. The second floor contains two family bedrooms plus a bonus room for future expansion.

SECOND FLOOR

HOME PLAN

HPK2700249

Style: New American

First Floor: 2,249 sq. ft.

Second Floor: 620 sq. ft.

Total: 2,869 sq. ft.

Bonus Space: 308 sq. ft.

Bedrooms: 4

Bathrooms: 3 ½

Width: 69' - 6"

Depth: 52' - 0"

eplans.com

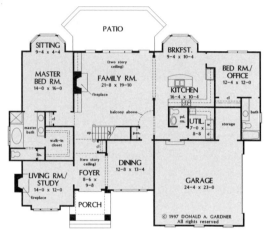

FIRST FLOOR

HOME PLAN

HPK2700250

Style: New American

First Floor: 2,247 sq. ft.

Second Floor: 637 sq. ft.

Total: 2,884 sq. ft.

Bonus Space: 235 sq. ft.

Bedrooms: 4

Bathrooms: 4

Width: 64' - 0"

Depth: 55' - 2"

Foundation: Crawlspace, Unfinished Walkout Basement

eplans.com

FIRST FLOOR

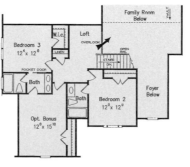

SECOND FLOOR

THIS ASTONISHING TRADITIONAL HOME LOOKS GREAT WITH ITS GABLES, muntin windows, keystone lintels, and turret-style bay. Inside, the heart of the home is the vaulted family room with a fireplace. The kitchen conveniently connects to the dining room, breakfast room, and garage. The master bath leads into a walk-in closet. The home office or nursery near the hall bath is illuminated by a bayed wall of windows and could become an additional family bedroom. Family bedrooms upstairs share a loft that overlooks the family room.

FIRST FLOOR

SECOND FLOOR

HPK2700251

Style: Neoclassical

First Floor: 1,993 sq. ft.

Second Floor: 894 sq. ft.

Total: 2,887 sq. ft.

Bonus Space: 176 sq. ft.

Bedrooms: 3

Bathrooms: 2 ½

Width: 55' - 0"

Depth: 78' - 6"

Foundation: Crawlspace

HOME PLAN

eplans.com

HERE'S A COUNTRY HOME THAT OFFERS LOTS OF DOWN-HOME APPEAL but steps out with upscale style. The grand foyer leads to a spacious great room with an extended-hearth fireplace and access to the rear covered porch. Open planning allows the windowed breakfast nook to enjoy the glow of the fireplace, and the secluded formal dining room has its own hearth. The master suite offers private access to the rear covered porch, and a spacious bath that boasts two walk-in closets, twin vanities, and a windowed, whirlpool tub. Two upstairs bedrooms share a full bath in the balcony hall, which leads to a onus room with a walk-in closet.

© Larry E. Belk Designs

COPYRIGHT LARRY E. BELK

DRIVING UP TO THE PORTE-COCHERE ENTRY OF THIS HOME, visitors will remark on its visually dynamic elevation. Interior views are just as notable. Beyond the covered entryway, the foyer leads into the wide, glass-walled living room. To the right, the formal dining room features a tiered pedestal ceiling. To the left is the master suite wing of the home. The master suite, with its curved glass wall, has access to the patio area and overlooks the pool. The master bath, with its huge walk-in closet, comes complete with a columned vanity area, a soaking tub, and a shower.

HOME PLAN

HPK2700252

Style: Italianate
First Floor: 2,212 sq. ft.
Second Floor: 675 sq. ft.
Total: 2,887 sq. ft.
Bedrooms: 3
Bathrooms: 3
Width: 70' - 8"
Depth: 74' - 10"
Foundation: Slab

eplans.com

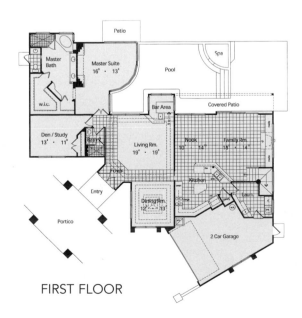

FIRST FLOOR

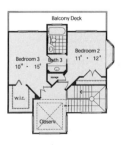

SECOND FLOOR

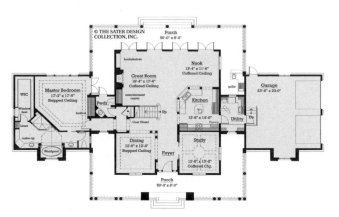

FIRST FLOOR

SECOND FLOOR

A WIDE, WELCOMING PORCH AND PLENTY OF STONE ACCENTS highlight the facade of this charming symmetrical design. Inside, coffered ceilings enhance the study, great room, and breakfast nook; the dining room and master suite both boast stepped ceilings. From the great room, four sets of French doors open to a wraparound rear porch with a grilling area. The master bedroom, also with porch access, includes built-in shelves, a walk-in closet with a window seat, and a luxurious bath with a whirlpool tub. On the second floor, two family bedrooms share a full bath with a whirlpool tub; a loft area and a bonus room offer extra space.

HOME PLAN

HPK2700253

Style: Farmhouse

First Floor: 2,151 sq. ft.

Second Floor: 738 sq. ft.

Total: 2,889 sq. ft.

Bonus Space: 534 sq. ft.

Bedrooms: 3

Bathrooms: 2 ½

Width: 99' - 0"

Depth: 56' - 0"

Foundation: Crawlspace

eplans.com

HOME PLAN

HPK2700254

Style: New American

First Floor: 2,036 sq. ft.

Second Floor: 866 sq. ft.

Total: 2,902 sq. ft.

Bedrooms: 4

Bathrooms: 3 ½

Width: 65' - 0"

Depth: 53' - 4"

Foundation: Crawlspace, Slab, Unfinished Basement

eplans.com

FIRST FLOOR

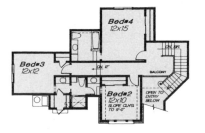

SECOND FLOOR

FIELDSTONE AND SHINGLES GIVE THIS EXTERIOR AN UPLAND COUNTRY COTTAGE LOOK. The impressive entrance leads to a two-story foyer, filled with natural light. A gallery with a ten-foot ceiling leads further into the living room, which has rear-property views. The left side of the plan is devoted to a family room with a fireplace, the island kitchen, utility room and breakfast area. The first-floor master suite boasts a vaulted ceiling, a private patio, His and Hers walk-in closets, and dual basins. The second floor is home to three additional bedrooms, two full baths, and a balcony that looks to the foyer below.

THIS CLASSICAL HOME, REMINISCENT OF THE NEW ORLEANS FRENCH QUARTER, is designed for the owner who enjoys the finer things. Wrought-iron details, arch-top windows, and intriguing court-yards at the front and back make this home ideal for temperate climates. His and Hers bathrooms in the master suite are luxurious and practical. The open kitchen and breakfast area are casual and relaxed, while the family room and dining area could be used for more formal entertainment. Two bedrooms upstairs are accessed by merry-go-round-style steps with multiple landing areas. Large storage areas make this home as practical as it is elegant.

FIRST FLOOR

HPK2700255

Style: Norman

First Floor: 2,262 sq. ft.

Second Floor: 646 sq. ft.

Total: 2,908 sq. ft.

Bedrooms: 3

Bathrooms: 2 ½

Width: 49' - 9"

Depth: 106' - 9"

Foundation: Slab

SECOND FLOOR

eplans.com

HOME PLAN

HPK2700256

Style: Farmhouse

First Floor: 1,913 sq. ft.

Second Floor: 997 sq. ft.

Total: 2,910 sq. ft.

Bonus Space: 377 sq. ft.

Bedrooms: 4

Bathrooms: 3 ½

Width: 63' - 0"

Depth: 59' - 4"

Foundation: Crawlspace, Unfinished Basement

eplans.com

THIS ENCHANTING FARMHOUSE BRINGS THE PAST TO LIFE WITH PLENTY OF MODERN AMENITIES. An open-flow kitchen/breakfast area and family room combination is the heart of the home, opening up to the screened porch and offering the warmth of a fireplace. For more formal occasions, the foyer is flanked by a living room on the left and a dining room on the right. An elegant master bedroom, complete with a super-sized walk-in closet, is tucked away quietly behind the garage. Three more bedrooms reside upstairs, along with two full baths and a future recreation room.

FIRST FLOOR

SECOND FLOOR

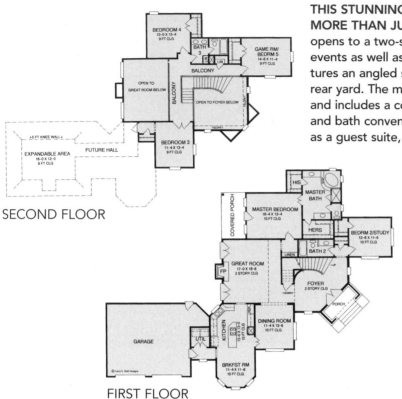

SECOND FLOOR

FIRST FLOOR

THIS STUNNING EUROPEAN-STYLE HOME IS SO MUCH MORE THAN JUST A PRETTY FACE. The two-story foyer opens to a two-story great room that's ready for planned events as well as comfortable gatherings. The kitchen features an angled sink with a window above for views to the rear yard. The master suite opens to a covered rear porch and includes a corner whirlpool tub. A secondary bedroom and bath conveniently located on the first floor can be used as a guest suite, nursery, or home office/study.

HOME PLAN

HPK2700257

Style: Tudor

First Floor: 2,009 sq. ft.

Second Floor: 913 sq. ft.

Total: 2,922 sq. ft.

Bonus Space: 192 sq. ft.

Bedrooms: 5

Bathrooms: 3

Width: 86' - 10"

Depth: 65' - 6"

Foundation: Crawlspace, Slab, Unfinished Basement

eplans.com

©The Sater Design Collection, Inc.

CLEAN, SIMPLE LINES DEFINE THIS VICTORIAN-STYLE HOME, which opens through double doors to a spacious grand room. Adornments here include a coffered ceiling and triple French doors to the covered porch at the back. Both the dining room and the master bedroom feature stepped ceilings. Two walk-in closets and a fine bath with a separate tub and shower further enhance the master suite. Both family bedrooms upstairs have walk-in closets and built-ins. A bonus room can become an additional bedroom later, with space for a full bath.

HOME PLAN

HPK2700258

Style: Country
First Floor: 2,215 sq. ft.
Second Floor: 708 sq. ft.
Total: 2,923 sq. ft.
Bonus Space: 420 sq. ft.
Bedrooms: 3
Bathrooms: 3
Width: 76' - 4"
Depth: 69' - 10"
Foundation: Crawlspace

eplans.com

SECOND FLOOR

FIRST FLOOR

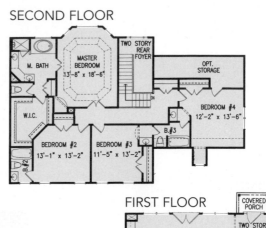

SECOND FLOOR

FIRST FLOOR

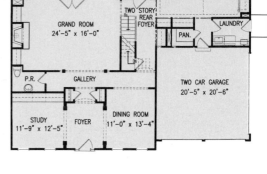

HPK2700259

Style: Greek Revival

First Floor: 1,602 sq. ft.

Second Floor: 1,334 sq. ft.

Total: 2,936 sq. ft.

Bedrooms: 4

Bathrooms: 3 ½

Width: 54' - 0"

Depth: 45' - 8"

Foundation: Unfinished Walkout Basement

eplans.com

THE COZY COVERED PORCH WILL ENTICE YOU TO THE FRONT DOOR of this Colonial gem, but once inside, the huge country kitchen will have you calling this place home. Upstairs the master suite, enhanced by a tray ceiling, is outfitted with a dual-sink vanity, garden tub, separate shower, private toilet, and large walk-in closet. Three family bedrooms, two full baths, and an optional storage area complete this plan.

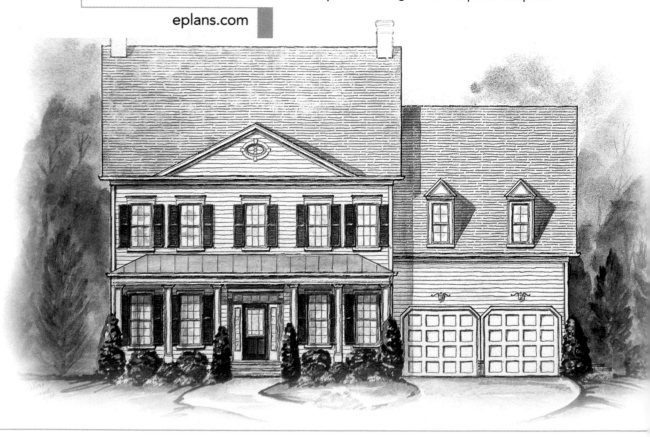

HPK2700260

HOME PLAN #

Style: Farmhouse

First Floor: 1,976 sq. ft.

Second Floor: 970 sq. ft.

Total: 2,946 sq. ft.

Bedrooms: 4

Bathrooms: 3 ½

Width: 58' - 8"

Depth: 66' - 4"

eplans.com

© 1993 Donald A. Gardner Architects, Inc.

FIRST FLOOR

SECOND FLOOR

THIS STYLISH COUNTRY FARMHOUSE OFFERS PLENTY OF LIVING SPACE. Bay windows fill the interior with light and picturesque views. A loft/study on the second floor overlooks the elegant foyer and great room below. Sit by the warming fire in the great room or join in the outdoor fun via sliding glass doors to the rear deck. The master bedroom and breakfast area admit natural light through bay windows and skylights. Private covered porches are accessible from the master bedroom and the living room. Three bedrooms and two full baths occupy the second floor.

FIRST FLOOR

SECOND FLOOR

THE NEARLY OCTAGONAL SHAPE OF THE KITCHEN, WITH ITS LONG WORK ISLAND, will please the family's gourmet cook. The breakfast room, which opens to the back through a French door, flows into the two-story family room; to one side there's a butler's pantry leading to the dining room. The formal living room is on the other side of the two-story foyer. A bedroom with a private bath and walk-in closet could be an in-law suite, study, or home office. The other four bedrooms are upstairs of a balcony overlooking the family room. The laundry room is also on this floor. The master suite includes a sitting room, a walk-in closet, and a luxurious bath.

HOME PLAN

HPK2700261

Style: New American

First Floor: 1,463 sq. ft.

Second Floor: 1,490 sq. ft.

Total: 2,953 sq. ft.

Bedrooms: 5

Bathrooms: 4 ½

Width: 54' - 0"

Depth: 51' - 6"

Foundation: Crawlspace, Slab, Unfinished Walkout Basement

eplans.com

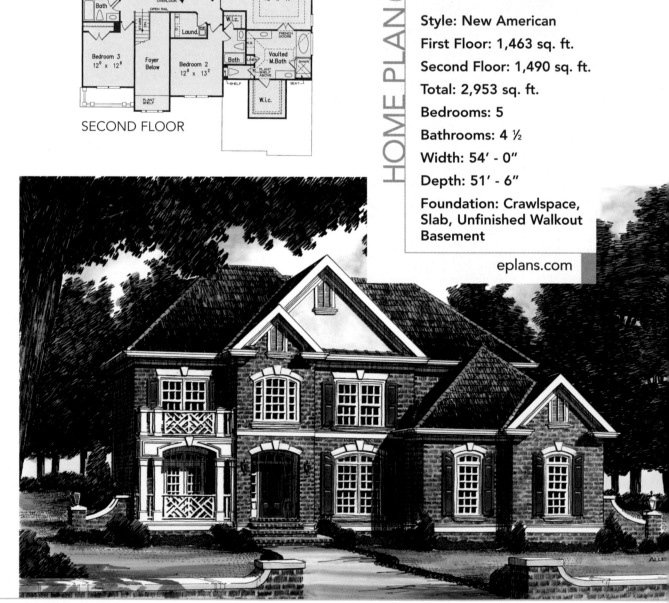

© 2000 Donald A. Gardner, Inc.

HIPPED ROOFLINES, SUNBURST WINDOWS, AND FRENCH-STYLE SHUTTERS are the defining elements of this home's exterior. Inside, the foyer is flanked by the dining room and the study. Further on, the lavish great room can be entered by walking between two stately columns and is complete with a fireplace, built-in shelves, a vaulted ceiling, and views to the rear patio. The island kitchen easily accesses a pantry and a desk and flows into the bayed breakfast area. The first-floor master bedroom enjoys a fireplace, two walk-in closets, and an amenity-filled private bath. Two additional bedrooms reside upstairs, along with a sizable bonus room.

HOME PLAN

HPK2700262

Style: New American

First Floor: 2,270 sq. ft.

Second Floor: 685 sq. ft.

Total: 2,955 sq. ft.

Bonus Space: 563 sq. ft.

Bedrooms: 3

Bathrooms: 2 ½

Width: 75' - 1"

Depth: 53' - 6"

eplans.com

FIRST FLOOR

SECOND FLOOR

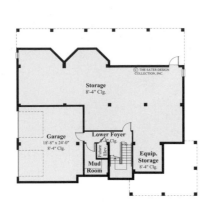

FIRST FLOOR

SECOND FLOOR

HOME PLAN

HPK2700263

Style: New American

First Floor: 2,096 sq. ft.

Second Floor: 892 sq. ft.

Total: 2,988 sq. ft.

Bedrooms: 3

Bathrooms: 3 ½

Width: 56' - 0"

Depth: 54' - 0"

Foundation: Unfinished Walkout Basement

eplans.com

SIDING AND SHINGLES GIVE THIS HOME A CRAFTSMAN LOOK while columns and gables suggest a more traditional style. The foyer opens to a short flight of stairs that leads to the great room, which features a lovely coffered ceiling, a fireplace, built-ins, and French doors to the rear veranda. To the left, the open, island kitchen enjoys a pass-through to the great room and easy service to the dining bay. The secluded master suite has two walk-in closets, a luxurious bath, and veranda access. Upstairs, two family bedrooms enjoy their own full baths and share a loft area.

©The Sater Design Collection, Inc.

© William E. Poole Designs, Inc.

HOME PLAN

HPK2700264

Style: Country

First Floor: 2,014 sq. ft.

Second Floor: 976 sq. ft.

Total: 2,990 sq. ft.

Bonus Space: 390 sq. ft.

Bedrooms: 4

Bathrooms: 3 ½

Width: 73' - 9"

Depth: 55' - 5"

Foundation: Crawlspace, Unfinished Basement

eplans.com

FIRST FLOOR

SECOND FLOOR

WIDE STEPS LEAD UP TO A COVERED FRONT PORCH, inviting one to step inside and appreciate the welcome expressed by this fine four-bedroom home. The two-story foyer is flanked by the formal dining room to the left and the formal living room to the right. A pocket door leads from the living room into the spacious family room, where a fireplace waits to warm cool fall evenings. The L-shaped island kitchen offers an adjacent breakfast area, as well as a pantry and built-in desk. The first-floor master suite is designed to pamper, with a huge walk-in closet, a whirlpool tub, corner shower, and private outdoor access. Upstairs, three family bedrooms, two full baths, and a large future recreation room complete the plan.

FIRST FLOOR

SECOND FLOOR

A FRENCH COUNTRY FLAIR DISTINGUISHES THIS HOME.
The two-story foyer opens to both the formal dining room and the formal living room. The kitchen, breakfast room, and family room are grouped for great casual living. A nearby bedroom and bath would make a nice guest suite. The master suite is designed for privacy and relaxation. An amenity-filled bath features His and Hers walk-in closets and vanities, a corner whirlpool tub, and a separate shower. Two bedrooms and a bath with two private vanity areas are located upstairs. A large game room offers a loft overlooking the foyer. An expandable area can be finished as needed.

HOME PLAN

 # HPK2700265

Style: French Country

First Floor: 2,134 sq. ft.

Second Floor: 863 sq. ft.

Total: 2,997 sq. ft.

Bedrooms: 4

Bathrooms: 3

Width: 60' - 6"

Depth: 68' - 0"

Foundation: Crawlspace, Slab

eplans.com

HOME PLAN
HPK2700266

Style: New American
First Floor: 2,154 sq. ft.
Second Floor: 845 sq. ft.
Total: 2,999 sq. ft.
Bedrooms: 4
Bathrooms: 3
Width: 65' - 4"
Depth: 66' - 4"
Foundation: Crawlspace, Slab

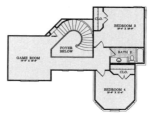

FIRST FLOOR

SECOND FLOOR

HOME PLAN
HPK2700267

Style: New American
First Floor: 1,716 sq. ft.
Second Floor: 1,300 sq. ft.
Total: 3,016 sq. ft.
Bedrooms: 6
Bathrooms: 4 ½
Width: 60' - 0"
Depth: 47' - 8"
Foundation: Crawlspace

FIRST FLOOR

SECOND FLOOR

Treat Yourself to One of These Luxurious Designs

Above: **DECORATIVE CEILING ELEMENTS** and a private balcony elevate this master bedroom above the ordinary. Below: **A STUDY LINED** with built-in shelves becomes a personal library.

These plans were designed to suit the love of luxury in all of us. A home of this size includes the rooms found in previously showcased plans—a combination of formal and informal spaces—with the addition of some extra rooms often not found in a home less than 3,000 square feet.

Entertainment becomes a main focus in these homes. Not only do they include dining rooms and living rooms for formal occasions, as well as the breakfast nooks and family rooms for casual events, there is now room for some higher-end amenities. Whether it's called a hearth room, family room, or great room, such a space in these homes is bound to include a built-in entertainment center or shelves flanking a warming fireplace. The kitchen gets pampered as well, with walk-in pantries, working islands, and more than enough counter space. Other added amenities in this area may include a butler's pantry leading to the dining room, or a built-in bar for cocktails.

Venture upstairs and you may find a play room for the kids, or maybe one for the adults that's large enough for a pool table, big-screen TV, or bar. A sitting or reading loft may accommodate more quiet forms of entertainment. Guests and family members will also appreciate the extra square footage when each bedroom is equipped with its own private bath and a walk-in closet. Outdoor space may also get special attention here with balconies and upper decks accessible from the common rooms or even the bedroom suites.

Whether located upstairs or downstairs—or one on each floor!—the master bedroom gets a V.I.P. treatment. A sitting room may overlook the backyard and a rear terrace—perhaps with outdoor fireplace or summer kitchen. A large bedroom area will accommodate a wide bed with furniture

A WINE ROOM in the basement is just one of many extra rooms these plans have to offer.

Below: Many of the homes in this section include SPACIOUS WALK-IN CLOSETS in the master suite.

nd surrounding space, all below a decorative eiling. Beyond, one or two walk-in closets could e the size of small rooms. The master bath ncludes amenities with couples in mind: twin anities, separate shower and tub, and a com- artmented toilet.

Beyond all of the little extras and lavish menities, the homes in this section provide the me quality of design, layout, and appearance ut with luxurious taste and a desire to meet the omeowner's every need. In short, these homes re the very best our designers have to offer.

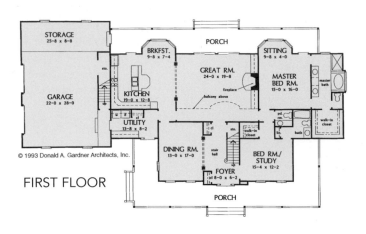

FIRST FLOOR

© 1993 Donald A. Gardner Architects, Inc.

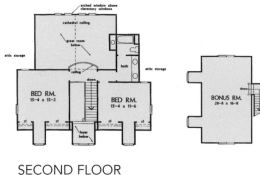

SECOND FLOOR

HOME PLAN

#HPK2700268

Style: Farmhouse

First Floor: 2,316 sq. ft.

Second Floor: 721 sq. ft.

Total: 3,037 sq. ft.

Bonus Space: 545 sq. ft.

Bedrooms: 4

Bathrooms: 3 ½

Width: 95' - 4"

Depth: 54' - 10"

eplans.com

THREE DORMERS TOP A COVERED WRAPAROUND PORCH on this attractive country home. The entrance with Palladian clerestory window lends an abundance of natural light into the foyer. The great room further this feeling of airiness with a balcony above the great room and two sets of sliding glass doors leading to the back porch. For privacy, the master suite occupies the right side of the first floor. With a sitting bay and all the amenities of a modern master bath, this lavish retreat will be a welcome haven for the homeowner. Two family bedrooms reside upstairs, sharing a full hall bath.

© 1993 Donald A. Gardner Architects, Inc.

FIRST FLOOR

HOME PLAN

HPK2700269

Style: Colonial Revival

First Floor: 2,121 sq. ft.

Second Floor: 920 sq. ft.

Total: 3,041 sq. ft.

Bedrooms: 4

Bathrooms: 3

Width: 63' - 0"

Depth: 63' - 0"

Foundation: Crawlspace, Slab

eplans.com

SECOND FLOOR

A STRIKING COMBINATION OF BRICK AND SIDING COMPLEMENTS MULTIPANE WINDOWS AND A COLUMNED ENTRY to create a fresh face on this classic design. The two-story foyer opens to the formal living and dining rooms set off by columned archways. Casual living space includes a spacious family area open to the breakfast room—bright with windows—and the kitchen. The main-level master suite boasts two walk-in closets, an angled whirlpool tub, a separate shower, and additional linen storage. A guest suite or family bedroom with a full bath is positioned for privacy on the opposite side of the plan. Each of the two family bedrooms on the upper level boasts a walk-in closet. The bedrooms share a full bath with separate dressing areas and are open to a gallery hall that leads to a sizable game room with attic access.

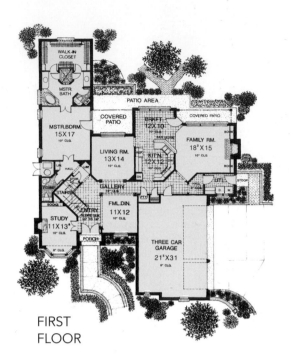

FIRST
FLOOR

HPK2700270

Style: French Country

First Floor: 2,144 sq. ft.

Second Floor: 920 sq. ft.

Total: 3,064 sq. ft.

Bonus Space: 212 sq. ft.

Bedrooms: 4

Bathrooms: 3 ½

Width: 59' - 0"

Depth: 79' - 3"

Foundation: Crawlspace, Slab

eplans.com

HOME PLAN

SECOND
FLOOR

FIELDSTONE, STUCCO, AND BRICK GIVE THIS COTTAGE HARMONY IN VARIETY. The foyer opens to a private study with bay windows and fireplace. The formal dining room is just down the hall and opens through column accents to the living room. The kitchen serves both the formal and casual spaces. The family room is as cozy with a fireplace and rear-window display. The master suite is really a work of luxury and features His and Hers walk-in closet entrances, vanities, and compartmented toilet. The second level houses three additional bedrooms, two full baths, and bonus space.

FIRST FLOOR

SECOND FLOOR

HOME PLAN

HPK2700271

Style: French Country

First Floor: 2,429 sq. ft.

Second Floor: 654 sq. ft.

Total: 3,083 sq. ft.

Bonus Space: 420 sq. ft.

Bedrooms: 3

Bathrooms: 3 ½

Width: 63' - 6"

Depth: 71' - 4"

Foundation: Crawlspace, Slab, Unfinished Walkout Basement

eplans.com

KEYSTONES THAT CAP EACH WINDOW, A TERRACE THAT DRESSES UP THE ENTRANCE, and a bay-windowed turret add up to the totally refined exterior of this home. Inside, open planning employs columns to define the foyer, dining room, and two-story family room. The first-floor master suite is designed with every amenity to answer your needs. Rounding out the first floor are the kitchen, breakfast nook, and keeping room. The second floor contains two bedrooms, each with a private bath and walk-in closet, and an optional bonus room.

FIRST FLOOR

SECOND FLOOR

HOME PLAN

HPK2700272

Style: New American

First Floor: 2,200 sq. ft.

Second Floor: 889 sq. ft.

Total: 3,089 sq. ft.

Bedrooms: 4

Bathrooms: 3

Width: 60' - 6"

Depth: 68' - 0"

Foundation: Crawlspace, Slab

eplans.com

MULTIPANE WINDOWS, VARIED ROOF LINES AND A STUCCO FACADE combine to give this home a wonderful European flavor. A two-story foyer ushers you into the formal areas of the living room and dining room. The large kitchen works well with the cozy family room and sunny breakfast room, with a pass-through to the family room. A nearby bedroom has access to a full bath and can be used as a guest suite. The luxurious master bedroom with its lavish bath and His and Hers walk-in closets rounds out this level. Dominating the second floor, the large game room is accessible to the two family bedrooms. Each bedroom has a walk-in closet and a shared full bath.

HOME PLAN

HPK2700273

Style: Contemporary

First Floor: 1,725 sq. ft.

Second Floor: 1,364 sq. ft.

Total: 3,089 sq. ft.

Bedrooms: 4

Bathrooms: 3

Width: 64' - 4"

Depth: 50' - 4"

Foundation: Crawlspace, Unfinished Basement

eplans.com

GLASS-FILLED, HIPPED DORMERS AND CORNER QUOINS lend this four-bedroom home great curb appeal. Skylights illuminate the vaulted foyer and curved staircase. The formal dining room has a niche for a buffet and French doors leading to the rear deck. Decorative columns help define the living room, which offers a fireplace. A quiet den provides a bay window and a nearby full bath. The gourmet kitchen overlooks the family room that has a hearth. A luxurious master suite and three secondary bedrooms fill the second floor.

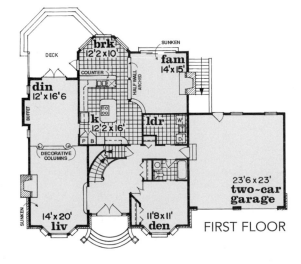

FIRST FLOOR

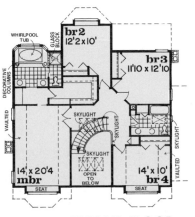

SECOND FLOOR

FIRST FLOOR

SECOND FLOOR

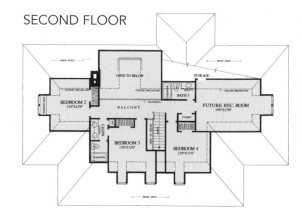

IMAGINE DRIVING UP TO THIS COTTAGE BEAUTY AT THE END OF A LONG WEEK. The long wraparound porch, hipped rooflines, and shuttered windows will transport you. Inside, the foyer is flanked by a living room on the left and a formal dining room on the right. Across the gallery hall, the hearth-warmed family room will surely become the hub of the home. To the right, the spacious kitchen boasts a worktop island counter, ample pantry space, and a breakfast area. A short hallway opens to the utility room and the two-car garage. The master suite takes up the entire left wing of the home, enjoying an elegant private bath and a walk-in closet that goes on and on. Upstairs three more bedrooms reside, sharing two full baths. Expandable future space awaits on the right.

HPK2700274

Style: Farmhouse
First Floor: 2,142 sq. ft.
Second Floor: 960 sq. ft.
Total: 3,102 sq. ft.
Bonus Space: 327 sq. ft.
Bedrooms: 4
Bathrooms: 3 ½
Width: 75' - 8"
Depth: 53' - 0"
Foundation: Crawlspace

eplans.com

HOME PLAN

HPK2700275

Style: New American

First Floor: 1,919 sq. ft.

Second Floor: 1,190 sq. ft.

Total: 3,109 sq. ft.

Bonus Space: 286 sq. ft.

Bedrooms: 4

Bathrooms: 3 ½

Width: 64' - 6"

Depth: 55' - 10"

Foundation: Crawlspace, Slab, Unfinished Basement

eplans.com

FIRST FLOOR

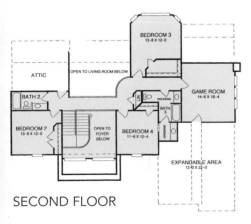

SECOND FLOOR

FLOWER BOXES, ARCHES, AND MULTIPANE WINDOWS COMBINE TO CREATE THE ELEGANT FACADE of this four-bedroom home. Inside, the two-story foyer introduces a formal dining room to its right and leads to a two-story living room that is filled with light. An efficient kitchen has a bayed breakfast room and shares a snack bar with a cozy family room. Located on the first floor for privacy, the master suite is graced with a luxurious bath. Upstairs, three secondary bedrooms share two full baths and access a large game room. For future growth there is an expandable area accessed through the game room.

FIRST FLOOR

PORCH
PATIO
BREAKFAST
13-4 x 10-0
pantry
GREAT RM.
17-6 x 17-10
(two story ceiling)
MASTER
BED RM.
14-0 x 18-0
(cathedral ceiling)
KITCHEN
13-4 x 13-0
master bath
shelves
lin.
balcony above
pd. rm.
niche
fireplace
sto.
up
walk-in closet
walk-in closet
STUDY
12-0 x 15-0
DINING RM.
12-0 x 13-8
UTIL.
w
d
storage
FOYER
12-8 x 8-4
PORCH
GARAGE
22-0 x 22-8

storage

SECOND FLOOR

BED RM.
14-0 x 13-4
(cathedral ceiling)
bath
great room below
walk-in closet
lin.
bath
attic access
(raised ceiling)
cl
cl
(cathedral ceiling)
15-6 x 8-4
attic access
BED RM.
12-0 x 15-0
(cathedral ceiling)
down
railing
cl
cl
foyer below
BED RM.
12-0 x 11-4
(cathedral ceiling)
BONUS RM.
14-8 x 20-8
attic access
attic access

STATELY AND SOPHISTICATED, THIS HOME SHOWCASES DRAMA IN THE ENTRYWAY WITH BOLD COLUMNS AND A BARREL-VAULT ARCH that leads to the double front door. Elliptical transoms and a bonneted roof over the upper foyer soften the facade, contrasting with the hipped roof and gables. Upon entrance, the study and dining room flank a grand staircase. A see-through fireplace, bay window, and walk-in pantry add elegance and convenience. With the kitchen as the heart of the home, a center island allows room for two cooks. All bedrooms feature cathedral ceilings and Palladian windows. The master suite includes twin walk-in closets and a spacious master bath with lush amenities. Note the additional bonus room and garage storage.

HPK2700276

HOME PLAN

Style: Country

First Floor: 2,160 sq. ft.

Second Floor: 951 sq. ft.

Total: 3,111 sq. ft.

Bonus Space: 491 sq. ft.

Bedrooms: 4

Bathrooms: 3 ½

Width: 61' - 11"

Depth: 63' - 11"

eplans.com

HPK2700277

Style: Pueblo

First Floor: 2,422 sq. ft.

Second Floor: 714 sq. ft.

Total: 3,136 sq. ft.

Bedrooms: 4

Bathrooms: 4

Width: 77' - 6"

Depth: 62' - 0"

Foundation: Slab

eplans.com

REAR EXTERIOR

THIS SOUTHWESTERN CONTEMPORARY HOME offers a distinctive look for any neighborhood—both inside and out. The formal living areas are concentrated in the center of the plan, perfect for entertaining. To the right, the kitchen and family room function well together as a working and living area. The first-floor sleeping wing includes a guest suite and a master suite. Upstairs, two family bedrooms are reached by a balcony overlooking the living room. Each bedroom has a walk-in closet and a dressing area with a vanity; they share a compartmented bath that includes a linen closet.

HOMES OVER 3,000 SQUARE FEET

FIRST FLOOR

SECOND FLOOR

FIRST FLOOR

SECOND FLOOR

HPK2700278

HOME PLAN

Style: Farmhouse

First Floor: 2,086 sq. ft.

Second Floor: 1,077 sq. ft.

Total: 3,163 sq. ft.

Bonus Space: 403 sq. ft.

Bedrooms: 4

Bathrooms: 3 ½

Width: 81' - 10"

Depth: 51' - 8"

eplans.com

THIS BEAUTIFUL FARMHOUSE, WITH ITS PROMINENT TWIN GABLES AND BAYS, adds just the right amount of country style. The master suite is quietly tucked away downstairs with no rooms directly above. The family cook will love the spacious U-shaped kitchen and adjoining bayed breakfast nook. A bonus room awaits expansion on the second floor, where three large bedrooms share two full baths. Storage space abounds with walk-ins, half-shelves, and linen closets. A curved balcony borders a versatile loft/study, which overlooks the stunning two-story family room.

HOME PLAN

HPK2700279

Style: Farmhouse

First Floor: 2,194 sq. ft.

Second Floor: 973 sq. ft.

Total: 3,167 sq. ft.

Bonus Space: 281 sq. ft.

Bedrooms: 4

Bathrooms: 3 ½

Width: 71' - 11"

Depth: 54' - 4"

eplans.com

FIRST FLOOR

SECOND FLOOR

THIS UPDATED FARMHOUSE HAS BEEN GIVEN ADDITIONAL CUSTOM-STYLED FEATURES. Twin gables, sidelights, and an arched entryway accent the facade; decorative ceiling treatments, bay windows, and French doors adorn the interior. From an abundance of counter space and large walk-in pantry to the built-ins and storage areas, this design makes the most of space. Supported by columns, a curved balcony overlooks the stunning two-story great room. The powder room is easily accessible from the common rooms, and angled corners soften the dining room. The well-equipped private bath and twin closets in the master suite are welcome luxuries.

FIRST FLOOR

SECOND FLOOR

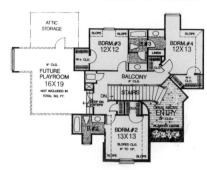

HPK2700280

HOME PLAN

Style: Chateauesque
First Floor: 2,237 sq. ft.
Second Floor: 931 sq. ft.
Total: 3,168 sq. ft.
Bonus Space: 304 sq. ft.
Bedrooms: 4
Bathrooms: 3 ½
Width: 68' - 0"
Depth: 55' - 6"
Foundation: Slab

THIS MAJESTIC ESTATE HAS PALATIAL INSPIRA-TION, with a plan any modern family will love. A hardwood entry leads to brick flooring in the kitchen and breakfast nook, for vintage appeal. The family room and vaulted living room warm heart and soul with extended-hearth fireplaces. For a quiet retreat, the study opens with French doors from the hall and leads out to the walled lanai courtyard through another set of French doors. The vaulted master suite is impressive, with a bay window, a sumptuous bath, and His and Hers walk-in closets. Upstairs, three ample bedrooms will access the future playroom.

eplans.com

FIRST FLOOR

SECOND FLOOR

HOME PLAN

HPK2700281

Style: Georgian

First Floor: 2,086 sq. ft.

Second Floor: 1,094 sq. ft.

Total: 3,180 sq. ft.

Bonus Space: 372 sq. ft.

Bedrooms: 4

Bathrooms: 4 ½

Width: 64' - 4"

Depth: 61' - 10"

Foundation: Crawlspace, Unfinished Basement

eplans.com

TAKE ONE LOOK AT THIS COLONIAL HAVEN AND YOU WILL CALL IT HOME. A columned front porch and an upstairs deck were built for lazy summer days; the extended-hearth fireplace will warm your heart on chilly winter nights. The living room—with fireplace—and formal dining room are perfect for entertaining. In the bumped-out kitchen and bayed breakfast area, natural light will be the order of the day. The first-floor master suite includes an enormous walk-in closet and a private bath. Upstairs, three generous bedrooms, three baths, and space for expansion will please everyone.

A WIDE, WELCOMING FRONT PORCH AND THREE DORMER WINDOWS LEND SOUTHERN FLAIR to this charming farmhouse. Inside, three fireplaces—found in the living, dining, and family rooms—create a cozy atmosphere. The family room opens to the covered rear porch, and the breakfast area opens to a small side porch. Sleeping quarters include a luxurious first-floor master suite—with a private bath and two walk-in closets—as well as three family bedrooms upstairs.

FIRST FLOOR

HOME PLAN

HPK2700282

Style: Federal - Adams

First Floor: 2,200 sq. ft.

Second Floor: 1,001 sq. ft.

Total: 3,201 sq. ft.

Bonus Space: 674 sq. ft.

Bedrooms: 4

Bathrooms: 3 ½

Width: 70' - 4"

Depth: 74' - 4"

Foundation: Crawlspace

eplans.com

SECOND FLOOR

© 2000 Donald A. Gardner, Inc.

HPK2700283

Style: Craftsman

First Floor: 2,477 sq. ft.

Second Floor: 742 sq. ft.

Total: 3,219 sq. ft.

Bonus Space: 419 sq. ft.

Bedrooms: 4

Bathrooms: 4

Width: 99' - 10"

Depth: 66' - 2"

eplans.com

THIS DESIGN BRINGS BACK THE SOPHISTICATION AND ELEGANCE OF DAYS GONE BY, yet its modern layout creates a natural traffic flow for easy living. Columns partition space without enclosing it, while built-ins in the great room and counter space in the utility/mud room add convenience. The family-efficient floor plan can be witnessed in the kitchen's handy pass-through, and the kitchen has access to the rear porch for outdoor entertaining. Cathedral ceilings highlight the master bedroom and bedroom/study, while vaulted ceilings top the breakfast area and loft/study. The bonus room can be used as a home theater, playroom, or gym, and its position allows the room to keep recreational noise away from the rest of the house.

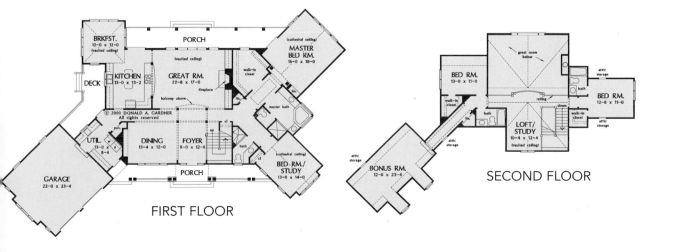

FIRST FLOOR

SECOND FLOOR

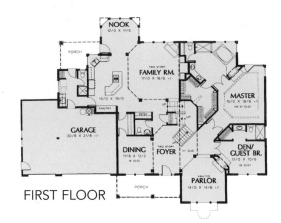

FIRST FLOOR

SECOND FLOOR

IN THIS FOUR-BEDROOM DESIGN, THE CASUAL AREAS ARE FREE-FLOWING, OPEN, AND SOARING, and the formal areas are secluded and well defined. The two-story foyer with a clerestory window leads to a quiet parlor with a vaulted ceiling and a Palladian window. The formal dining room opens from the foyer through decorative columns and is served by a spacious gourmet kitchen. The family room, defined by columns, has an angled corner hearth and is open to the kitchen and breakfast nook. The master suite is full of interesting angles, from the triangular bedroom and multi-angled walk-in closet to the corner tub in the sumptuous master bath. A nearby den has its own bathroom and could serve as a guest room. Upstairs, two additional bedrooms share a full bath and a balcony hall.

HOME PLAN

(#) HPK2700284

Style: Country
First Floor: 2,642 sq. ft.
Second Floor: 603 sq. ft.
Total: 3,245 sq. ft.
Bonus Space: 255 sq. ft.
Bedrooms: 4
Bathrooms: 4 ½
Width: 80' - 0"
Depth: 61' - 0"
Foundation: Crawlspace

eplans.com

A PEDIMENTED ENTRY, SHINGLE ACCENTS, AND SHUTTERS BLEND MODERN AND TRADITIONAL LOOKS on this Southern design. The foyer features a two-story ceiling and opens to the formal dining room, which has a lovely tray ceiling. A gallery hall connects the formal living room with all areas of the home. French doors open the living space to the back property. The master wing includes two walk-in closets, an angled garden tub, a separate shower with a seat, and a knee-space vanity. Second-floor sleeping quarters are connected by a balcony hall that leads to a sizable game room.

HOME PLAN

#HPK2700285

Style: Greek Revival

First Floor: 2,055 sq. ft.

Second Floor: 1,229 sq. ft.

Total: 3,284 sq. ft.

Bedrooms: 4

Bathrooms: 3 ½

Width: 65' - 0"

Depth: 60' - 10"

Foundation: Crawlspace, Slab

eplans.com

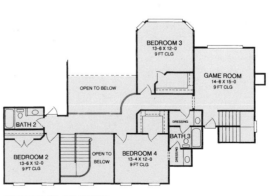

FIRST FLOOR

SECOND FLOOR

FIRST FLOOR

SECOND FLOOR

HOME PLAN

HPK2700286

Style: Mediterranean

First Floor: 2,397 sq. ft.

Second Floor: 887 sq. ft.

Total: 3,284 sq. ft.

Bedrooms: 4

Bathrooms: 3 ½

Width: 107' - 10"

Depth: 84' - 2"

Foundation: Slab

eplans.com

THIS STUNNING HOME IS A GRACIOUS REPRESENTATION OF THE OWNER'S OWN HOSPITALITY, from the elegant receiving rooms to the quaint guest quarters. Enter the grand foyer that opens straight through onto the expansive veranda, and proceed to the left to the parlor, and to the right into the formal dining room. The casual area centers around the oversized, gourmet kitchen. A breakfast nook offers a casual place to dine while the leisure room with built-in entertainment center is the perfect family gathering place. The master suite is secluded at the rear of the plan and is fashioned with veranda doors, detailed ceiling, spa-style bath, and a huge, walk-in closet. At the top of the stairs, a loft open to the grand foyer gives access to the deck. Two large family bedrooms share a full hall bath. Joined to the main house by the veranda is a lovely guest suite.

HOME PLAN

HPK2700287

Style: Mediterranean

First Floor: 2,188 sq. ft.

Second Floor: 1,110 sq. ft.

Total: 3,298 sq. ft.

Bedrooms: 4

Bathrooms: 3 ½

Width: 69' - 0"

Depth: 64' - 8"

Foundation: Slab

eplans.com

FIRST FLOOR

SECOND FLOOR

THIS EUROPEAN-STYLE BRICK-AND-STUCCO HOME SHOWCASES AN ARCHED ENTRY and presents a commanding presence from the curb. Inside, the living room, the dining room, and the family room are located at the rear of the home to provide wide-open views of the rear grounds beyond. A colonnade with connecting arches defines the space for a living room with a fireplace and the dining room. The spacious master suite features a relaxing sitting area, His and Hers closets, and an extravagant bath. Take special note of the private His and Hers bathrooms. On the second floor, three bedrooms, two baths, and a game room complete the home.

FIRST FLOOR

SECOND FLOOR

THIS DELIGHTFUL TWO-STORY HOME OFFERS FORMAL AND INFORMAL SPACES. The enchanting foyer features a gracefully curved staircase and Colonial columns that lead to the living room and formal dining room beyond. Pocket doors introduce you to the spacious hearth room where a fireplace is flanked by matching windows. Triple windows across the rear wall allow daylight to flow through this favorite gathering place. An island with seating defines the functional kitchen, which serves the breakfast area and dining room with equal ease. A library completes the first floor. Highlighting the second floor is an expansive balcony that wraps around to a secondary bedroom with a private bath and walk-in closet. Two additional bedrooms with large closets share a common bath. The spacious master suite boasts a tray ceiling and a deluxe dressing room.

HOME PLAN

HPK2700288

Style: Neoclassical

First Floor: 1,670 sq. ft.

Second Floor: 1,641 sq. ft.

Total: 3,311 sq. ft.

Bedrooms: 4

Bathrooms: 3 ½

Width: 60' - 0"

Depth: 45' - 6"

Foundation: Unfinished Basement

eplans.com

FIRST FLOOR

SECOND FLOOR

STATELY COLUMNS AND A COVERED PORCH invite visitors and family alike to partake of this home. Attractive angles in the large kitchen help to tie this room into the nearby family and breakfast rooms. The master suite offers walk-in closets, a double-bowl vanity, a garden tub, and a separate shower. The formal living and dining rooms are convenient to one another for ease in entertaining. A secondary bedroom is also located on this level. Upstairs, two large family bedrooms share a hall bath and have access to a game room.

HPK2700289

HOME PLAN

Style: Country

First Floor: 2,361 sq. ft.

Second Floor: 974 sq. ft.

Total: 3,335 sq. ft.

Bedrooms: 4

Bathrooms: 3

Width: 68' - 0"

Depth: 64' - 10"

Foundation: Crawlspace, Slab

eplans.com

FIRST FLOOR

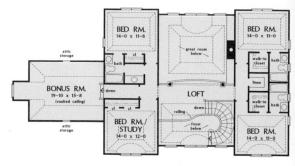

SECOND FLOOR

HOME PLAN

HPK2700290

Style: Norman

First Floor: 2,062 sq. ft.

Second Floor: 1,279 sq. ft.

Total: 3,341 sq. ft.

Bonus Space: 386 sq. ft.

Bedrooms: 5

Bathrooms: 4 ½

Width: 73' - 8"

Depth: 50' - 0"

eplans.com

A TWO-STORY CHATEAU-STYLE HOME may be exactly what you are looking for to entertain guests in grand style and accommodate a growing family. When visitors pass through the elegant columns on the front porch into the foyer with its spiral staircase and art niche, they know this is a special place. To the left is the formal dining room and straight ahead is the spacious, two-story high great room with a centered fireplace flanked by built-in shelves. The huge kitchen with an island counter and handy pantry easily serves the dining room and the sunlit breakfast nook. The absolutely magnificent master suite assumes the entire right wing of the plan. Upstairs, four bedrooms (make one a study) and three baths offer plenty of comfort. A balcony overlooks the great room.

HOME PLAN

HPK2700291

Style: Farmhouse

First Floor: 2,357 sq. ft.

Second Floor: 995 sq. ft.

Total: 3,352 sq. ft.

Bonus Space: 545 sq. ft.

Bedrooms: 4

Bathrooms: 3 ½

Width: 95' - 4"

Depth: 54' - 10"

eplans.com

FROM THE TWO-STORY FOYER WITH A PALLADIAN CLERESTORY WINDOW AND GRACEFUL STAIRWAY to the large great room with a cathedral ceiling and curved balcony, impressive spaces prevail in this open plan. A columned opening from the great room introduces the spacious family kitchen with a center island and breakfast bay. The master suite, privately located at the opposite end of the first floor, features a sitting bay, an extra-large walk-in closet, and a bath with every possible luxury. Three bedrooms and two full baths make up the second floor, perfect for friends and family. A bonus room and attic storage offer expansion opportunities for the future.

SECOND FLOOR

FIRST FLOOR

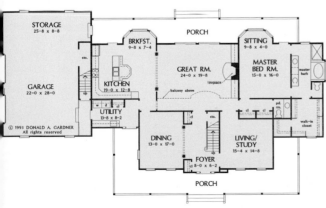

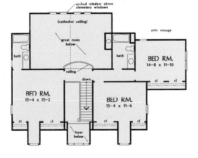

FIRST FLOOR

SECOND FLOOR

WITH AN ABUNDANCE OF NATURAL LIGHT AND AMENITIES, this home is sure to please. The sunporch doubles as a delightful area to enjoy meals with a view. A mudroom off the utility room accesses a side porch and serves as a place to hang coats or shed dirty shoes before entering the kitchen or family room. The master bedroom, family room, and living room/library each boast a private fireplace. Upstairs houses three additional bedrooms, two sharing a full bath and one with an attached full bath. Future expansion space completes the second floor. Extra storage space in the garage is an added convenience.

HPK2700292

Style: Greek Revival

First Floor: 2,337 sq. ft.

Second Floor: 1,016 sq. ft.

Total: 3,353 sq. ft.

Bonus Space: 394 sq. ft.

Bedrooms: 4

Bathrooms: 3 ½

Width: 66' - 2"

Depth: 71' - 2"

Foundation: Crawlspace

HOME PLAN

eplans.com

© William E. Poole Designs, Inc.

HPK2700293

Style: Neoclassical

First Floor: 1,759 sq. ft.

Second Floor: 1,607 sq. ft.

Total: 3,366 sq. ft.

Bedrooms: 5

Bathrooms: 4

Width: 68' - 8"

Depth: 56' - 8"

Foundation: Unfinished Walkout Basement

eplans.com

THIS LUXURIOUS TWO-STORY HOME COMBINES A STATELY WILLIAMSBURG EXTERIOR STYLE with a large, functional floor plan. Natural light radiates through the multiple rear windows to flood the great room, breakfast area, and kitchen. Secluded to the rear of this home is an optional library or bedroom, which can serve as a comfortable guest room. Built-in bookshelves flank the entrance to the second-floor master bedroom where a lavish retreat offers a large sitting area surrounded by windows. Three additional bedrooms, each with large closets and private access to a bath, complete this family-friendly home.

FIRST FLOOR

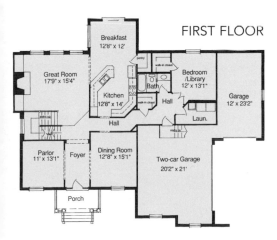

SECOND FLOOR

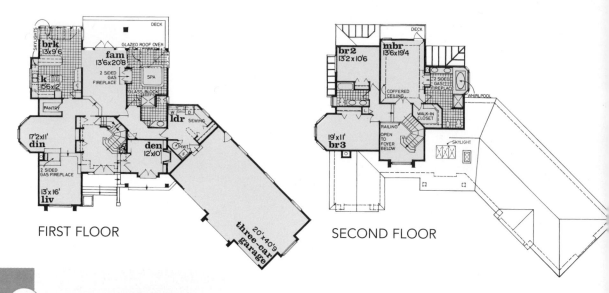

FIRST FLOOR

SECOND FLOOR

HPK2700294

Style: Contemporary

First Floor: 2,132 sq. ft.

Second Floor: 1,295 sq. ft.

Total: 3,427 sq. ft.

Bedrooms: 3

Bathrooms: 3

Width: 91' - 6"

Depth: 75' - 6"

Foundation: Crawlspace, Unfinished Basement

eplans.com

SAND-FINISHED STUCCO, DISTINCTIVE COLUMNS, AND OVERSIZED CIRCLE-TOP WINDOWS grace this luxurious three bedroom home. A sunken living room features a two-sided gas fireplace that it shares with the formal dining room. The den is warmed by a fireplace and features double doors to the front porch. The family room is also sunken and shares a two-sided fireplace with an indoor spa and a glazed roof overhead. Two secondary bedrooms and a master suite are on the second floor. The master suite enjoys a through-fireplace between the bath and the bedroom.

ORDER BLUEPRINTS ANYTIME AT EPLANS.COM OR 1-800-521-6797

HPK2700295

Style: Chateauesque

First Floor: 2,446 sq. ft.

Second Floor: 1,013 sq. ft.

Total: 3,459 sq. ft.

Bonus Space: 187 sq. ft.

Bedrooms: 5

Bathrooms: 4 ½

Width: 73' - 0"

Depth: 68' - 0"

Foundation: Slab

eplans.com

LIVE LIKE ROYALTY IN YOUR OWN EUROPEAN CHATEAU! A commanding arch frames the entryway to a two-story foyer. Take the angled stairs to reach three of the five bedrooms, or walk straight ahead to the gallery. From here, enter the great room with central fireplace. The space is open to the breakfast nook and kitchen, with easily acesses the dining room for formal meals. Continue down the gallery for the highlight of this plan--the master suite. In here, the bedroom includes a bayed sitting area as well as a well-appointed bath and a large walk-in closet for two. Guests can enjoy the convenience of a second first-floor suite nearby.

FIRST FLOOR

SECOND FLOOR

FIRST FLOOR

SECOND FLOOR

TWO GUEST SUITES—ONE ON EACH FLOOR—ENHANCE THE INTERIOR OF THIS MAGNIFICENT STUCCO HOME. A grand entrance provides passage to a foyer that opens to the study on the left, the formal dining room on the right, and the formal living room straight ahead. The casual living area combines a kitchen with an island cooktop, a sun-filled breakfast nook, and a spacious leisure room. Arched openings lead into the master bedroom and a lavish bath that enjoys a private garden. The second-floor guest suite includes a loft and a large observation deck.

REAR EXTERIOR

HOME PLAN

 # HPK2700296

Style: Mediterranean
First Floor: 2,894 sq. ft.
Second Floor: 568 sq. ft.
Total: 3,462 sq. ft.
Bedrooms: 3
Bathrooms: 3 ½
Width: 67' - 0"
Depth: 102' - 0"
Foundation: Slab

eplans.com

© William E. Poole Designs, Inc.

HPK2700297

Style: Plantation

First Floor: 2,033 sq. ft.

Second Floor: 1,447 sq. ft.

Total: 3,480 sq. ft.

Bonus Space: 411 sq. ft.

Bedrooms: 3

Bathrooms: 3 ½

Width: 67' - 10"

Depth: 64' - 4"

Foundation: Crawlspace, Unfinished Basement, Unfinished Walkout Basement

HOME PLAN

eplans.com

FIRST FLOOR

SECOND FLOOR

SOUTHERN GRANDEUR IS EVIDENT IN THIS WONDERFUL TWO-STORY DESIGN with its magnificent second-floor balcony. The formal living spaces—dining room and living room—flank the impressive foyer with its stunning staircase. The family room resides in the rear, opening to the terrace. The sunny breakfast bay adjoins the island kitchen for efficient planning. The right wing holds the two-car garage, utility room, a secondary staircase, and a study that can easily be converted to a guest suite with a private bath. The master suite and Bedrooms 2 and 3 are placed on the second floor.

A TWO-STORY FOYER WELCOMES FRIENDS AND FAMILY TO THIS FOUR-BEDROOM COLONIAL HOME. The formal living and dining rooms are perfectly situated for fine dinner parties. An angled kitchen is adjacent to a breakfast area and the large family room, which is complete with a warming fireplace. Located on the first floor for privacy, the master bedroom suite is sure to please with two walk-in closets, a corner whirlpool tub, and a separate shower. Venture upstairs to find three bedrooms--two with walk-in closets--and a spacious game room.

FIRST FLOOR

HOME PLAN

HPK2700298

Style: Colonial Revival

First Floor: 2,129 sq. ft.

Second Floor: 1,359 sq. ft.

Total: 3,488 sq. ft.

Bonus Space: 216 sq. ft.

Bedrooms: 4

Bathrooms: 3 ½

Width: 65' - 0"

Depth: 57' - 11"

Foundation: Crawlspace, Slab

eplans.com

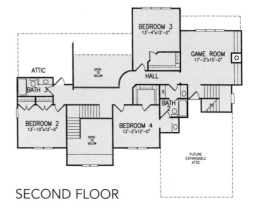

SECOND FLOOR

1998 Donald A. Gardner, Inc.

ORMERS, GABLES WITH WOOD BRACKETS, A DOUBLE-OOR ENTRY, and a stone-and-siding exterior lend charm nd sophistication to this Craftsman estate. Cathedral ceil- gs and fireplaces are standard in the living room, family oom, and master bedroom; the living room, family room, nd study feature built-in bookshelves. The spacious kitchen ith a cooktop island and walk-in pantry opens completely o the family room and breakfast area. The master suite xcels with a private sitting room, access to its own porch, wo oversized walk-in closets, and a lavish bath. Overlooking oth the foyer and the living room, the second-floor balcony onnects two bedrooms, a library, and a bonus room.

REAR EXTERIOR

FIRST FLOOR

HOME PLAN

HPK2700299

Style: Craftsman

First Floor: 2,755 sq. ft.

Second Floor: 735 sq. ft.

Total: 3,490 sq. ft.

Bonus Space: 481 sq. ft.

Bedrooms: 3

Bathrooms: 3 ½

Width: 92' - 6"

Depth: 69' - 10"

eplans.com

SECOND FLOOR

FIRST FLOOR

SECOND FLOOR

THIS GORGEOUS HOME IS TAILOR-MADE FOR A CORNER OR PIE-SHAPED LOT. Featuring mirror-image gables on both sides, this elevation is stunning from any direction. A two-story entry and a great room command attention upon entering the home. The master suite includes a masonry fireplace situated between the sitting area and the bedroom. A study, conveniently located off the foyer, can be used as a bedroom. A gourmet kitchen with a triangular work island, a corner sink, and a large pantry is located on the opposite side of the home. Upstairs, one bedroom with a private outside balcony is ideal for an office. A game room, a bath, and another bedroom with a private outside balcony provide the finishing touches to this elegant home.

HPK2700300

Style: Neoclassical
First Floor: 2,515 sq. ft.
Second Floor: 978 sq. ft.
Total: 3,493 sq. ft.
Bedrooms: 4
Bathrooms: 3 ½
Width: 69' - 5"
Depth: 81' - 1"
Foundation: Slab

eplans.com

FIRST FLOOR

SECOND FLOOR

HOME PLAN

HPK2700301

Style: New American

First Floor: 2,469 sq. ft.

Second Floor: 1,025 sq. ft.

Total: 3,494 sq. ft.

Bonus Space: 320 sq. ft.

Bedrooms: 4

Bathrooms: 3 ½

Width: 67' - 8"

Depth: 74' - 2"

Foundation: Crawlspace, Slab, Unfinished Basement

eplans.com

A LOVELY DOUBLE ARCH GIVES THIS EUROPEAN-STYLE HOME A COMMANDING PRESENCE. Once inside, a two-story foyer provides an open view directly through the formal living room to the rear grounds beyond. The spacious kitchen with a work island and the bayed breakfast area share space with the family room. The private master suite features dual sinks, twin walk-in closets, a corner garden tub, and a separate shower. A large game room completes this wonderful family home.

AN ABUNDANCE OF WINDOWS AND AN ATTRACTIVE BRICK FACADE enhance the exterior of this traditional two-story home. Inside, a study and formal dining room flank the two-story foyer. Fireplaces warm both the great room and first-floor master suite. The suite also provides a separate sitting room, two walk-in closets, and a private bath. The island kitchen extends into the breakfast room. The second floor features three additional family bedrooms, two baths, and a bonus room fit for a home office.

FIRST FLOOR

SECOND FLOOR

HOME PLAN

HPK2700302

Style: New American
First Floor: 2,511 sq. ft.
Second Floor: 1,062 sq. ft.
Total: 3,573 sq. ft.
Bonus Space: 465 sq. ft.
Bedrooms: 4
Bathrooms: 3 ½
Width: 84' - 11"
Depth: 55' - 11"

eplans.com

HOME PLAN

HPK2700303

Style: French Country

First Floor: 2,654 sq. ft.

Second Floor: 1,013 sq. ft.

Total: 3,667 sq. ft.

Bedrooms: 4

Bathrooms: 3 ½

Width: 75' - 4"

Depth: 74' - 2"

Foundation: Crawlspace, Slab, Unfinished Basement

eplans.com

FIRST FLOOR

SECOND FLOOR

EUROPEAN ACCENTS SHAPE THE EXTERIOR OF THIS STRIKING FAMILY HOME. Inside, the foyer is open to the dining room on the right and the living room straight ahead. Here, two sets of double doors open to the rear covered porch. Casual areas of the home include a family room warmed by a fireplace and an island kitchen open to a bayed breakfast room. The first-floor master retreat is a luxurious perk, which offers a bayed sitting area, a whirlpool bath, and large His and Hers walk-in closets. The first-floor bedroom—with its close proximity to the master suite—is perfect for a nursery or home office. Upstairs, two more family bedrooms boast walk-in closets and share a bath. Future space is available just off the game room.

FIRST FLOOR

SECOND FLOOR

THIS MANOR HOME LOOKS AS IF IT WAS NESTLED IN THE FRENCH COUNTRYSIDE. The combination of brick, stone, and rough cedar, and multiple chimneys add to the charm of the facade. The gracious two-story entry leads to all areas of the home. A beautiful curving staircase leads to an upper balcony overlooking the entry. The second floor consists of three bedrooms, each with connecting baths and walk-in closets. Space for a future playroom is located above the garage. Downstairs, the family area with a cathedral ceiling is open to the large kitchen and breakfast area. A large pantry is located near the kitchen. The cozy study has its own marble fireplace and a vaulted ceiling.

HOME PLAN

HPK2700304

Style: French Country

First Floor: 2,700 sq. ft.

Second Floor: 990 sq. ft.

Total: 3,690 sq. ft.

Bonus Space: 365 sq. ft.

Bedrooms: 4

Bathrooms: 3 ½

Width: 76' - 0"

Depth: 74' - 1"

Foundation: Crawlspace, Slab, Unfinished Basement

eplans.com

A STATELY HIPPED ROOF CROWNS THIS IMPRESSIVE EXECUTIVE HOME'S BRICK EXTERIOR, which includes arch-topped windows, keystones and a covered entry with a balustrade. The spacious floor plan boasts formal and casual living areas. A two-story ceiling in the foyer and family room highlights an exciting curved balcony on the second floor. The generously proportioned kitchen includes a center island sink and plenty of work space. Distinctive shelving is built into either end of the home's center hall. The master suite and a guest suite, each with tray ceilings and private baths, are located on the first floor. Two vaulted bedrooms, two full baths, and a bonus room can be found upstairs.

HOME PLAN

HPK2700305

Style: Colonial

First Floor: 2,908 sq. ft.

Second Floor: 790 sq. ft.

Total: 3,698 sq. ft.

Bonus Space: 521 sq. ft.

Bedrooms: 4

Bathrooms: 4 ½

Width: 86' - 11"

Depth: 59' - 5"

eplans.com

FIRST FLOOR

SECOND FLOOR

A TRULY GRAND ENTRY—absolutely stunning on a corner lot—sets the eclectic yet elegant tone of this four-bedroom home. The foyer opens to a dramatic circular stair, then on to the two-story great room that's framed by a second-story balcony. An elegant dining room is set to the side, distinguished by a span of arches. The gourmet kitchen features wrapping counters, a cooktop island, and a breakfast room. A front study and a secondary bedroom are nice accompaniments to the expansive master suite. A through-fireplace, a spa-style bath, and a huge walk-in closet highlight this area. Upstairs, a loft opens to two balconies overlooking the porch and leads to two family bedrooms and a game room.

FIRST FLOOR

HOME PLAN # HPK2700306

Style: Neoclassical

First Floor: 2,772 sq. ft.

Second Floor: 933 sq. ft.

Total: 3,705 sq. ft.

Bedrooms: 4

Bathrooms: 4 ½

Width: 74' - 8"

Depth: 61' - 10"

Foundation: Crawlspace, Slab

eplans.com

SECOND FLOOR

© William E. Poole Designs, Inc.

HOME PLAN

HPK2700307

Style: Farmhouse

First Floor: 2,442 sq. ft.

Second Floor: 1,286 sq. ft.

Total: 3,728 sq. ft.

Bonus Space: 681 sq. ft.

Bedrooms: 4

Bathrooms: 3 ½ + ½

Width: 84' - 8"

Depth: 60' - 0"

Foundation: Crawlspace

eplans.com

WITH A GAZEBO-STYLE CORNER AND CAREFUL EXTERIOR DETAILS, you can't help but imagine tea parties, porch swings, and lazy summer evenings spent on this covered porch. Inside, a living room/library will comfort with its fireplace and built-ins. The family room is graced with a fireplace and a curved, two-story ceiling with an overlook above. The master bedroom is a private retreat with a lovely bath, twin walk-in closets, and rear-porch access. Upstairs, three bedrooms with sizable closets—one bedroom would make an excellent guest suite or alternate master suite—share access to expandable space.

FIRST FLOOR

SECOND FLOOR

FIRST FLOOR

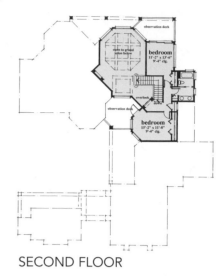

SECOND FLOOR

A UNIQUE COURTYARD PROVIDES A HAPPY MEDIUM FOR INDOOR/OUTDOOR LIVING IN THIS DESIGN. Inside, the foyer opens to a grand salon with a wall of glass, providing unobstructed views of the backyard. Informal areas include a leisure room with an entertainment center and glass doors that open to a covered poolside lanai. An outdoor fireplace enhances casual gatherings. The master suite is filled with amenities that include a bayed sitting area, access to the rear lanai, His and Hers closets, and a soaking tub. Upstairs, two family bedrooms—both with private decks—share a full bath. A detached guest house has a cabana bath and an outdoor grill area.

REAR EXTERIOR

HOME PLAN

HPK2700308

Style: Mediterranean
First Floor: 2,853 sq. ft.
Second Floor: 939 sq. ft.
Total: 3,792 sq. ft.
Bedrooms: 4
Bathrooms: 3 ½
Width: 80' - 0"
Depth: 96' - 0"
Foundation: Slab

eplans.com

HPK2700309

A SOUTHERN, TRADITIONAL-STYLE PLAN WITH WHEEL-CHAIR-ACCESSIBLE FEATURES, this home has something for everyone. Imagine welcoming friends and family on the full-length front porch with beautiful columns. Inside, the feeling of grandeur is evident with the spacious great room, while a computer center nearby keeps the space modern and convenient. A charming wraparound window seat in the breakfast room provides a place for conversation over coffee. The master suite features a personal exercise or hobby room as well as an opulent bath and two walk-in closets. Upstairs, discover the children's bedrooms, an office, and a home theater room.

Style: Farmhouse
First Floor: 2,484 sq. ft.
Second Floor: 1,336 sq. ft.
Total: 3,820 sq. ft.
Bedrooms: 4
Bathrooms: 3 ½
Width: 65' - 6"
Depth: 108' - 6"
Foundation: Crawlspace, Slab

eplans.com

FIRST FLOOR

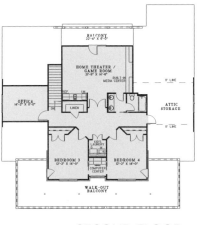

SECOND FLOOR

FIRST FLOOR

SECOND FLOOR

HPK2700310

Style: New American

First Floor: 2,520 sq. ft.

Second Floor: 1,305 sq. ft.

Total: 3,825 sq. ft.

Bedrooms: 4

Bathrooms: 3 ½

Width: 73' - 8"

Depth: 58' - 6"

Foundation: Slab

eplans.com

DISTINCTIVE TOUCHES TO THIS ELEGANT EUROPEAN-STYLE HOME make an inviting first impression. The two-story foyer is graced by a lovely staircase and a balcony overlook from the upstairs. To the right is the formal dining room; to the left, a study. The great room directly leads to the two-story double bay windows that introduce the kitchen and keeping room. A huge walk-in pantry and adjacent butler's pantry connect the dining room to the kitchen. A marvelous owners suite features a sitting room and pampering bath. Upstairs, three bedrooms and two full baths complete the plan.

HOME PLAN

(#) HPK2700311

Style: New American

First Floor: 2,319 sq. ft.

Second Floor: 1,570 sq. ft.

Total: 3,889 sq. ft.

Bedrooms: 4

Bathrooms: 3 ½

Width: 72' - 0"

Depth: 58' - 0"

Foundation: Crawlspace

eplans.com

FINE BRICK DETAILING, MULTIPLE ARCHES AND GABLES, and a grand entry give this four-bedroom home plenty of charm. The graceful, window-filled entry leads to a foyer flanked by a formal dining room and a study perfect for a home office. The great room, directly ahead, offers a fireplace and access to outside. A butler's pantry is located between the kitchen and dining room. The master suite is on the first floor. On the second floor, three family bedrooms, each with a walk-in closet, share two baths and a game room.

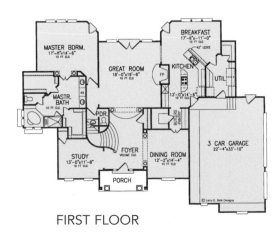

FIRST FLOOR

SECOND FLOOR

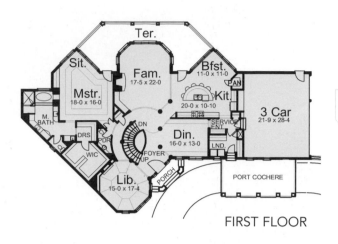

FIRST FLOOR

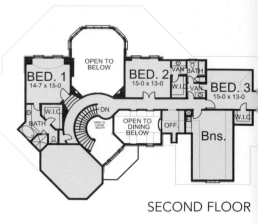

SECOND FLOOR

LOVELY STUCCO COLUMNS AND A COPPER STANDING-SEAM ROOF HIGHLIGHT THIS STONE-AND-BRICK FACADE. An elegant New World interior starts with a sensational winding staircase, a carved handrail, and honey-hued hardwood floor. An open, two-story formal dining room enjoys front-property views and leads to the gourmet kitchen through the butler's pantry, announced by an archway. Beyond the foyer, tall windows brighten the two-story family room and bring in a sense of the outdoors; a fireplace makes the space cozy and warm. The center food-prep island counter overlooks a breakfast niche that offers wide views through walls of windows and access to the rear porch.

REAR EXTERIOR

HOME PLAN

HPK2700312

Style: Chateauesque

First Floor: 2,612 sq. ft.

Second Floor: 1,300 sq. ft.

Total: 3,912 sq. ft.

Bonus Space: 330 sq. ft.

Bedrooms: 4

Bathrooms: 3 ½

Width: 95' - 6"

Depth: 64' - 0"

Foundation: Unfinished Basement

eplans.com

© 1998 Donald A. Gardner, Inc.

REAR EXTERIOR

IDING AND STONE EMBELLISH THE EXTERIOR OF THIS FIVE-
BEDROOM TRADITIONAL ESTATE for an exciting, yet stately
appearance. A two-story foyer creates an impressive entry. An equally impressive two-story great room features a fireplace, built-ins, and
back-porch access. The first-floor master suite enjoys an elegant tray
ceiling, back-porch access, and a lavish bath with all the amenities,
including an enormous walk-in closet. Down the hall, a second first-
floor bedroom easily converts to a study. The island kitchen easily
serves the dining and breakfast rooms. A fireplace warms the casual
family room. The breakfast room accesses the screened porch. Three
additional bedrooms are on the second floor. The bonus room above
the garage is great for attic storage, a home office, or a guest suite.

HPK2700313

Style: French Country
First Floor: 2,908 sq. ft.
Second Floor: 1,021 sq. ft.
Total: 3,929 sq. ft.
Bonus Space: 328 sq. ft.
Bedrooms: 5
Bathrooms: 4
Width: 85' - 4"
Depth: 70' - 4"

eplans.com

FIRST FLOOR

SECOND FLOOR

FIRST FLOOR

SECOND FLOOR

THE GRANDIOSE ENTRANCE IS REMINISCENT OF HOMES FROM EARLY AMERICA and the exquisite interior does not disappoint. Formal living areas give way to the informal openness of the family room and adjoining breakfast area and island kitchen. Access to the rear terrace from this area makes alfresco meals an option. Upstairs houses three additional family bedrooms—two share a Jack-and-Jill bath—the third boasts a private, full bath. A future rec room completes this level.

HOME PLAN

HPK2700314

Style: Federal - Adams
First Floor: 2,767 sq. ft.
Second Floor: 1,179 sq. ft.
Total: 3,946 sq. ft.
Bonus Space: 591 sq. ft.
Bedrooms: 4
Bathrooms: 3 ½ + ½
Width: 79' - 11"
Depth: 80' - 6"
Foundation: Crawlspace

eplans.com

© William E. Poole Designs, Inc

© Larry E. Belk Designs

A DISTINCTIVELY FRENCH FLAIR IS THE HALLMARK OF THIS EUROPEAN DESIGN. Inside, the two-story foyer provides views to the huge great room beyond. A well-placed study off the foyer provides space for a home office. The kitchen, breakfast room, and sunroom are adjacent and lend a spacious feel. The great room is visible from this area through decorative arches. The master suite includes a roomy sitting area and a lovely bath with a centerpiece whirlpool tub flanked by half-columns. Upstairs, Bedrooms 2 and 3 share a bath that includes separate dressing areas.

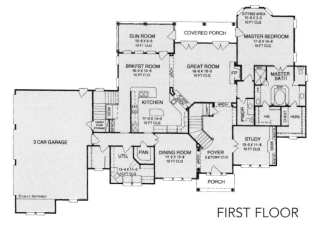

FIRST FLOOR

HOME PLAN

HPK2700315

Style: Beaux Arts

First Floor: 2,608 sq. ft.

Second Floor: 1,432 sq. ft.

Total: 4,040 sq. ft.

Bedrooms: 4

Bathrooms: 3 ½

Width: 89' - 10"

Depth: 63' - 8"

Foundation: Crawlspace, Slab

eplans.com

SECOND FLOOR

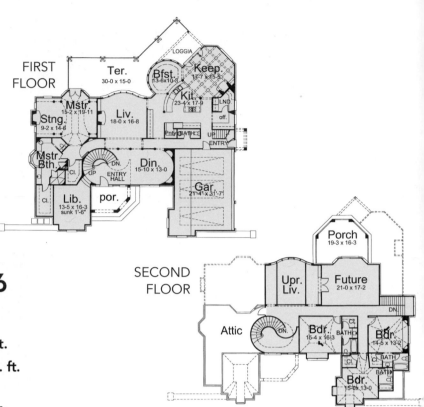

FIRST FLOOR

SECOND FLOOR

HPK2700316

Style: Chateauesque

First Floor: 2,901 sq. ft.

Second Floor: 1,140 sq. ft.

Total: 4,041 sq. ft.

Bonus Space: 522 sq. ft.

Bedrooms: 4

Bathrooms: 4 ½

Width: 80' - 0"

Depth: 70' - 0"

Foundation: Finished Walkout Basement

eplans.com

THIS STATELY CHATEAUESQUE HOME IS AS MAGNIFICENT INSIDE as its exterior would suggest. Columns throughout the home are well placed to draw out the spacious grandeur of this plan. The heavenly master suite is a fairy tale come true. His and Hers walk-in closets, a sitting room with a fireplace, and French-door access to the rear veranda guarantee comfort; the extraordinary bath, complete with a huge tub set in a bay overlooking gardens, is sure to pamper. A circular breakfast bay enjoys views of the veranda and the loggia. Upstairs, three bedrooms come with separate lavish baths. Additional space is available to add a guest apartment. A sunken floor separates the downstairs front library from other rooms.

HPK2700317

HOME PLAN #

Style: New American

First Floor: 2,095 sq. ft.

Second Floor: 1,954 sq. ft.

Total: 4,049 sq. ft.

Bedrooms: 5

Bathrooms: 4 ½

Width: 56' - 0"

Depth: 63' - 0"

Foundation: Crawlspace, Unfinished Walkout Basement

eplans.com

FIRST FLOOR

SECOND FLOOR

THE DISTINGUISHED FACADE OF THIS LOVELY DESIGN HINTS AT THE ENCHANTING AMENITIES FOUND WITHIN. A two-story foyer welcomes you inside. To the right, a bayed living room is separated from the formal dining room by graceful columns. A butler's pantry leads to the gourmet island kitchen. The breakfast room accesses a rear covered porch and shares a casual area with the two-story family room. Here, a fireplace flanked by built-ins adds to the relaxing atmosphere. Bedroom 5, with a private bath, converts to an optional study. Upstairs, the master suite offers palatial elegance. Here, the sitting room is warmed by a fireplace flanked by built-ins and the suite accesses a private second-floor porch. A dressing room leads to the vaulted master bath and enormous His and Hers walk-in closets. Three additional bedrooms are available on the second floor.

FIRST FLOOR

SECOND FLOOR

HERE IS A TWO-STORY COUNTRY HOME THAT HAS EQUAL PORTIONS OF CHARM AND LIVABILITY. The two-story foyer with its handsome staircase is flanked by a living room/study and a dining room. The expansive and well-equipped kitchen lies between the dining room and a breakfast nook, which features a window seat and direct access to the covered porch. The focus of the first floor is the grand room with its fireplace, built-ins, coffered ceiling, and the 21-foot bow window. Five bedrooms and three full baths reside on the second level. The master suite occupies the right side of this plan and contains a sitting area, a huge bath with a tray ceiling, and two walk-in closets.

HPK2700318

HOME PLAN

Style: Country

First Floor: 1,839 sq. ft.

Second Floor: 2,320 sq. ft.

Total: 4,159 sq. ft.

Bedrooms: 5

Bathrooms: 3 ½

Width: 61' - 6"

Depth: 61' - 0"

Foundation: Crawlspace, Unfinished Walkout Basement

eplans.com

FIRST FLOOR

Ext. Storage

Garage
21'4"x45'8"

Patio

Utility

Screened
Porch

Bedroom
12'9"x12'2"

Master
Bedroom
15'2"x25'5"

WIC

Family
19'11"x25'7"

Kitchen
15'3"x19'8"

Master
Bath

Breakfast
13'7"x14'2"

Dining
11'3"x14'

Study
11'5"x
12'1"

WIC

Foyer

Porch

SECOND FLOOR

Gameroom
20'x29'8"

WIC

Media
Room
12'8"x11'1"

WIC

WIC

Bedroom
11'5"x
16'11"

Sitting

Bedroom
11'5"x
16'1"

HOME PLAN

HPK2700319

Style: Neoclassical

First Floor: 3,129 sq. ft.

Second Floor: 1,058 sq. ft.

Total: 4,187 sq. ft.

Bonus Space: 551 sq. ft.

Bedrooms: 4

Bathrooms: 4 ½

Width: 68' - 0"

Depth: 117' - 10"

Foundation: Slab

eplans.com

ONCE INSIDE THE WELCOMING FACADE, an open floor plan between the foyer, the dining room, and the family room leads directly out to the screened porch and patio in the rear of the house. The L-shaped kitchen includes an island and a walk-in pantry, and nearby breakfast nook. A secondary bedroom, with its own private bath, and a utility room leads to the three-car garage. The luxurious master suite includes two walk-in closets, a fireplace, and access to the back porch. The second floor boasts two bedrooms and baths and a media room.

FIRST FLOOR

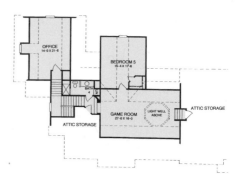

SECOND FLOOR

HOME PLAN

HPK2700320

Style: French Country

First Floor: 3,328 sq. ft.

Second Floor: 868 sq. ft.

Total: 4,196 sq. ft.

Bedrooms: 5

Bathrooms: 4

Width: 108' - 2"

Depth: 61' - 6"

Foundation: Crawlspace, Slab

eplans.com

THE COMBINATION OF STUCCO, STACKED STONE, AND BRICK adds texture and character to this French Country home. The foyer offers views to the study, dining room, and living room. Double French doors open to the study with built-in bookcases and a window seat overlooking the rear deck. The breakfast room, family room, and spacious kitchen make a nice backdrop for family living. The master suite is enhanced by a raised corner fireplace and a bath with an exercise room. Upstairs, two family bedrooms—or make one an office—and a full bath are balanced by a large game room.

HOME PLAN

(#) HPK2700321

Style: New American

First Floor: 3,098 sq. ft.

Second Floor: 1,113 sq. ft.

Total: 4,211 sq. ft.

Bonus Space: 567 sq. ft.

Bedrooms: 4

Bathrooms: 3 ½

Width: 112' - 0"

Depth: 69' - 9"

Foundation: Crawlspace

eplans.com

THE MAGNIFICENT ENTRY OF THIS ELEGANT TRADITIONAL HOME MAKES A GRAND IMPRESSION. The soaring ceiling of the foyer looks over a curved staircase that leads to secondary sleeping quarters. The first-floor master suite offers an expansive retreat for the homeowner, with mitered windows and a see-through fireplace shared with the spacious spa-style bath. Formal rooms open from the foyer, and a gallery hall leads to the casual living area, with a two-story family room and French doors to the outside. The three-car garage offers wardrobe space for coats.

FIRST FLOOR

SECOND FLOOR

FIRST FLOOR

SECOND FLOOR

AN ELEGANT EUROPEAN MANOR WITH FAMILY APPEAL, THIS BEAUTIFUL FOUR-BEDROOM PLAN will be a joy to own for generations to come. The two-story foyer presents a dramatic curved staircase that leads to two bedroom suites and a game room. Continue to the great room full of natural light and warmed by a cozy hearth. A unique shape in the kitchen maximizes counter space and offers easy access to the breakfast nook and a butler's pantry to the dining room. A nearby bedroom is perfect as a guest suite or live-in help's quarters. The master suite is located for privacy, exquisite with a sitting bay and a lavish bath that features a prominent step-up tub. The plan is completed by a three-car garage and two-car porte cochere.

HOME PLAN

HPK2700322

Style: French Country

First Floor: 2,950 sq. ft.

Second Floor: 1,278 sq. ft.

Total: 4,228 sq. ft.

Bedrooms: 4

Bathrooms: 4 ½

Width: 91' - 8"

Depth: 71' - 10"

Foundation: Crawlspace, Slab, Unfinished Basement

eplans.com

HPK2700323

Style: New American

First Floor: 2,639 sq. ft.

Second Floor: 1,625 sq. ft.

Total: 4,264 sq. ft.

Bedrooms: 4

Bathrooms: 3 ½

Width: 73' - 8"

Depth: 58' - 6"

Foundation: Crawlspace, Slab, Unfinished Basement

eplans.com

THIS HOME OFFERS BOTH LUXURY AND PRACTICALITY. A study and dining room flank the foyer, and the great room offers a warming fireplace and double French-door access to the rear yard. A butler's pantry acts as a helpful buffer between the kitchen and the columned dining room. Double bays at the rear of the home form the keeping room and the breakfast room on one side and the master bedroom on the other. Three family bedrooms and two baths grace the second floor. A game room is perfect for casual family time.

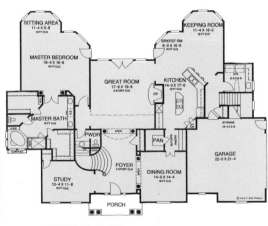

FIRST FLOOR

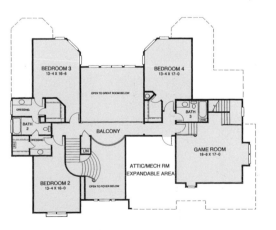

SECOND FLOOR

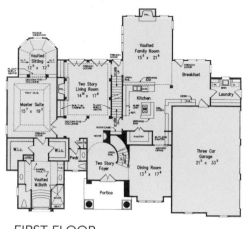

FIRST FLOOR

SECOND FLOOR

HPK2700324

Style: Neoclassical

First Floor: 2,764 sq. ft.

Second Floor: 1,598 sq. ft.

Total: 4,362 sq. ft.

Bedrooms: 4

Bathrooms: 3 ½

Width: 74' - 6"

Depth: 65' - 10"

Foundation: Crawlspace, Unfinished Walkout Basement

eplans.com

GREEK-INSPIRED PORTICO COLUMNS AND FRENCH COUNTRY ROOFLINES MAKE THIS HOME TRULY UNIQUE. At the heart of this magnificent design is the two-story living room with its fireplace and built-in bookshelves. To the right rear of the plan are the more casual rooms—the vaulted family room, island kitchen, and breakfast nook. A formal dining room, with kitchen access through the butler's pantry, awaits elegant meals at the front of the plan. The private master wing features a bayed sitting area and a deluxe vaulted bath with His and Hers wardrobes and vanity sinks. A curved staircase in the foyer gracefully winds its way up to the second floor. Here, three bedrooms, each with a walk-in closet, share two full baths, a loft and a gallery that overlooks the first floor.

HPK2700325

Style: New American

First Floor: 3,218 sq. ft.

Second Floor: 1,240 sq. ft.

Total: 4,458 sq. ft.

Bonus Space: 656 sq. ft.

Bedrooms: 4

Bathrooms: 3 ½

Width: 76' - 0"

Depth: 73' - 10"

Foundation: Unfinished Walkout Basement

eplans.com

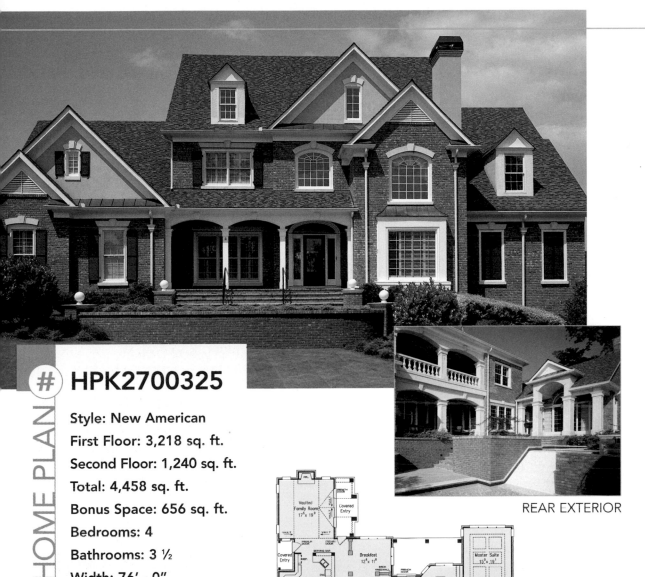

REAR EXTERIOR

FIRST FLOOR

SECOND FLOOR

THIS DESIGN FEATURES A BREATHTAKING FACADE WITH AN UPPER REAR BALCONY, four covered porches, and an inconspicuous side garage. The foyer is flanked by the dining room and the two-story library, which includes a fireplace and built-in bookcases. The elegant master bath provides dual vanities, a bright radius window, and a separate leaded-glass shower. A unique double-decker walk-in closet provides plenty of storage. Nearby, a home office offers stunning views of the backyard. Upstairs, two family bedrooms share a compartmented bath and a covered porch; a third offers a private bath. A bonus room is included for future expansion.

FIRST FLOOR

SECOND FLOOR

A COUNTRY-STYLE WRAPAROUND PORCH PROVIDES A CHEERFUL WELCOME to this distinguished farmhouse design. Formal spaces are magnificent: the dining room, living room, and family room (featuring a coffered ceiling) elevate the main part of the home. The kitchen boasts a serving bar and a walk-in pantry, as well as a butleris pantry. A first-floor bedroom with a walk-in closet can double as a study. The master suite, with a sitting area, vaulted bath, and access to a private covered porch, dominates the second floor. Three additional bedrooms all offer tray ceilings and walk-in closets. A large playroom, with wide views of the rear landscape, completes the plan.

HOME PLAN

HPK2700326

Style: Farmhouse

First Floor: 2,092 sq. ft.

Second Floor: 2,372 sq. ft.

Total: 4,464 sq. ft.

Bedrooms: 5

Bathrooms: 4 ½

Width: 75' - 5"

Depth: 64' - 0"

Foundation: Crawlspace, Unfinished Walkout Basement

eplans.com

FIRST FLOOR

Three-car Garage
21' x 31'10"

Hearth Room
16'4" x 14'

Terrace

Dressing

Hall

Breakfast
24' x 26' lrr

Master Bedroom
17' x 28'

Laun.
11' x 14'

Bath

Kitchen

Great Room
18'9' x 15'6"

Gallery

Bath

Dining Room
16' x 15'2"

Foyer

Library
16' x 14'

Porch

FIRST FLOOR

SECOND FLOOR

Bedroom
12'8" x 15'6"

Bath

Hall

walk in closet

Bedroom
12' x 13'6"

Balcony

Bedroom
15' x 15'2"

SECOND FLOOR

HOME PLAN

HPK2700327

Style: New American

First Floor: 3,300 sq. ft.

Second Floor: 1,170 sq. ft.

Total: 4,470 sq. ft.

Bedrooms: 4

Bathrooms: 3 ½ + ½

Width: 87' - 0"

Depth: 82' - 0"

Foundation: Unfinished Basement

eplans.com

THE GRACIOUS EXTERIOR OF THIS CLASSIC EUROPEAN-STYLE HOME is accentuated by dual boxed windows, dramatically curved stairs and a glassed entry decorated with tall columns. A grand foyer showcases the dining room and great room, which offers a fireplace and French doors opening to a rear terrace. A gourmet kitchen adjoins the breakfast room, also open to the terrace; just beyond, a corner fireplace warms the hearth room. The luxurious master suite provides a spacious walk-in closet and an opulent bath. Upstairs, a balcony overlooks the foyer and gallery. Three secondary bedrooms all provide walk-in closets; one offers a private bath.

FIRST FLOOR

SECOND FLOOR

HOME PLAN

#HPK2700328

Style: New American

First Floor: 2,954 sq. ft.

Second Floor: 1,534 sq. ft.

Total: 4,488 sq. ft.

Bedrooms: 4

Bathrooms: 3 ½ + ½

Width: 87' - 4"

Depth: 60' - 4"

Foundation: Crawlspace, Slab

eplans.com

ALMOST 4,500 SQUARE FEET OF LUXURIOUS LIVING AWAIT YOU IN THIS TWO-STORY TRADITIONAL DESIGN. A lavish entry welcomes you into this four-bedroom home with fantastic amenities such as an enormous master suite, private home office, upper-level exercise room, and state-of-the-art home theater with game area. Formal living and dining rooms with columned entries are evenly placed at the front of the home, setting a very formal tone. The great room has a built-in media center and shares a large bar seating area with a direct view into the gourmet-style kitchen. In addition to a large laundry room with hobby area, a nearby mudroom with built-in storage, and plenty of deep storage closets throughout this design make this the perfect family home.

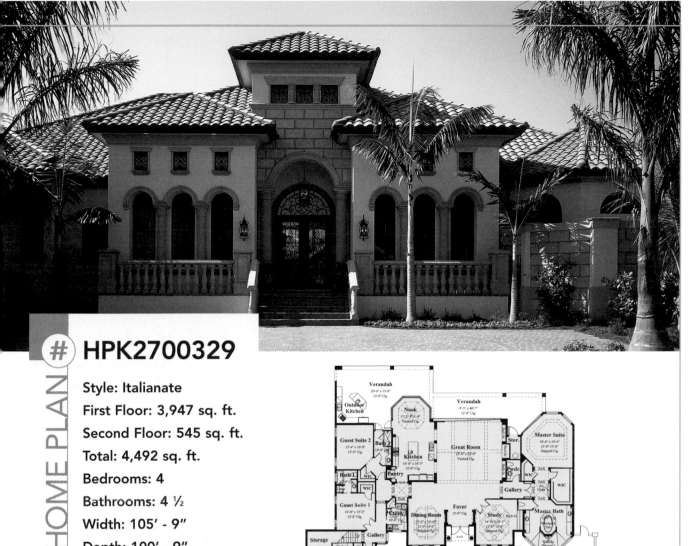

HPK2700329

Style: Italianate

First Floor: 3,947 sq. ft.

Second Floor: 545 sq. ft.

Total: 4,492 sq. ft.

Bedrooms: 4

Bathrooms: 4 ½

Width: 105' - 9"

Depth: 100' - 9"

Foundation: Slab

eplans.com

FIRST FLOOR

SECOND FLOOR

REPEATING ARCHES HINT OF A SEASIDE RESORT IN THIS FABULOUS MEDITERRANEAN MANOR. The triple arches of the facade are creatively repeated inside as pass-through points between the ultra-elegant kitchen and great room. An entire wall of glass pocket doors adds volumes of fresh-air living opportunities to this charming family space. Floor-to-ceiling glass panels also enhance the master suite, where they embrace a sitting nook and slide open to a private end of the veranda. A spa-style tub sits center stage in the master bath. Behind the curved wall is a walk-in shower with views to a private garden. The idyllic courtyard—with its stunning stone fireplace and gazebo-style, open-beamed canopy—has an arbor-like ambiance perfect for a cool drink and warm friends. A twilight glow highlights the indoor-outdoor connections of this home as the public and private rooms cast their personalities outside to the meandering veranda and glittering pool.

REAR EXTERIOR

FIRST FLOOR

SECOND FLOOR

THIS MAJESTIC STORYBOOK COTTAGE, FROM THE MAGICAL SETTING OF RURAL EUROPE, provides the perfect home for any large family—with a wealth of modern comforts within. A graceful staircase cascades from the two-story foyer. To the left, a sophisticated study offers a wall of built-ins. To the right, a formal dining room is easily served from the island kitchen. The breakfast room accesses the rear screened porch. Fireplaces warm the great room and keeping room. Two sets of double doors open from the great room to the rear covered porch. The master bedroom features private porch access, a sitting area, lavish bath, and two walk-in closets. Upstairs, three additional family bedrooms offer walk-in closet space galore! The game room is great entertainment for both family and friends. A three-car garage with golf-cart storage completes the plan.

HOME PLAN

HPK2700330

Style: French Country

First Floor: 3,033 sq. ft.

Second Floor: 1,545 sq. ft.

Total: 4,578 sq. ft.

Bedrooms: 4

Bathrooms: 3 ½ + ½

Width: 91' - 6"

Depth: 63' - 8"

Foundation: Crawlspace, Slab, Unfinished Basement

eplans.com

HOME PLAN

HPK2700331

Style: Chateauesque

First Floor: 2,453 sq. ft.

Second Floor: 2,138 sq. ft.

Total: 4,591 sq. ft.

Bedrooms: 5

Bathrooms: 4

Width: 80' - 0"

Depth: 67' - 0"

Foundation: Unfinished Basement

eplans.com

FIRST FLOOR

Solr.
15-4 x 11-8

Bfst.
11-8 x 11-8

Liv.
15-4 x 16-8

Kit.
19-4 x 15-0

Gst.
12-4 x 12-8

Keep.
17-4 x 13-8

BATH

LOGGIA

UP

Din.
14-0 x 16-0

ENTRY
HALL

Lib.
15-8 x 11-0

UP

DN.

3 Car
21-4 x 31-4

LND.

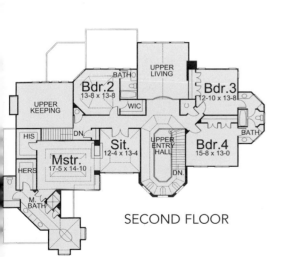

SECOND FLOOR

UPPER
LIVING

BATH

Bdr.2
13-8 x 13-8

Bdr.3
12-10 x 13-8

WIC

UPPER
KEEPING

HIS

DN.

BATH

Sit.
12-4 x 13-4

UPPER
ENTRY
HALL

Bdr.4
15-8 x 13-0

HERS

Mstr.
17-5 x 14-10

DN.

M.
BATH

ACCOMMODATE YOUR LIFE'S DIVERSE PATTERN OF FORMAL OCCASIONS AND CASUAL TIMES with this spacious home. The exterior of this estate presents a palatial bearing, while the interior is both comfortable and elegant. Formal areas are graced with amenities to make entertaining easy. Casual areas are kept intimate, but no less large. The solarium serves both with skylights and terrace access. Guests will appreciate a private guest room and a bath with loggia access on the first floor. Family bedrooms and the master suite are upstairs. Note the gracious ceiling treatments in the master bedroom, its sitting room, and Bedroom 2.

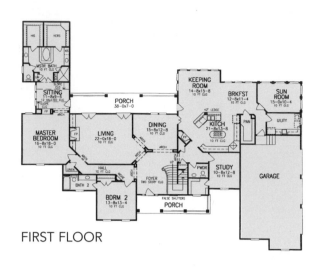

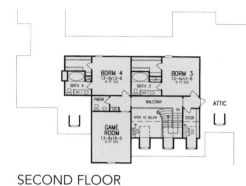

FIRST FLOOR

SECOND FLOOR

HOME PLAN

HPK2700332

Style: Country

First Floor: 3,471 sq. ft.

Second Floor: 1,221 sq. ft.

Total: 4,692 sq. ft.

Bedrooms: 4

Bathrooms: 4 ½ + ½

Width: 100' - 2"

Depth: 82' - 6"

Foundation: Crawlspace

eplans.com

MULTIPLE DORMERS AND A COVERED FRONT PORCH are sure signs that family friends are welcome to this four-bedroom home. The two-story foyer leads through arches into the formal dining room, living room, and hallway to the first floor sleeping wing. Here, a deluxe master suite has many amenities to offer: a two-sided fireplace, a sitting room, His and Hers walk-in closets, and a lavish bath. On the other end of the home, a spacious kitchen features a cook-top island and has direct access to the adjacent keeping and breakfast rooms. Note the huge walk-in pantry and the sun room. A private study offers a walk-in closet. Upstairs are two more family bedrooms, two-and-a-half baths, and a large game room.

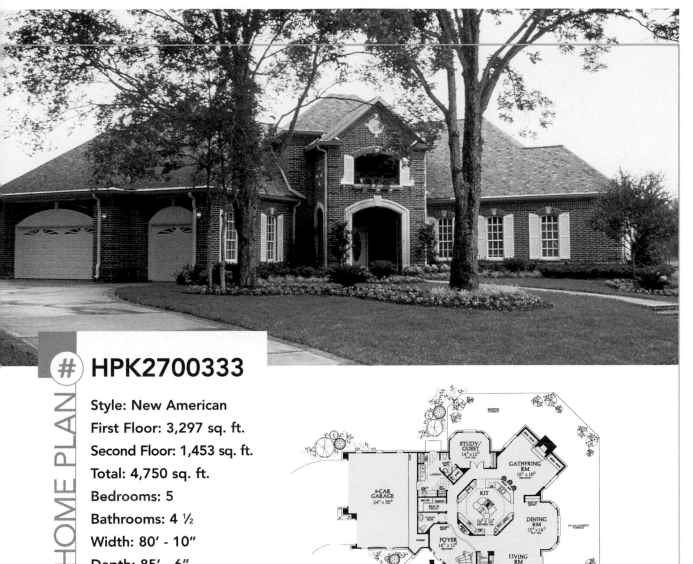

HOME PLAN

HPK2700333

Style: New American

First Floor: 3,297 sq. ft.

Second Floor: 1,453 sq. ft.

Total: 4,750 sq. ft.

Bedrooms: 5

Bathrooms: 4 ½

Width: 80' - 10"

Depth: 85' - 6"

Foundation: Slab

eplans.com

FIRST FLOOR

SECOND FLOOR

THIS ELEGANT HOME COMBINES A TRADITIONAL EXTERI-OR WITH A CONTEMPORARY INTERIOR and provides a delightful setting for both entertaining and individual solitude. A living room and bay-windowed dining room provide an open area for formal entertaining, which can spill outside to the entertainment terrace or to the nearby gathering room with its dramatic fireplace. On the opposite side of the house, French doors make it possible for the study/guest room to be closed off from the rest of the first floor. The master suite is also a private retreat, offering a fireplace as well as an abundance of natural light, and a bath designed to pamper. The entire family will enjoy the second-floor media loft from which a balcony overlooks the two-story gathering room below.

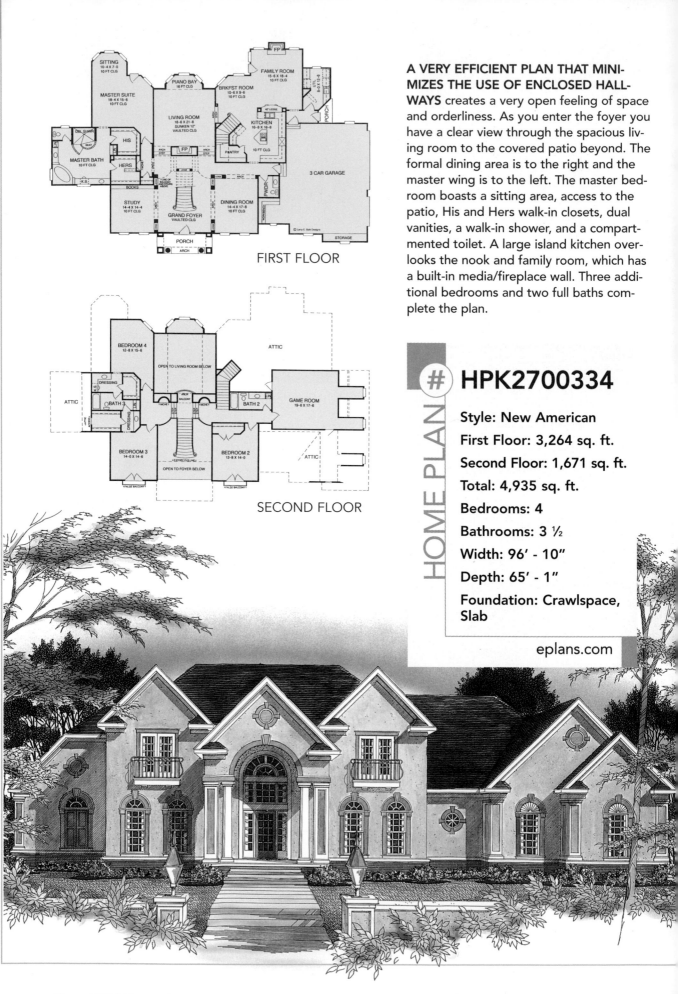

FIRST FLOOR

SECOND FLOOR

A VERY EFFICIENT PLAN THAT MINI-MIZES THE USE OF ENCLOSED HALL-WAYS creates a very open feeling of space and orderliness. As you enter the foyer you have a clear view through the spacious living room to the covered patio beyond. The formal dining area is to the right and the master wing is to the left. The master bedroom boasts a sitting area, access to the patio, His and Hers walk-in closets, dual vanities, a walk-in shower, and a compartmented toilet. A large island kitchen overlooks the nook and family room, which has a built-in media/fireplace wall. Three additional bedrooms and two full baths complete the plan.

HPK2700334

HOME PLAN

Style: New American

First Floor: 3,264 sq. ft.

Second Floor: 1,671 sq. ft.

Total: 4,935 sq. ft.

Bedrooms: 4

Bathrooms: 3 ½

Width: 96' - 10"

Depth: 65' - 1"

Foundation: Crawlspace, Slab

eplans.com

HPK2700335

Style: Craftsman
First Floor: 3,253 sq. ft.
Second Floor: 1,747 sq. ft.
Total: 5,000 sq. ft.
Bedrooms: 4
Bathrooms: 4 ½
Width: 112' - 9"
Depth: 89' - 10"
Foundation: Crawlspace

eplans.com

THIS IMPRESSIVE TWO-STORY CRAFTSMAN DESIGN FEATURES A MODERN LAYOUT filled with abundant rooms and amenities. A wide front porch welcomes you inside to an entry flanked on either side by formal living and dining rooms. Built-ins enhance the dining room, while the living room shares a see-through fireplace with the library/study. The island kitchen offers a utility room and food pantry nearby, and it overlooks the breakfast and family rooms. The mudroom accesses the rear porch and sun room. The luxurious master suite contains a sitting area, His and Hers walk-in closets, a private bath, and an exercise room. At the rear, planters enhance the raised patio area. The second floor features three additional bedrooms. A study between Bedrooms 3 and 4 is perfect for the kids. A game room, sleep loft, and rear balcony complete this floor.

FIRST FLOOR

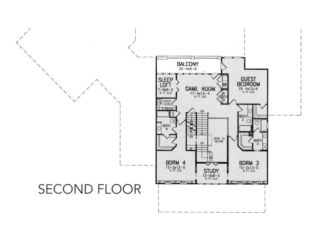

SECOND FLOOR

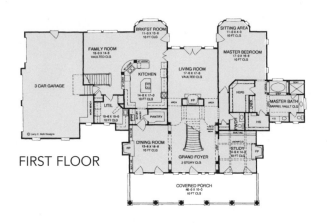

FIRST FLOOR

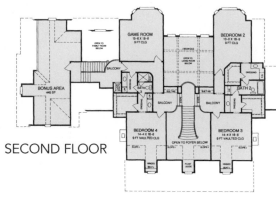

SECOND FLOOR

HPK2700336

Style: Federal - Adams

First Floor: 3,170 sq. ft.

Second Floor: 1,914 sq. ft.

Total: 5,084 sq. ft.

Bonus Space: 445 sq. ft.

Bedrooms: 4

Bathrooms: 3 ½

Width: 100' - 10"

Depth: 65' - 5"

Foundation: Crawlspace

eplans.com

THIS ELEGANTLY APPOINTED HOME IS A BEAUTY INSIDE AND OUT. A centerpiece stair rises gracefully from the two-story grand foyer. The kitchen, breakfast room, and family room provide open space for the gathering of family and friends. The beam-ceilinged study and the dining room flank the grand foyer, and each includes a fireplace. The master bedroom features a cozy sitting area and a luxury master bath with His and Hers vanities and walk-in closets. Three large bedrooms and a game room complete the second floor. A large expandable area is available at the top of the rear stair.

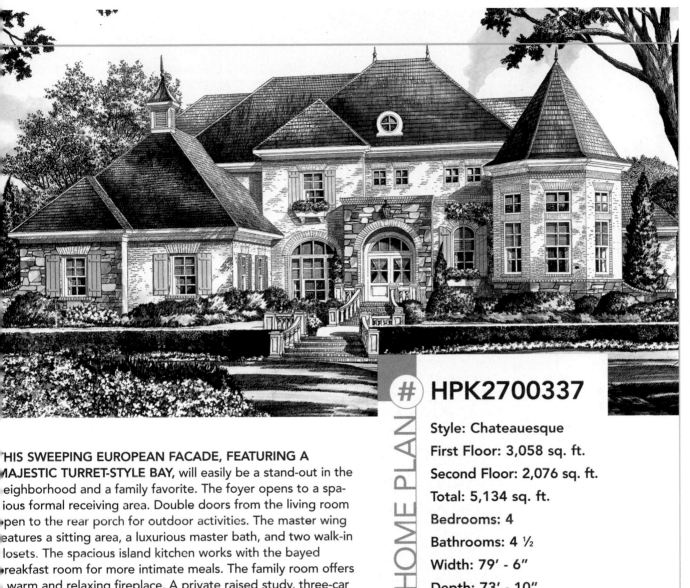

HOME PLAN #

HPK2700337

Style: Chateauesque

First Floor: 3,058 sq. ft.

Second Floor: 2,076 sq. ft.

Total: 5,134 sq. ft.

Bedrooms: 4

Bathrooms: 4 ½

Width: 79' - 6"

Depth: 73' - 10"

Foundation: Crawlspace, Slab, Unfinished Basement

eplans.com

THIS SWEEPING EUROPEAN FACADE, FEATURING A MAJESTIC TURRET-STYLE BAY, will easily be a stand-out in the neighborhood and a family favorite. The foyer opens to a spacious formal receiving area. Double doors from the living room open to the rear porch for outdoor activities. The master wing features a sitting area, a luxurious master bath, and two walk-in closets. The spacious island kitchen works with the bayed breakfast room for more intimate meals. The family room offers a warm and relaxing fireplace. A private raised study, three-car garage, and utility room complete the first floor. Upstairs, three additional family bedrooms share the second floor with a music loft, hobby room, and game room.

FIRST FLOOR

SECOND FLOOR

FIRST FLOOR

SECOND FLOOR

THIS HOME IS ELEGANTLY STYLED IN THE FRENCH COUNTRY TRADITION. A large dining room and a study open off the two-story grand foyer. The large formal living room accesses the covered patio. A more informal family room is conveniently located off the kitchen and breakfast room. The roomy master suite includes a sitting area, a luxurious private bath, and its own entrance to the study. The second floor can be reached from the formal front stair or a well-placed rear staircase. Three large bedrooms and a game room are located on this floor. The walkout basement can be expanded to provide more living space.

HOME PLAN

HPK2700338

Style: French Country

First Floor: 3,261 sq. ft.

Second Floor: 1,920 sq. ft.

Total: 5,181 sq. ft.

Bedrooms: 4

Bathrooms: 3 ½

Width: 86' - 2"

Depth: 66' - 10"

Foundation: Crawlspace, Unfinished Basement

eplans.com

ORDER BLUEPRINTS ANYTIME AT EPLANS.COM OR 1-800-521-679?

HOME PLAN

HPK2700339

Style: New American

First Floor: 3,599 sq. ft.

Second Floor: 1,621 sq. ft.

Total: 5,220 sq. ft.

Bonus Space: 537 sq. ft.

Bedrooms: 4

Bathrooms: 5 ½

Width: 108' - 10"

Depth: 53' - 10"

Foundation: Slab, Unfinished Basement

eplans.com

A GRAND FACADE DETAILED WITH BRICK CORNER QUOINS, STUCCO FLOURISHES, ARCHED WINDOWS, and an elegant entrance presents this home. A spacious foyer is accented by curving stairs and flanked by a formal living room and a formal dining room. For cozy times, a through-fireplace is located between a large family room and a quiet study. The master bedroom is designed to pamper, with two walk-in closets, a two-sided fireplace, a bayed sitting area, and a lavish private bath. Upstairs, three secondary bedrooms each have a private bath and a walk-in closet. Also on this level is a spacious recreation room, perfect for a game room or children's playroom.

FIRST FLOOR

SECOND FLOOR

SECOND FLOOR

FIRST FLOOR

HOME PLAN

#HPK2700340

Style: Mediterranean

First Floor: 4,716 sq. ft.

Second Floor: 619 sq. ft.

Total: 5,335 sq. ft.

Bedrooms: 4

Bathrooms: 5 ½

Width: 95' - 0"

Depth: 134' - 6"

Foundation: Slab

eplans.com

A TALL ENTRY AND BROAD FOOTPRINT GIVE THIS EUROPEAN HOME A COMMANDING PRESENCE. Upon entering, a large foyer gives way to a loggia beyond, the master wing on the left, and the remaining rooms to the right. The master bedroom's built-ins provide a place to display treasures and a sitting room for relaxing while surrounded by slender windows with backyard views. His and Hers closets flank the hallway leading to the master bath with a corner tub, dual vanity sinks, and a built-in window seat. The right wing of the home opens with a formal dining room on the right and a kitchen entrance past the wet bar on the left. The open island kitchen overlooks the breakfast and leisure rooms. Across the hall, a butterfly garden brings nature indoors and a guest study provides a private space off the solana and outdoor kitchen. Three guest suites—one upstairs, two down—provide excellent quarters for visitors.

HPK2700341

Style: New American

First Floor: 3,745 sq. ft.

Second Floor: 1,643 sq. ft.

Total: 5,388 sq. ft.

Bonus Space: 510 sq. ft.

Bedrooms: 5

Bathrooms: 4 ½ + ½

Width: 100' - 0"

Depth: 70' - 1"

Foundation: Crawlspace, Slab, Unfinished Basement

eplans.com

FIRST FLOOR

SECOND FLOOR

TEEP ROOFLINES AND PLENTY OF WINDOWS CREATE A SOPHISTICATED AURA AROUND THIS HOME. Columns support the balconies above as well s the entry below. An angled family room featuring a replace is great for rest and relaxation. Snacks and unlight are just around the corner with the nearby reakfast room and island kitchen. A ribbon of windows in the living room makes for an open feel. A bay-windowed study/library has two sets of French doors—ne to the living room and one to the master suite. The naster bedroom offers a bath with dual vanities and a pacious walk-in closet. Three family bedrooms are ocated on the upper level with a recreation/media oom and an optional bonus room.

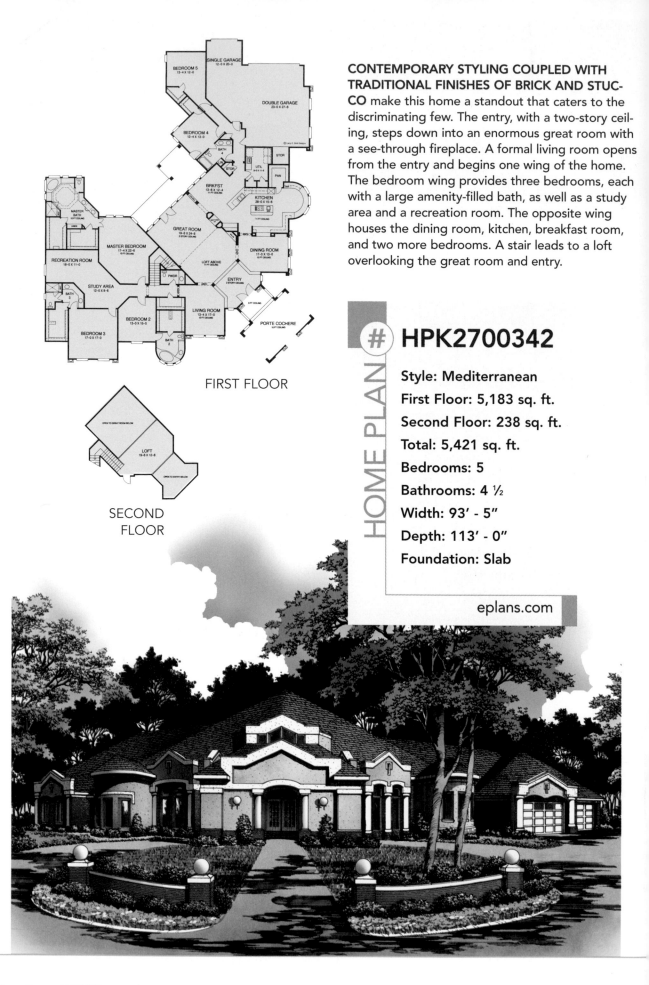

FIRST FLOOR

SECOND FLOOR

CONTEMPORARY STYLING COUPLED WITH TRADITIONAL FINISHES OF BRICK AND STUC- CO make this home a standout that caters to the discriminating few. The entry, with a two-story ceiling, steps down into an enormous great room with a see-through fireplace. A formal living room opens from the entry and begins one wing of the home. The bedroom wing provides three bedrooms, each with a large amenity-filled bath, as well as a study area and a recreation room. The opposite wing houses the dining room, kitchen, breakfast room, and two more bedrooms. A stair leads to a loft overlooking the great room and entry.

HOME PLAN

HPK2700342

Style: Mediterranean

First Floor: 5,183 sq. ft.

Second Floor: 238 sq. ft.

Total: 5,421 sq. ft.

Bedrooms: 5

Bathrooms: 4 ½

Width: 93' - 5"

Depth: 113' - 0"

Foundation: Slab

eplans.com

ORDER BLUEPRINTS ANYTIME AT EPLANS.COM OR 1-800-521-6797

HOME PLAN

HPK2700343

Style: Farmhouse

First Floor: 2,732 sq. ft.

Second Floor: 2,734 sq. ft.

Total: 5,466 sq. ft.

Bedrooms: 5

Bathrooms: 5 ½ + ½

Width: 85' - 0"

Depth: 85' - 6"

Foundation: Crawlspace, Slab, Unfinished Walkout Basement

eplans.com

FIRST FLOOR

SECOND FLOOR

A WRAPAROUND COVERED PORCH ADDS PLENTY OF OUTDOOR SPACE to this already impressive home. Built-in cabinets flank the fireplace in the grand room; a fireplace also warms the hearth room. The gourmet kitchen includes an island counter, large walk-in pantry, and serving bar. A secluded home office, with a separate entrance nearby, provides a quiet work place. A front parlor provides even more room for entertaining or relaxing. The master suite dominates the second floor, offering a spacious sitting area with an elegant tray ceiling, a dressing area, and a luxurious bath with two walk-in closets, double vanities, and a raised garden tub. The second floor is also home to an enormous exercise room and three additional bedrooms.

TIMELESS BRICK EXTERIOR SHOWCASES SLAT-... SHUTTERS AND MULTIPANED, OVERSIZED WIN-... ...s. The brick portico with contrasting arches and a ...ony adds pizazz to this stately facade. The designer ...ghtfully utilizes space and includes amenities such as ...alk-in pantry, an exercise room, numerous built-ins, a computer room, and skylights over the screened and covered porches. Let guests bring their kids along to play in the upstairs game room/home theater!

FIRST FLOOR

HOME PLAN

(#) **HPK2700344**

Style: New American

First Floor: 3,276 sq. ft.

Second Floor: 2,272 sq. ft.

Total: 5,548 sq. ft.

Bedrooms: 5

Bathrooms: 4 ½

Width: 81' - 6"

Depth: 93' - 2"

Foundation: Crawlspace, Slab, Unfinished Basement

eplans.com

SECOND FLOOR

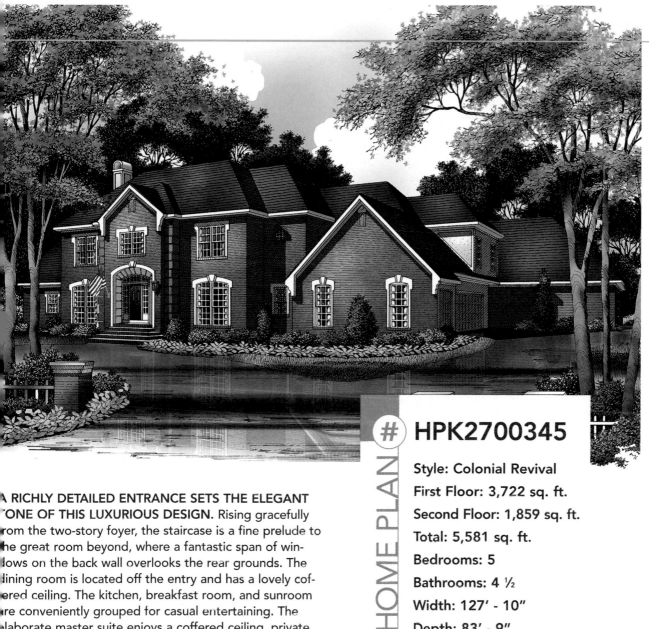

A RICHLY DETAILED ENTRANCE SETS THE ELEGANT TONE OF THIS LUXURIOUS DESIGN. Rising gracefully from the two-story foyer, the staircase is a fine prelude to the great room beyond, where a fantastic span of windows on the back wall overlooks the rear grounds. The dining room is located off the entry and has a lovely coffered ceiling. The kitchen, breakfast room, and sunroom are conveniently grouped for casual entertaining. The elaborate master suite enjoys a coffered ceiling, private sitting room, and spa-style bath. The second level consists of four bedrooms with private baths and a large game room featuring a rear stair.

HOME PLAN

HPK2700345

Style: Colonial Revival
First Floor: 3,722 sq. ft.
Second Floor: 1,859 sq. ft.
Total: 5,581 sq. ft.
Bedrooms: 5
Bathrooms: 4 ½
Width: 127' - 10"
Depth: 83' - 9"
Foundation: Slab

eplans.com

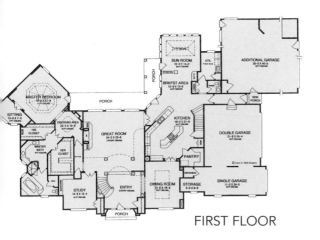

FIRST FLOOR

SECOND FLOOR

FIRST FLOOR

SECOND FLOOR

LOOKING FOR A STYLE SUPERLATIVE? Look no further than this quietly elegant design. A columned entry and Palladian windows add panache and grace. The floor plan was decidedly created for family living. A great room with fireplace and curved staircase, a breakfast area and adjoining family room, the upstairs game room, and the more formal dining and music rooms lend space for all occasions. The master suite is on the first floor but has a loft overlook above. It has such fine appointments as an exercise room, a fireplace, and a cedar closet. Two of four family bedrooms are also on the first floor. The additional two bedrooms are upstairs. Each has a private bath and walk-in closet.

HOME PLAN

HPK2700346

Style: New American
First Floor: 4,383 sq. ft.
Second Floor: 1,544 sq. ft.
Total: 5,927 sq. ft.
Bedrooms: 5
Bathrooms: 4 ½ + ½
Width: 113' - 4"
Depth: 84' - 5"
Foundation: Slab

eplans.com

THE DISTINCTIVE COVERED ENTRY TO THIS STUNNING MANOR, flanked by twin turrets, leads to a gracious foyer. The foyer opens to a formal dining room, a study, and a step-down gathering room. The spacious kitchen includes numerous amenities, including an island work station and a built-in desk. The adjacent morning room and the gathering room, with a wet bar and a raised-hearth fireplace, are bathed in light and open to the terrace. The secluded master suite offers two walk-in closets, a dressing area, and an exercise area with a spa. The second floor features four bedrooms and an oversized activities room with a fireplace and a balcony. Unfinished attic space can be completed to your specifications.

HOME PLAN

HPK2700347

Style: Chateauesque
First Floor: 3,736 sq. ft.
Second Floor: 2,264 sq. ft.
Total: 6,000 sq. ft.
Bedrooms: 5
Bathrooms: 5 ½ + ½
Width: 133' - 4"
Depth: 65' - 5"
Foundation: Slab

eplans.com

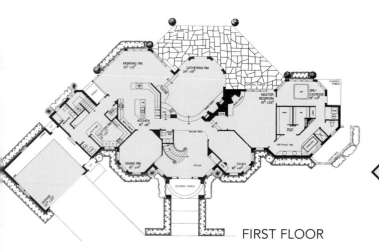

FIRST FLOOR

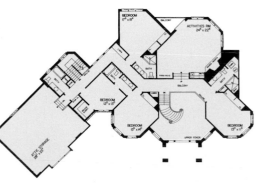

SECOND FLOOR

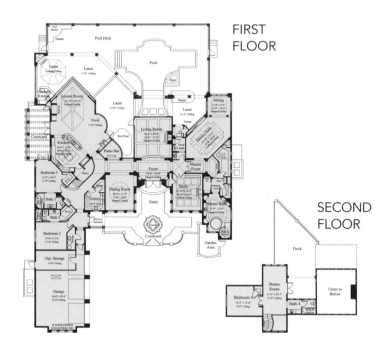

FIRST FLOOR

SECOND FLOOR

HPK2700348

Style: Italianate
First Floor: 5,265 sq. ft.
Second Floor: 746 sq. ft.
Total: 6,011 sq. ft.
Bedrooms: 4
Bathrooms: 4 ½
Width: 100' - 0"
Depth: 140' - 0"
Foundation: Slab

HOME PLAN

eplans.com

PASSING THE COURTYARD AND BEAUTIFULLY ARCHED ENTRY, VISITORS WILL MARVEL AT THE INTERSECTING FOYER, which leads ahead to the living room and connects the left and right wings of the plan. The dining room and study flank the entryway, establishing the home's formal spaces. Ahead, the living room features one of the home's several fireplaces and a row of accent windows placed just below the astonishing 22-foot ceiling. A dramatic array of windows frames the amazing view of the plan's garden lanai and pool. Two bedrooms at the left of the plan are attended by full baths and walk-in closets. But the star of the show is the resplendent master suite, which incorporates all the luxury amenities appropriate to a home of this magnitude.

REAR EXTERIOR

FRONT PERSPECTIVE

FIRST FLOOR

SECOND FLOOR

HOME PLAN

HPK2700349

Style: Italianate
First Floor: 4,742 sq. ft.
Second Floor: 1,531 sq. ft.
Total: 6,273 sq. ft.
Bedrooms: 4
Bathrooms: 4 ½ + ½
Width: 96' - 0"
Depth: 134' - 8"
Foundation: Slab

eplans.com

THE MAJESTIC ENTRANCE IS JUST THE BEGINNING OF THIS MAGNIFICENT ESTATE. A short hallway to the right of the foyer leads into the master suite that comprises the entire right side of the plan downstairs. The master bath offers dual vanities, a large shower, and a tub with an enclosed view of a privacy garden. His and Hers walk-in closets lead from the dressing area, which flows easily into the bedroom. Within the bedroom, a sitting room offers a quiet retreat. The left side of the plan belongs to a spacious gourmet kitchen with an island snack bar, plenty of counter space, a breakfast nook, and a large leisure area. Adjacent to the kitchen is a guest bedroom with a private full bath. Upstairs there are two additional bedrooms, each with a full bath and walk-in closet, one with a balcony. A media room is the finishing touch on this masterpiece.

HOMES OVER 3,000 SQUARE FEET

THIS ELEGANT FRENCH COUNTRY ESTATE FEATURES A PLUSH WORLD OF LUXURY WITHIN. A beautiful curved staircase cascades into the welcoming foyer that is flanked by a formal living room and the dining room with a fireplace. A butler's pantry leads to the island kitchen, which is efficiently enhanced by a walk-in storage pantry. The kitchen easily serves the breakfast room. The covered rear porch is accessed from the media/family room and the great room warmed by a fireplace. The master suite is a sumptuous retreat highlighted by its lavish bath and two huge walk-in closets. Next door, double doors open to a large study. All family bedrooms feature walk-in closets. Bedrooms 2 and 3 share a bath. Upstairs, Bedrooms 4 and 5 share another hall bath. A home office is located above the three-car garage.

FIRST FLOOR

HOME PLAN

HPK2700350

Style: French Country

First Floor: 5,394 sq. ft.

Second Floor: 1,305 sq. ft.

Total: 6,699 sq. ft.

Bonus Space: 414 sq. ft.

Bedrooms: 5

Bathrooms: 3 ½ + ½

Width: 124' - 10"

Depth: 83' - 2"

Foundation: Crawlspace

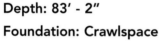

SECOND FLOOR

eplans.com

REAR EXTERIOR

THE GRAND ENTRANCE TO THIS ELEGANT EUROPEAN-STYLE HOME is flanked by window bays stacked two high. The two-story foyer opens immediately to a formal dining room and a study; straight ahead is the entry to the living room and a magnificent curved staircase to the second level. An opulent master suite, filled with amenities, is located on the main floor; three more bedrooms, two baths, a game room, and an immense storage area are upstairs. A three-car garage and guest house can be reached by a covered walk.

HOME PLAN

HPK2700351

Style: French Country

First Floor: 4,252 sq. ft.

Second Floor: 2,562 sq. ft.

Total: 6,814 sq. ft.

Bedrooms: 5

Bathrooms: 5 ½ + ½

Width: 143' - 0"

Depth: 86' - 11"

Foundation: Slab

eplans.com

FIRST FLOOR

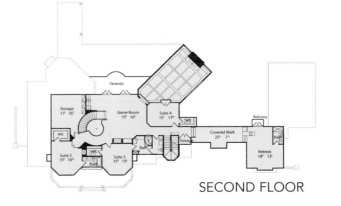

SECOND FLOOR

Outer Beauty—Dress Up the Surroundings of Your New Home

Now that you have your new house in order, it's time to address the exterior. A home alone on a flat stretch of yard may look nice, but luscious landscaping adds the "wow" factor that really impresses.

Already have a garage? Does it serve your entire family fleet? Perhaps you plan to use your attached garage for storage—a second garage will keep cars, SUVs, boats, and other vehicles out of the elements. Many designs include an apartment above the bays—use the upstairs for guest space and the downstairs for a spacious game room. With our variety of styles, you're sure to find a plan to suit your home's exterior.

Landscaping may sound daunting, but it can be as simple or extravagant as you desire. Choose a plan of finely pruned shrubs or a free-form gathering of wildflowers and bushes. Prefer autumn perennials to spring annuals? We make it easy for you to choose a design based on the time of year during which your garden will be in full bloom.

The perfect addition to a beautiful backyard is an outdoor structure in which to enjoy it. Add a gazebo to the lawn for a shady spot to read and sip tea amongst the flowers. Let vines of roses or ivy crawl their way up the sides of a decorative arbor for a whimsical look.

The garage, landscape, and project plans in this section allow you to make more of your property—it can become your very own secret garden. Start with one of our professionally drawn plans and see where your imagination takes you.

MANY OF OUR LANDSCAPE DESIGNS incorporate fanciful stone walks, patios, and ponds.

Opposite: **SHEDS DON'T HAVE TO BE UGLY!** Choose one of our attractive designs to house your gardening tools and other equipment. Right: **SURROUND A PATIO** with vivid blooms for a garden-party setting. Below: **SPRAWLING GREENERY** may add just the right touch to an outdoor masonry fireplace.

HPK2700352

Total: 1,031 sq. ft.
Width: 18' - 0"
Depth: 32' - 0"

HPK2700353

Total: 1,050 sq. ft.
Width: 20' - 0"
Depth: 30' - 0"

HPK2700354

Total: 336 sq. ft.
Width: 14' - 0"
Depth: 24' - 0"

HPK2700355

Total: 384 sq. ft.
Width: 16' - 0"
Depth: 24' - 0"

HPK2700356

Total: 704 sq. ft.
Width: 16' - 0"
Depth: 24' - 0"

HPK2700357

Total: 576 sq. ft.
Width: 24' - 0"
Depth: 24' - 0"

HPK2700358

Total: 656 sq. ft.
Width: 16' - 0"
Depth: 24' - 0"

HPK2700359

Total: 336 sq. ft.
Width: 14' - 0"
Depth: 24' - 0"

HPK2700360

Total: 910 sq. ft.
Width: 24' - 0"
Depth: 24' - 0"

HPK2700361

Total: 1,088 sq. ft.
Width: 22' - 0"
Depth: 25' - 0"

HPK2700362

Total: 1,400 sq. ft.
Width: 28' - 0"
Depth: 30' - 0"

HPK2700363

Total: 662 sq. ft.
Width: 28' - 0"
Depth: 26' - 0"

HPK2700364

Total: 741 sq. ft.
Width: 24' - 8"
Depth: 32' - 0"

HPK2700365

Total: 1,071 sq. ft.
Width: 34' - 0"
Depth: 24' - 0"

HPK2700366

Total: 713 sq. ft.
Width: 28' - 0"
Depth: 26' - 0"

HPK2700367

Total: 1,080 sq. ft.
Width: 24' - 0"
Depth: 42' - 0"

HPK2700368

Total: 1,456 sq. ft.
Width: 36' - 0"
Depth: 22' - 0"

HPK2700369

Width: 17' - 0"
Depth: 11' - 8"

HPK2700370

Width: 12' - 0"
Depth: 12' - 0"

HPK2700371

Width: 16' - 0"
Depth: 12' - 0"

HPK2700372

Width: 10' - 0"
Depth: 10' - 0"

HPK2700373

Square Footage: 144
Width: 12' - 0"
Depth: 16' - 0"

HPK2700374

Square Footage: 288
Width: 20' - 0"
Depth: 16' - 0"

HPK2700375

Width: 20' - 0"
Depth: 30' - 0"

HPK2700376

Square Footage: 64
Width: 8' - 0"
Depth: 8' - 0"

HPK2700377

Square Footage: 96
Width: 8' - 0"
Depth: 12' - 0"

HPK2700378

Square Footage: 144
Width: 12' - 0"
Depth: 12' - 0"

HPK2700379

Square Footage: 144
Width: 12' - 0"
Depth: 12' - 0"

HPK2700380

Square Footage: 160
Width: 16' - 0"
Depth: 12' - 0"

HPK2700381

Width: 8' - 0"
Depth: 8' - 0"

HPK2700382

Square Footage: 12
Width: 3' - 0"
Depth: 4' - 0"

HPK2700383

Width: 4' - 3"
Depth: 6' - 0"

HPK2700384

Square Footage: 96
Width: 8' - 0"
Depth: 16' - 0"

A ROMANTIC OLD-FASHIONED ROSE BORDER IS ALWAYS IN STYLE. The voluptuous fragrance and heavy-petaled blossoms of roses bring charm to any sunny garden. Here, the designer chooses old garden roses, which offer scent as well as ease of care, unlike modern hybrid tea roses. Although many of these cherished plants bloom only once during the season, their other charms far outweigh the repeat-blossoms of their modern cousins. Many have excellent summer and fall foliage and a heavy crop of glossy rose hips in autumn.

In this border design, these belles of the garden are mixed with classic perennial partners and bulbs to create months of color and interest. A circular bed is tucked into this pleasingly curved border and is separated by a ribbon-like strip of lawn. A rose-covered pergola in the border frames a classically inspired

PLAN

HPK2700385

Season: Summer

Design by:
Maria Morrison

eplans.com

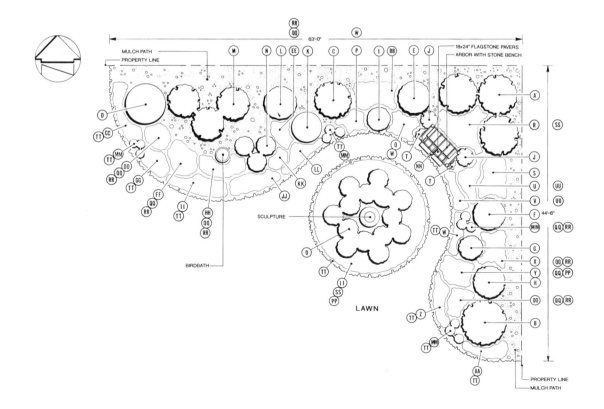

sculpture in the bed's center, creating two balanced focal points. A stone bench placed under the arbor provides a lovely spot to contemplate the wonders of this flower-filled haven. Mulched pathways at the back of the border allow easy access for maintenance and for cutting flowers for the house.

Designed to beautify the corner of a backyard, this rose-filled border can be easily turned into a free-standing bed and placed in the center of a lawn by rounding off the straight sides into a more free-flowing shape.

PLAN # HPK2700386

Season: Spring
Design by: Jim Morgan

eplans.com

WHEN SMALL TREES, FLOWERING SHRUBS, PERENNIALS AND GROUNDCOVERS ARE PLANTED TOGETHER, the result is a lovely mixed border that looks great throughout the year. The trees and shrubs—both evergreen and deciduous types—provide structure and form in winter, while also offering decorative foliage and flowers in other seasons. Perennials and bulbs occupy large spaces between groups of woody plants and contribute leaf texture and floral color to the scene.

Even though this border contains a lot of plants, it is easy to care for. That's part of the beauty of a mixed border—the woody plants are long-lived and need little pruning if allowed to grow naturally. By limiting the number of perennials and blanketing

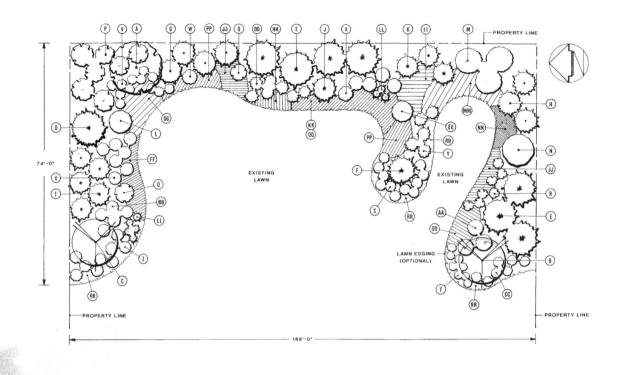

the ground with weed-smothering groundcovers, maintenance is kept to a minimum without sacrificing beauty.

You can install this mixed border in a sunny location almost anywhere on your property, though it's intended to run along the back of an average-sized lot. If your property is larger or smaller than the one in this plan, you can alter the design by either increasing or decreasing the number of plants in each grouping. Evergreen and deciduous shrubs and small trees, mixed with drifts of bulbs and flowering perennials, create an ever-changing border that's gorgeous every month of the year.

A FLOWER-FILLED GARDEN CREATED IN THE ROMANTIC STYLE OF AN ENGLISH BORDER need not demand much care, as this lovely design illustrates. The designer carefully selects unfussy bulbs and perennials and a few flowering shrubs, all of which are disease- and insect-resistant and noninvasive, and don't need staking or other maintenance. A balance of spring-, summer-, and fall-blooming plants keeps the border exciting throughout the growing season. Because English gardens are famous for their gorgeous roses, the designer includes several rosebushes, but chooses ones unharmed by bugs and mildew.

Hedges form a backdrop for most English flower gardens; the designer plants an informal one here to reduce pruning. A generous mulched path runs between the flowers and the hedge, so it's easy to tend them, while the edging keeps grass from invading and creating a

nuisance. Plant this border along any sunny side of your property. Imagine it along the back of the yard, where you can view it from a kitchen window or from a patio or deck, along one side of the front yard, or planted with the hedge bordering the front lawn and providing privacy from the street.

Brimming with easy-care flowers from spring through fall, this low-maintenance flower border evokes the spirit of an English garden, but doesn't require a staff to take care of it.

HPK2700387

Season: Summer

Design by: Maria Morrison

PLAN

eplans.com

ANY EXPOSURE

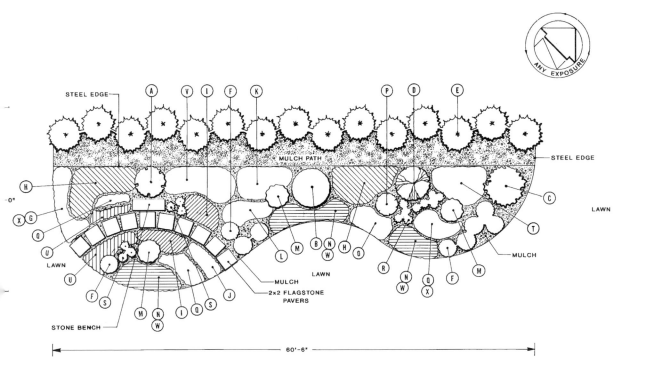

STEEL EDGE
A V I F K P D E
MULCH PATH
STEEL EDGE
LAWN
H
-0"
X G
Q
U
LAWN
U
F S
M N
W
I Q S
J
STONE BENCH
MULCH
2x2 FLAGSTONE PAVERS
L M B N H O
W
LAWN
R
N Q F
W X
M
C
T
MULCH
M

|← 60'-6" →|

IF YOU'D LIKE TO HAVE AN EASY-CARE GARDEN that offers more than a single burst of brilliant color, this season-spanning border packed with perennials is perfect for you. The designer selects a wide array of perennials that begin flowering in the spring, provide plenty of color throughout the summer, and continue blooming into the fall. All you'll need to do is remove spent blossoms from time to time and divide plants every few years.

A deciduous hedge curves around the back of the border, providing a pleasant foil for the perennials throughout the growing season. Before dropping its leaves in autumn, the hedge puts on its own show of dazzling color just as the perennials are beginning to slow down. Once the perennials

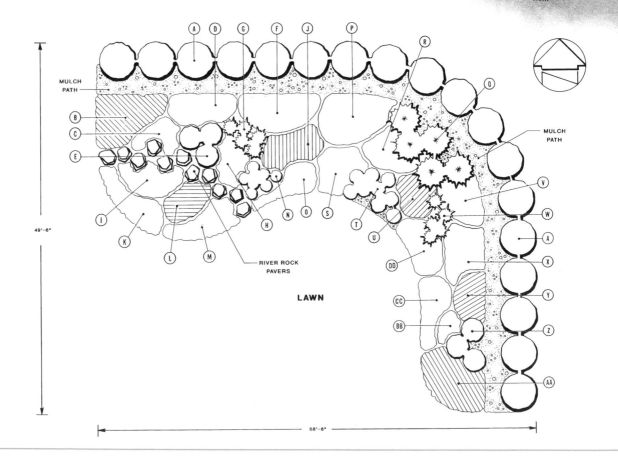

MULCH PATH

MULCH PATH

RIVER ROCK PAVERS

LAWN

49'-6"

58'-8"

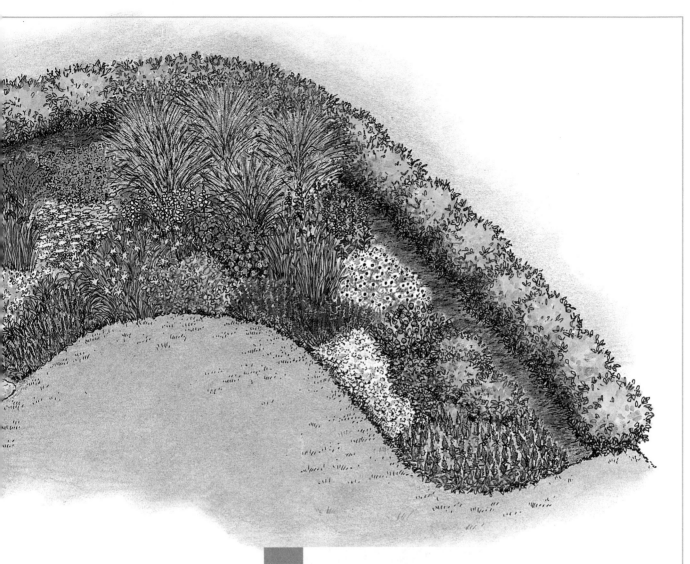

have finished blooming, you can leave the dried flower heads on the plants to add subtle beauty to the winter landscape.

The classic curved shape of this border will fit easily into a corner of your front- or back-yard. If you have a large yard, you may want to install this border on one side with its mirror image on the other and with a path set between them. This bed brims with flower color from spring through fall, so be sure to site it in a sunny location where you can enjoy the scene from both indoors and out.

HPK2700388

PLAN

Season: Summer

Design by: Maria Morrison

eplans.com

BLUE AND YELLOW FLOWERS PLANTED TOGETHER REWARD THE GARDENER with a naturally complementary color scheme that's as bright and pretty as any garden can be. It's hard to err when using these colors, because the pure blues and the lavender blues—whether dark or pastel—look just as pretty with the pale lemon yellows as with the bright sulfur yellows and the golden yellows. Each combination makes a different statement, some subtle and sweet as with the pastels, and others bold and demanding as with the deep vivid hues. But no combination fails to please.

The designer of this beautiful bed, which can be situated in any sunny spot, effectively orchestrated a

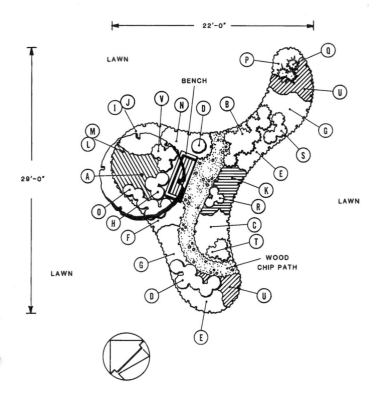

sequence of blue-and-yellow-flowering perennials so the garden blooms from spring through fall. The designer not only combined the floral colors beautifully together, but also incorporated various flower shapes and textures so they make a happy opposition. Fluffy, rounded heads of blossoms set off elegant spires, and mounded shapes mask the lanky stems of taller plants. Large, funnel-shaped flowers stand out against masses of tiny, feathery flowers like jewels displayed against a silk dress.

Although the unmistakable color scheme for this garden is blue and yellow, the designer sprinkled in an occasional spot of orange to provide a lovely jolt of brightly contrasting color. A few masses of creamy white flowers frost the garden, easing the stronger colors into a compatible union.

Natural color companions, blue and yellow flowers create a pleasing garden scene that looks great anywhere it's planted. This island bed works perfectly in an open sunny yard, but it could be modified to fit along the side of a house or to the back up against a fence or hedge along a property border.

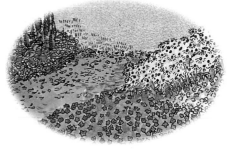

THIS BORDER INCLUDES EVERYTHING BIRDS NEED—FOOD, WATER AND NESTING SITES—and encourages them to become permanent residents of your yard. The design curves inward, creating a sense of enclosure and a sanctuary that appeals to even the shiest types of birds. The border's attractive design includes a pond, birdhouse, and birdbath, which act as focal points and make the garden irresistible to people as well.

The large variety of pretty fruiting shrubs offers birds natural nourishment throughout much of the year, but you can supplement the food supply with store-bought bird food if you wish. Deciduous and evergreen trees provide shelter and nesting places, while the mulched areas give birds a place to take dust baths and to poke around for insects and worms.

HPK2700390

Season: Summer

Design by: Michael J. Opisso

eplans.com

Because water is so important to birds, the garden includes two water features: a small naturalistic pond, and a birdbath set in a circular bed. Both offer spots for perching, bathing, and drinking. In cold-weather climates, consider adding a special heater to the birdbath to keep the water from freezing; water attracts birds in winter even more than birdseed.

NOTE: The pond is not included in the landscape plans.

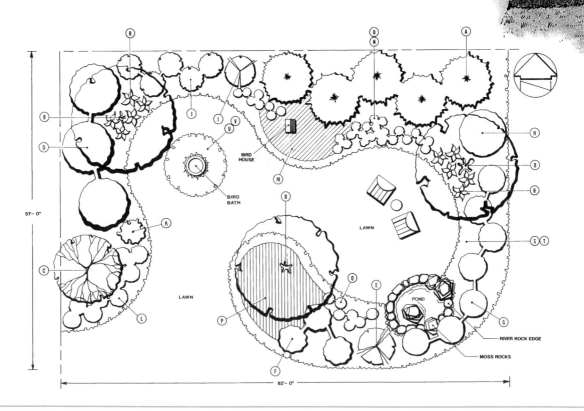

BIRDS FLOCK TO THIS BORDER, which provides them with ample supplies of food and water and locations for nesting and bathing. There's plenty of room for bird-watchers as well.

PLAN

HPK2700391

Season: Fall

Design by: Michael J. Opisso

eplans.com

THERE IS NO BETTER WAY TO WAKE UP IN THE MORNING THAN TO THE SOUND OF SONGBIRDS IN THE GARDEN. Wherever you live, you will be surprised at the number and variety of birds you can attract by offering them a few basic necessities—water, shelter, nesting spots, and food. Birds need water for drinking and bathing. They need shrubs and trees, especially evergreens, for shelter and nesting. Edge spaces—open areas with trees nearby for quick protection—provide ground feeders with foraging places, and plants with berries and nuts offer other natural sources of food. The garden presented here contains all the necessary elements to attract birds to the garden. The shrubs and trees are chosen

especially to provide a mix of evergreen and deciduous species.
All of these, together with the
masses of flowering perennials, bear seeds, nuts, or
berries that are known to
appeal to birds. The berry
show looks quite pretty, too,
until the birds gobble them up!
Planted densely enough for necessary
shelter, the bird-attracting plants create a lovely private backyard that's enjoyable throughout the seasons. The birdbath is
located in the lawn so it will be in the sun. A naturalistic pond
provides water in a more protected setting. The birdhouses
and feeders aren't really necessary—though they may be the
icing on the cake when it comes to luring the largest number
of birds—because the landscape provides abundant natural
food and shelter. Outside one of the main windows of the
house, a birdfeeder hangs from a small flowering tree, providing an up-close view of your feathered friends. Call Out:
Nature lovers will delight in the abundant number of birds
that will flock to this beautiful garden. An attractive collection
of berried plants and evergreens offers food and shelter for
the wildlife, while creating a handsome, pastoral setting.

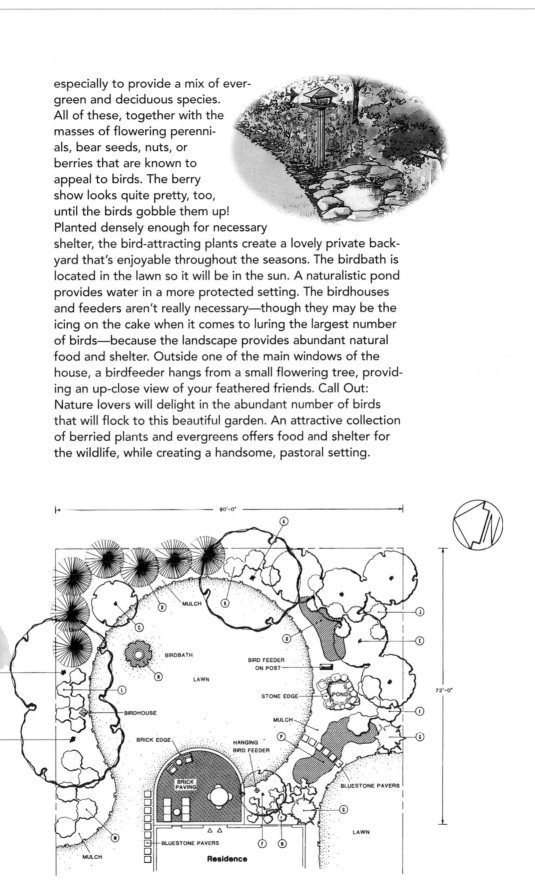

THIS NATURALISTIC GARDEN PLAN RELIES UPON SEVERAL DIFFERENT FEATURES to attract as many different species of birds as possible. A songbird's basic needs include food, water and shelter, but this backyard plan offers luxury accommodations not found in every yard, and also provides the maximum opportunity for birds and bird watchers to observe each other. Special features provide for specific birds; for example, the rotting log attracts woodpeckers and the dusting area will be used gratefully by birds to free themselves of parasites. In addition to plants that produce plentiful berries and seeds, the designer includes a ground feeder to lure morning doves, cardinals and other birds that prefer to eat off the ground. The birdhouse located in the shade of the specimen tree to the rear of the garden suits a wide variety of songbirds.

The angular deck nestles attractively into the restful circular shapes of the garden. The designer encloses the deck amidst the bird-attracting plantings to maximize close-up observation opportunities and create an intimate setting. Two other sitting areas welcome bird watchers into the garden. A bench positioned on a small patio under the shade of a graceful flowering tree provides a relaxing spot to sit and contemplate the small

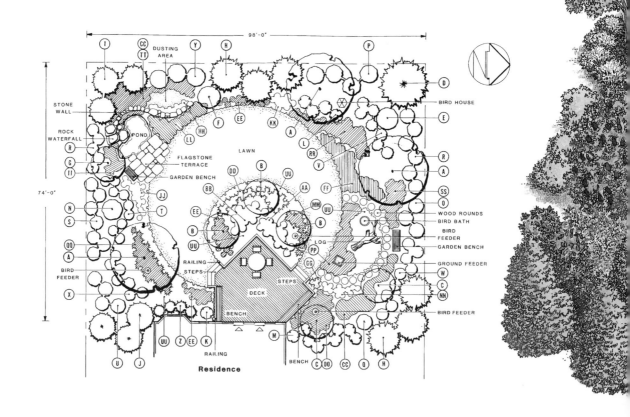

garden pool (not included in plan blueprints) and the melody of a low waterfall. Another bench—this one situated in the sun—may be reached by strolling along a path of wood-rounds on the opposite side of the yard. Both wildlife and people will find this backyard a very special retreat. This large, naturalistic backyard design creates a wonderful environment for attracting a wide range of bird species, because it offers a plentiful supply of natural food, water and shelter. The deck and garden benches invite people to observe and listen to the songbirds in comfort.

PLAN

HPK2700392

Season: Spring

Design by: David Poplawski

eplans.com

YOUR YARD WILL BE HOME TO JEWEL-TONED, QUICK-SILVER HUMMINGBIRDS once you install this colorful bed. A rich display of bright annuals and perennials, specially selected to attract hummingbirds, creates a delightful setting. All birds need water, and hummingbirds are particularly attracted to flowing water, so the birdbath in this design features a small bubbler device. ~~Informal flagstone pavers lead through the garden to a semicircular mulched area set with flagstones that surround the birdbath. The path to the wooden pergola (not included in plans), which creates a lovely sitting area, leads through the pretty flowers. Climbing vines and hanging planters attached to the pergola provide additional nectar and create a pleasant shady area where you can watch the hummers dart by.

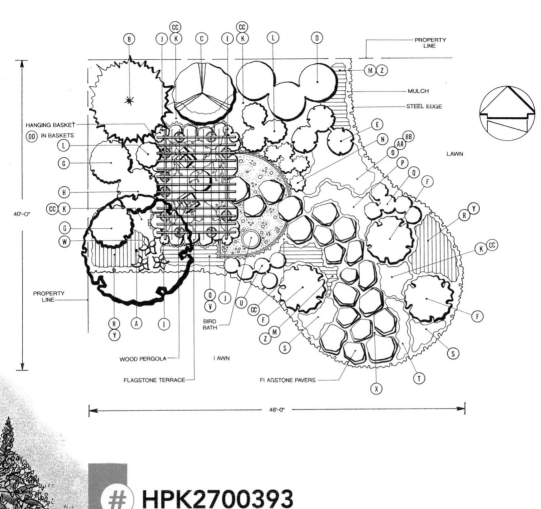

PROPERTY LINE

MULCH

STEEL EDGE

LAWN

HANGING BASKET
DD IN BASKETS

40'-0"

PROPERTY LINE

WOOD PERGOLA

FLAGSTONE TERRACE

BIRD BATH

LAWN

FLAGSTONE PAVERS

48'-0"

PLAN HPK2700393

Season: Summer

Design by: Patrick J. Duffe

eplans.com

Hang the pots so you can watch the birds at eye level from the sitting area. Neutral-colored plastic pots look best and cut down on evaporation, minimizing watering chores.

Site this design in a sunny location close to your house so you can observe the birds from indoors as well. Or, if you prefer, locate the bed in a quiet corner of your yard to enhance the tranquil atmosphere.Sit beneath the flower-draped pergola and enjoy glimpses of hummingbirds as they pause in midflight to drink nectar and splash in the birdbath.

FILLED WITH FRUITING SHRUBS, trees, ornamental grasses, and perennials that provide food for birds, this border is as beautiful as it is bird-friendly.

THIS ATTRACTIVE BORDER DOES DOUBLE DUTY, because it serves both as a beautiful landscape planting as well as an effective wildlife sanctuary. Offering natural food sources, shelter, and water, the planting brings birds to your property throughout the year, and its informal but tidy design looks right at home in any suburban setting. Although they serve a practical purpose as well, the birdhouses, bird feeders, and birdbath add interesting architectural elements to the design.

The shrubs and trees used in the border—and even many of the perennials and ornamental grasses—produce berries and seeds that attract birds. They are arranged informally and should be left unpruned to form a dense shelter for nesting sites. Because most berried

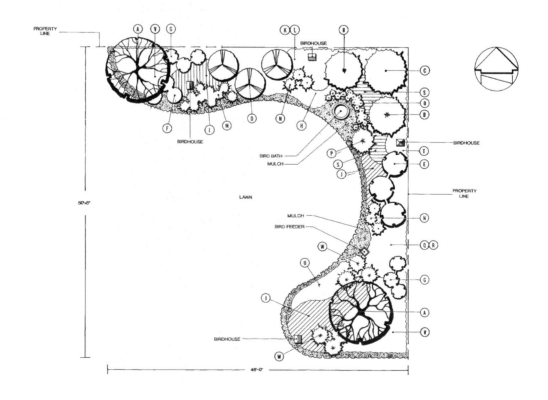

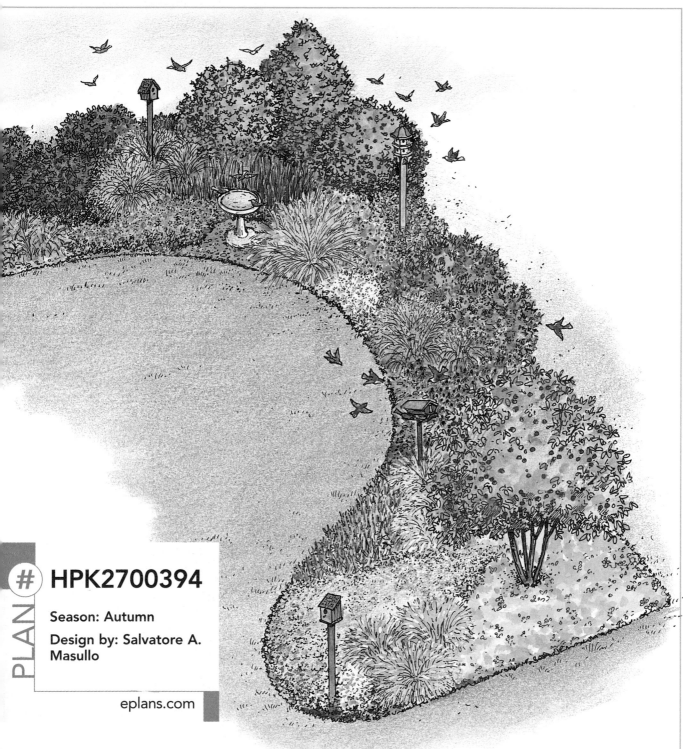

HPK2700394

Season: Autumn

Design by: Salvatore A. Masullo

eplans.com

PLAN #

...lants produce best when cross-pollinated by ...nother similar plant, the designer masses specimens ...gether and repeats plants.

...ou can site this border along the property lines in ...ither your front- or backyard, or round off its corners ...nd use it as an island planting. Then sit back and ...njoy the birds and birdsongs that fill your garden.

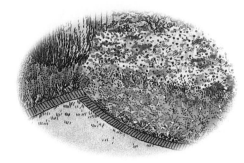

TO KEEP THE GRASS FROM SPREADING into the planting borders—and to reduce weeding and edging chores—the designer calls for a decorative brick mowing strip surrounding the lawn.

THIS DESIGN PROVES THAT "DROUGHT TOLERANT" AND "LOW MAINTENANCE" don't have to mean boring. This attractive backyard looks lush, colorful, and inviting but relies entirely on plants that flourish even if water is scarce. This means you won't spend any time tending to their watering needs once the plantings are established. Even the lawn is planted with a newly developed turf grass that tolerates long periods of drought.

The designer specifies buffalo grass, a native grass of the American West, for the lawn. The grass has fine-textured, grayish green leaf blades, tolerates cold, and needs far less water to remain green and healthy than most lawns. It goes completely dormant during periods of extended drought, but greens up with

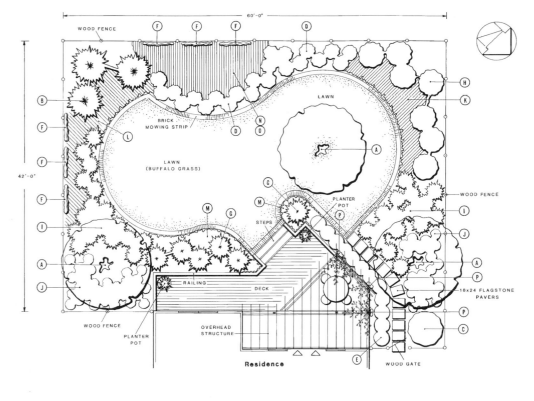

rain or irrigation. To keep the lawn green throughout summer, all you need do is water occasionally if rainfall doesn't cooperate. And mowing is an occasional activity, too! This slow-growing grass needs mowing only a few times in summer to about one inch high.

Deciduous and evergreen trees and shrubs interplanted with long-blooming flowering perennials—all drought-tolerant—adorn the yard, bringing color every season. Against the fence grow espaliered shrubs, which offer flowers in spring and berries in winter. The vine-covered trellis shades the roomy, angular deck, where you can sit in cool seclusion and relax while your beautiful backyard takes care of itself.

This environmentally sound landscape plan won't strain the local water supply or burden you with gardening chores, because all the plants used here—from grass to flowers to trees—are easy-care, trouble-free kinds that flourish without frequent rain or irrigation.

PLAN # HPK2700395

Season: Summer
Design by: Damon Scott

eplans.com

WHEN A BUSY COUPLE WANTS A LANDSCAPE THAT IS DISTINCTIVE and requires little maintenance, the Japanese-style garden and backyard pictured here are a perfect solution. The essence of a Japanese garden lies in emulating nature through simple, clean lines that do not look contrived. The low, tight hedges underscore the plantings behind them, while providing a contrast in form.

PLAN

(#) HPK2700396

Season: Summer

Design by: Michael J. Opisso

eplans.com

Looking straight out from the deck, the perimeter planting is a harmony of shades of green, with interest provided from contrasting textures.

Paving stones border the deck because in the Japanese garden, every element has both an aesthetic and a functional purpose. The stones alleviate the wear that would result from stepping directly onto the lawn from the deck, and provide a visual transition between the man-made deck and the natural grass. The pavers act as more than a path; they also provide a sight line to the stone lantern on the left side of the garden.

The deck, like the rest of the landscape, has clean, simple lines, and provides the transition from the home's interior to the garden. It surrounds a viewing garden, one step down. In the Japanese tradition, this miniature landscape mimics a natural scene. The one large moss rock plays an important role—it is situated at the intersection of the stepping-stone paths that lead through the garden. Here a decision must be made as to which way to turn. The stone water basin, a symbolic part of the Japanese tea ceremony, is located near the door to the house, signaling the entrance to a very special place.

THIS BEAUTIFUL JAPANESE-STYLE GARDEN provides space for outdoor living and entertaining in a tranquil setting. Featuring straight, simple lines, a small lawn, a large deck and extensive plantings of groundcovers and evergreens, the garden practically cares for itself.

MOSS ROCKS

STONE WATER
BASIN

RIVER ROCK
STEPPING STONE

Residence

DECK

GRAVEL

BLUESTONE PAVERS

LAWN

LAWN

LAWN

WOOD FENCE

STONE LANTERN

WOOD FENCE

PROPERTY LINE

BLUESTONE PAVERS

WOOD FENCE

PROPERTY LINE

PLAN # HPK2700397

Season: Summer

Design by: Salvatore A. Masullo

eplans.com

A COLORFUL, EASY-CARE FLOWER BED LIKE THIS PAISLEY-SHAPED RAISED BED can be located almost anywhere on your property—it is perfectly suitable as an entry garden, or as a transition between different levels in a backyard. The bed's curving, organic shape echoes the sinuous stone wall that divides its upper and lower sections. Flagstone steps further divide the bed and lead visitors from the lower, more symmetrical area to the upper, more asymmetrical section of the garden. The designer incorporates lovely low-growing flowering perennials to spill over the wall, creating a curtain of

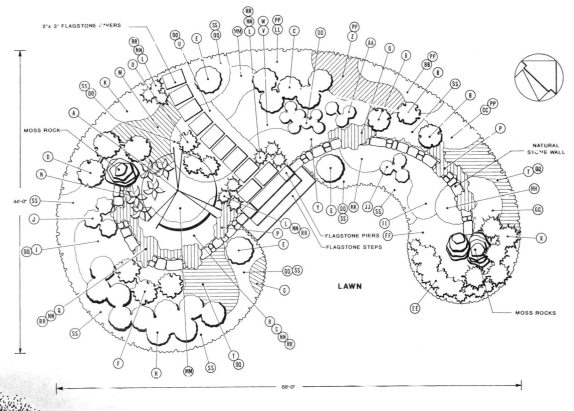

2'x 3' FLAGSTONE PAVERS

MOSS ROCK

44'-0"

NATURAL STONE WALL

FLAGSTONE PIERS
FLAGSTONE STEPS

LAWN

MOSS ROCKS

68'-0"

flowers. Twin flowering shrubs flank the entry steps, while a single specimen of the same type marks the exit. The rest of the bed is planted with a profusion of easy-care perennials, bulbs, ornamental grasses and flowering shrubs. This garden bed requires only a little of your precious time for routine maintenance. You'll need to remove spent blossoms, do a bit of cleanup in spring and fall and divide the perennials every few years. A curving stone retaining wall and small flowering tree give this flower garden dimension and form, which keep it attractive throughout the year.

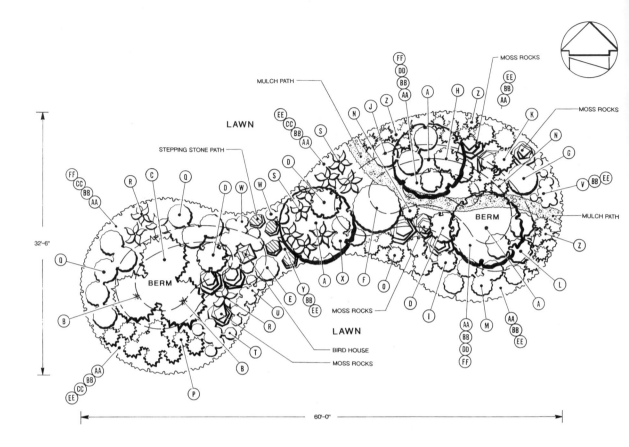

LAWN

MULCH PATH

MOSS ROCKS

MOSS ROCKS

STEPPING STONE PATH

MULCH PATH

BERM

BERM

32'-6"

60'-0"

MOSS ROCKS

LAWN

BIRD HOUSE

MOSS ROCKS

ONE OF THE GREAT JOYS OF A LOVELY LOW-MAINTENANCE GARDEN is having the time to really enjoy it. If you'd like a garden bed that is eye-catching as well as easy-care, this design is for you. This bow-tie-shaped bed contains a delightful variety of low-maintenance perennials, evergreens, deciduous trees and shrubs, and spring bulbs. Such a diverse blend of easy-care plants guarantees you'll have both year-round color and the time to take pleasure in every season's display. The berms at each end of the bed create a small valley that is traversed by a natural stone path. Trees screen the peak of the higher berm, adding a bit of mystery and encouraging visitors to explore. Two pathways—one of mulch, the other of stepping stones—make it easy to enjoy the plantings up close and to perform maintenance tasks, such as occasional deadheading and weeding. Moss rocks in three areas of the garden and a birdhouse near the stepping-stone path provide pleasing structure and interest. Locate this easy-care bed in an open area of lawn in the front- or backyard to create a pretty view that can be enjoyed from indoors and out.

HPK2700398

Season: Summer

Design by: Jeffery Diefenbach

eplans.com

HPK2700399

Season: Spring

Design by: Maria Morrison

PLAN

eplans.com

THE ROUGHLY C-SHAPED DESIGN OF THIS SHADY BED creates an eye-pleasing curve. The garden's undulating interior edge forms all kinds of interesting nooks and crannies, which invite visitors to explore. Site this bed under the spread of high-canopied trees, which offer filtered shade—the kind that allows many types of shade-loving plants to flourish.

Shade-loving shrubs dominate the bed, with drifts of spring-flowering bulbs, colonies of ferns, and groups of perennials interspersed throughout to add more color. Bulbs dot the mulched areas between the shrubs in spring. Once the bulbs finish their display and go

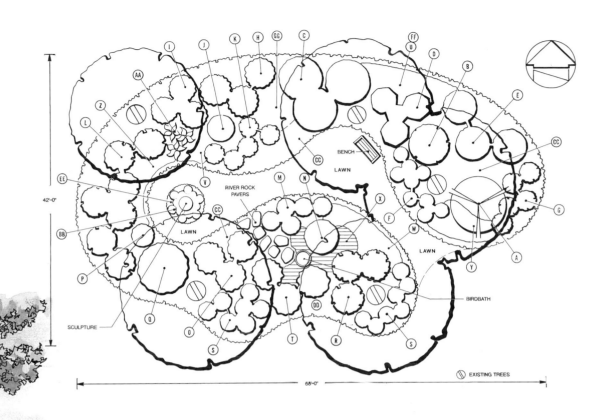

BENCH

LAWN

RIVER ROCK PAVERS

LAWN

LAWN

CC

SCULPTURE

BIRDBATH

42'-0"

68'-0"

⊘ EXISTING TREES

dormant, the mulch serves as pathways into the rest of the bed.

Many of the shrubs have lovely flowers during spring and summer, followed by showy berries that appear in fall and persist through winter. The designer adds a birdbath to accommodate the birds attracted by the berry-producing shrubs. Structural elements include a garden sculpture and a stepping-stone path that leads to a rustic bench, where visitors can sit and enjoy the naturalistic setting.

A shady front- or backyard can be transformed into a lovely garden setting by planting this undulating border beneath the existing trees. Modify the plan to suit the locations of your existing trees and dig planting holes for shrubs only where you will not sever tree roots that are thicker than one inch in diameter.

A SEMICIRCULAR FLAG-STONE PATH leads to a bench, enticing visitors to sit in the cool shade.

A SHADE GARDEN NEED NOT DEPEND ON FLOWERS—which usually need some sun to perform well—for color. You can enliven a shady area with a border that relies on a rainbow of foliage color to provide subtle, yet engaging beauty. This design contains an artful mix of foliage plants with colors and textures that range from understated to bold.

PLAN

 # HPK2700400

Season: Summer

Design by: Michael J. Opisso and Anne Rode

eplans.com

In this gently curving border, the designer combines a variety of deciduous and evergreen shrubs and trees with perennials to provide year-round foliage color. Many of the plants also add floral accents to the design. Designed for a location where sunlight is insufficient to support most free-flowering plants, this showy border derives its color from an array of shade-loving shrubs and perennials featuring variegated, golden, or purplish-red leaves.

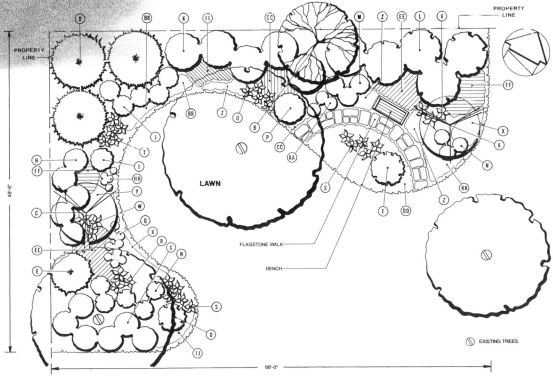

FLAGSTONE WALK

BENCH

LAWN

PROPERTY LINE

PROPERTY LINE

48'-6"

66'-0"

EXISTING TREES

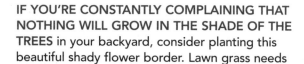

IF YOU'RE CONSTANTLY COMPLAINING THAT NOTHING WILL GROW IN THE SHADE OF THE TREES in your backyard, consider planting this beautiful shady flower border. Lawn grass needs full sun and struggles to grow under trees, so why not plant something that flourishes in the shade and looks much prettier! This charming flower border features shade-loving perennials and ferns, fits under existing trees, and blooms from spring through fall. In this design, flowering perennials grow through a low evergreen groundcover, which keeps the garden pretty even in winter, when the perennials are dormant.

Also providing year-round interest are rocks and boulders, as well as a bench that invites you to sit and enjoy the pretty scene. The designer shows this garden against a fence along the property border, but you could plant it in front of a hedge or other shrubbery and place it anywhere in your yard. If your property is smaller, you can easily eliminate

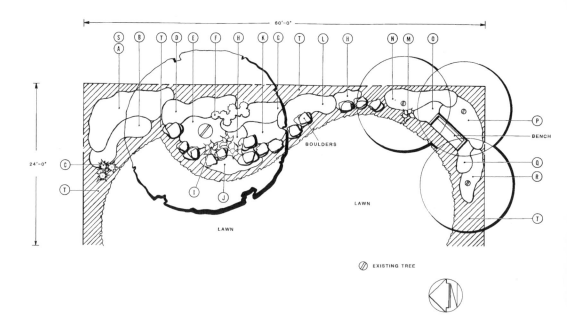

the corner containing the bench and end the border with the group of three rocks to the left of the bench.

This garden of shade-loving plants flourishes under trees where grass struggles to survive. Be sure to keep the plants healthy by providing plenty of water and fertilizer, especially if the garden plants compete for moisture and nutrients with thirsty tree roots.

 HPK2700401

Season: Summer

Design by: Michael J. Opisso

PLAN

eplans.com

HPK2700402

Season: Summer
Design by: Damon Scott

eplans.com

IF YOU LOOK AT THIS LANDSCAPE DESIGN AND ASK YOURSELF, "IS THAT REALLY A SWIMMING POOL?" then the designer is to be congratulated because he succeeded in his intention. Yes, it is a swimming pool, but the pool looks more like a natural pond and waterfall—one that you might discover in a clearing in the woods during a hike in the wilderness. ~~Although the pool is not included in the blueprints for this design, the surrounding landscape lends itself to its placement. Leave the pool out for a pleasing rock garden, play area, or romantic gazebo hideaway. ~~The designer achieves an aesthetically pleasing, natural look by employing several techniques. Large boulders form the waterfalls, one of which falls from a holding pond set among the boulders. If you do not choose to build a pool here, the boulders could empty into a pond or calming fountain. River-rock paving—the type of water-worn rocks that

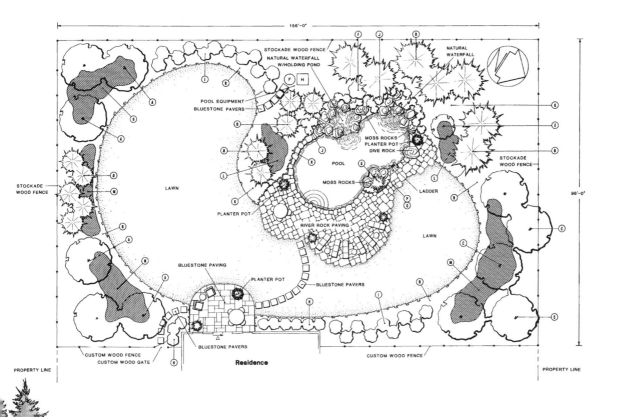

156'-0"

98'-0"

STOCKADE WOOD FENCE
NATURAL WATERFALL W/HOLDING POND

NATURAL WATERFALL

POOL EQUIPMENT
BLUESTONE PAVERS

MOSS ROCKS
PLANTER POT
DIVE ROCK

STOCKADE WOOD FENCE

STOCKADE WOOD FENCE

POOL

LAWN

MOSS ROCKS

LADDER

PLANTER POT

LAWN

RIVER ROCK PAVING

BLUESTONE PAVING

PLANTER POT

BLUESTONE PAVERS

PROPERTY LINE

CUSTOM WOOD FENCE
CUSTOM WOOD GATE

BLUESTONE PAVERS

Residence

CUSTOM WOOD FENCE

PROPERTY LINE

line the cool water of a natural spring or a rushing stream—adds a touch of wilderness. ~~The beautiful grassy areas of the landscape offer a serene setting with abundant floral and foliage interest throughout the year. For security reasons, a wooden stockade fence surrounds the entire backyard, yet the plantings camouflage it well. The irregular kidney shape of the lawn is pleasing to look at and beautifully integrates this naturalistic landscaping into its man-made setting.

ABUNDANT FLORAL AND FOLIAGE
interest year-round, river-rock paving, and border plantings bring a wonderful, natural setting to your own backyard.

LOW IN MAINTENANCE REQUIREMENTS AND HIGH IN NATURAL APPEAL, this garden of ornamental grasses delights the senses all year with subdued foliage colors, sparkling flower plumes, and rustling leaves.

MANY CULTURES SEEM TO HAVE AN IDENTIFIABLE GARDEN STYLE—there are formal Italian fountain gardens, French parterres, English perennial borders, and Japanese contemplation gardens. For many years, we didn't have an American-style garden. Now, a new trend has arisen which the originators have dubbed the 'New American Garden.' This style of landscaping is naturalistic and relies on sweeps of ornamental grasses to create the feel of the prairies that once dominated much of the American landscape.

The backyard garden presented here follows that theme. The grasses used vary from low-growing plants hugging the borders to tall plants reaching six feet or more. Some of the grasses are bold and upright; others arching and graceful. When the grasses flower, they produce plumes that dance in the wind and sparkle in the sun. Foliage colors include bright green, blue-green, variegated, and even blood-red. During autumn, foliage and flowers dry in place, forming a stunning scene of naturalistic hues in varying shades of straw, almond, brown, and rust.

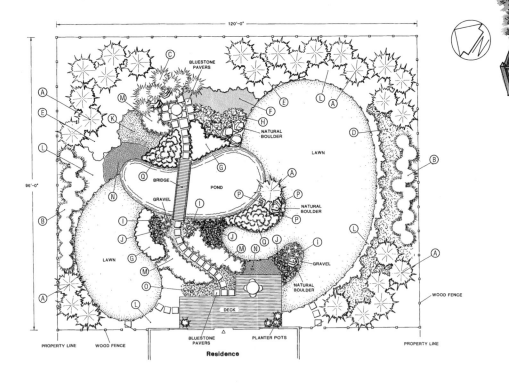

Most of the grasses remain interesting to look at all winter, unless heavy snow flattens them to the ground. In early spring, the dried foliage must be cut off and removed to make way for the new growth—but this is the only maintenance chore required by an established garden of ornamental grasses!

The design includes a large, realistic-looking pond (not included in the plan blueprints), which can be made from a vinyl-liner or concrete. At the end of the path leading from the bridge, a small seating area provides retreat.

#

HPK2700403

Season: Summer
Design by: Damon Scott

PLAN

eplans.com

PLAN

(#) HPK2700404

Season: Spring

Design by: Salvatore A. Masullo

eplans.com

DESIGNED TO BE AN OASIS IN THE SHADE, these garden beds surround a dramatic, yet naturalistic focal point—a small pond. The three lobes of the centrally located pond dictate the rhythm and design concept of the surrounding beds.

Visitors enter via one of three entrances that divide the garden into three distinct beds: a large semicircular bed to the northwest, a roughly S-shaped bed to the southwest ,and an island bed in the center, nearest the pond. Stepping-stones, set on a slightly sunken ridge, cut across the pond and allow visitors a panoramic view of the garden from the central stone.

Midsize evergreens ring the entire garden, giving it a sense of privacy and seclusion. A diverse mix of shade-loving flowering shrubs and trees, ferns and perennials provide varying texture and color throughout the year.

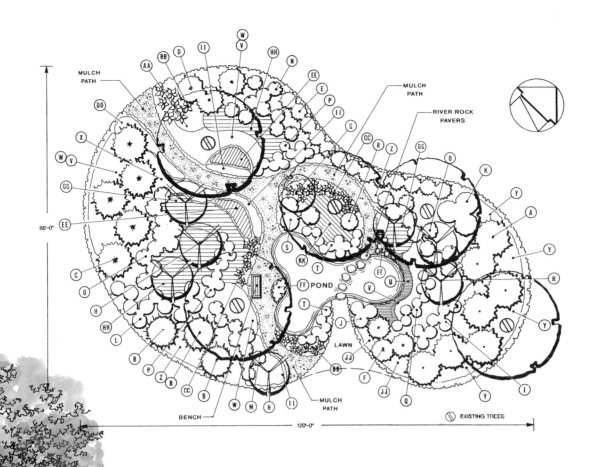

MULCH PATH

MULCH PATH

RIVER ROCK PAVERS

85'-0"

120'-0"

POND

LAWN

BENCH

MULCH PATH

EXISTING TREES

Site this garden under existing, high-canopied trees. To prevent fallen tree leaves from clogging the pond and fouling the water, cover the pond surface with bird netting in autumn. The black netting is almost invisible and allows you to easily catch and scoop out the leaves.

ALTHOUGH THE POND is not included in the blueprints for this design, the surrounding landscape lends itself to its placement. Plant this lovely pond garden where its shade-loving plants will flourish. You'll enjoy the beauty of this design all yearlong.

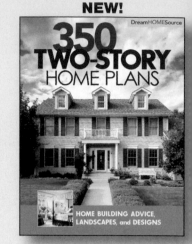

DREAM HOME SOURCE:
350 One-Story Home Plans

A compendium of exclusively one-story homes, for the homeowners that know what they are looking for. Plans run the gamut in both style and size, offering something for everyone.

$12.95 U.S.
ISBN-10: 1-931131-47-3
384 full-color pages

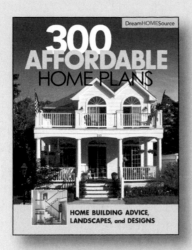

DREAM HOME SOURCE:
300 Affordable Home Plans

There's no need to sacrifice quality to meet any budget— no matter how small. Find stylish, time-proven designs, all in homes that fit small and modest budgets.

$12.95 U.S.
ISBN-10: 1-931131-59-7
ISBN-13 978-1-931131-59-9
384 full-color pages

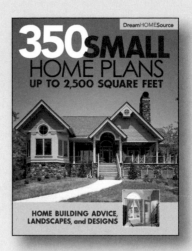

DREAM HOME SOURCE:
350 Small Home Plans

A reader-friendly resource is perfect for first-time buyers and small families looking for a starter home, this title will inspire and prepare readers to take the initial steps toward homeownership.

$12.95 U.S.
ISBN-10: 1-931131-42-2
384 full-color pages

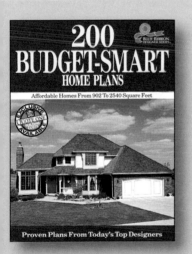

200 Budget-Smart Home Plans

Finally, a collection of homes in all sizes, styles, and types that today's homeowner can really afford to build. This complete selection of houses meets smaller and modest building budgets.

$8.95 U.S.
ISBN-10: 0-918894-97-2
224 pages

With more than 50 years of experience in the industry and millions of blueprints sold, Hanley Wood is a trusted source of high-quality, high-value pre-drawn home plans.

Using pre-drawn home plans is a **reliable, cost-effective way** to build your dream home, and our vast selection of plans is second-to-none. The nation's finest designers craft these plans that builders know they can trust. Meanwhile, our friendly, knowledgeable customer service representatives can help you every step of the way.

WHAT YOU'LL GET WITH YOUR ORDER

The contents of each designer's blueprint package is unique, but all contain detailed, high-quality working drawings. You can expect to find the following standard elements in most sets of plans:

I. FRONT PERSPECTIVE

This artist's sketch of the exterior of the house gives you an idea of how the house will look when built and landscaped.

2. FOUNDATION AND BASEMENT PLANS

This sheet shows the foundation layout including concrete walls, footings, pads, posts, beams, bearing walls, and foundation notes. If the home features a basement, the first-floor framing details may also be included on this plan. If your plan features slab construction rather than a basement, the plan shows footings and details for a monolithic slab. This page, or another in the set, may include a sample plot plan for locating your house on a building site. Additional sheets focus on foundation cross-sections and other details.

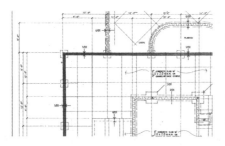

3. DETAILED FLOOR PLANS

These plans show the layout of each floor of the house. Rooms and interior spaces are carefully dimensioned, doors and windows located, and keys are given for cross-section details provided elsewhere in the plans.

4. HOUSE AND DETAIL CROSS-SECTIONS

Large-scale views show sections or cutaways of the foundation, interior walls, exterior walls, floors, stairways, and roof details. Additional cross-sections may show important changes in floor, ceiling, or roof heights, or the relationship of one level to another. These sections show exactly how the various parts of the house fit together and are extremely valuable during construction. Additional sheets may include enlarged wall, floor, and roof construction details.

5. FLOOR STRUCTURAL SUPPORTS

The floor framing plans provide detail for these crucial elements of your home. Each includes floor joist, ceiling joist, spacing, direction, span, and specifications. Beam and window headers, along with necessary details for framing connections, stairways, or dormers are also included.

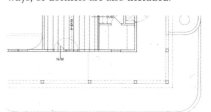

6. ELECTRICAL PLAN

The electrical plan offers suggested locations with notes for all lighting, outlets, switches, and circuits. A layout is provided for each level, as well as basements, garages, or other structures. This plan does not contain diagrams detailing how all wiring should be run, or how circuits should be engineered. These details should be designed by your electrician.

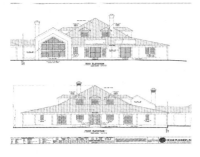

7. EXTERIOR ELEVATIONS

In addition to the front exterior, your blueprint set will include drawings of the rear and sides of your house as well. These drawings give notes on exterior materials and finishes. Particular attention is given to cornice detail, brick and stone accents, or other finish items that make your home unique.

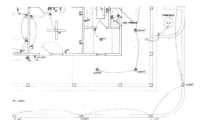

ROOF FRAMING PLANS — PLEASE READ

Some plans contain roof framing plans; however because of the wide variation in local requirements, many plans do not. If you buy a plan without a roof framing plan, you will need an engineer familiar with local building codes to create a plan to build your roof. Even if your plan does contain a roof framing plan, we recommend that a local engineer review the plan to verify that it will meet local codes.

BEFORE YOU CALL

You are making a terrific decision to use a pre-drawn house plan—it is one you can make with confidence, knowing that your blueprints are crafted by national-award-winning certified residential designers and architects, and trusted by builders.

Once you've selected the plan you want—or even if you have questions along the way—our experienced customer service representatives are available 24 hours a day, seven days a week to help you navigate the home-building process. To help them provide you with even better service, please consider the following questions before you call:

■ Have you chosen or purchased your lot?
If so, please review the building setback requirements of your local building authority before you call. You don't need to have a lot before ordering plans, but if you own land already, please have the width and depth dimensions handy when you call.

■ Have you chosen a builder?
Involving your builder in the plan selection and evaluation process may be beneficial. Luckily, builders know they can have confidence with pre-drawn plans because they've been designed for livability, functionality, and typically are builder-proven at successful home sites across the country.

■ Do you need a construction loan?
Construction loans are unique because they involve determining the value of something that is not yet constructed. Several lenders offer convenient contstruction-to-permanent loans. It is important to choose a good lending partner—one who will help guide you through the application and appraisal process. Most will even help you evaluate your contractor to ensure reliability and credit worthiness. Our partnership with IndyMac Bank, a nationwide leader in construction loans, can help you save on your loan, if needed.

■ How many sets of plans do you need?
Building a home can typically require a number of sets of blueprints—one for yourself, two or three for the builder and subcontractors, two for the local building department, and one or

more for your lender. For this reason, we offer 5- and 8-set plan packages, but your best value is the Reproducible Plan Package. Reproducible plans are accompanied by a license to make modifications and typically up to 12 duplicates of the plan so you have enough copies of the plan for everyone involved in the financing and construction of your home.

■ Do you want to make any changes to the plan?
We understand that it is difficult to find blueprints for a home that will meet all of your needs. That is why Hanley Wood is glad to offer plan Customization Services. We will work with you to design the modifications you'd like to see and to adjust your blueprint plans accordingly—anything from changing the foundation; adding square footage, redesigning baths, kitchens, or bedrooms; or most other modifications. This simple, cost-effective service saves you from hiring an outside architect to make alterations. Modifications may only be made to Reproducible Plan Packages that include the license to modify.

■ Do you have to make any changes to meet local building codes?
While all of our plans are drawn to meet national building codes at the time they were created, many areas required that plans be stamped by a local engineer to certify that they meet local building codes. Building codes are updated frequently and can vary by state, county, city, or municipality. Contact your local building inspection department, office of planning and zoning, or department of permits to determine how your local codes will affect your construction project. The best way to assure that you can make changes to your plan, if necessary, is to purchase a Reproducible Plan Package.

■ Has everyone—from family members to contractors—been involved in selecting the plan?
Building a new home is an exciting process, and using pre-drawn plans is a great way to realize your dreams. Make sure that everyone involved has had an opportunity to review the plan you've selected. While Hanley Wood is the only plans provider with an exchange policy, it's best to be sure all parties agree on your selection before you buy.

CALL TOLL-FREE 1-800-521-6797

Source Key
HPK27

CUSTOMIZE YOUR PLAN – HANLEY WOOD CUSTOMIZATION SERVICES

Creating custom home plans has never been easier and more directly accessible. Using state-of-the-art technology and top-performing architectural expertise, Hanley Wood delivers on a long-standing customer commitment to provide world-class home-plans and customization services. Our valued customers—professional home builders and individual home owners—appreciate the convenience and accessibility of this interactive, consultative service.

With the Hanley Wood Customization Service you can:

■ Save valuable time by avoiding drawn-out and frequently repetitive face-to-face design meetings

■ Communicate design and home-plan changes faster and more efficiently
■ Speed-up project turn-around time
■ Build on a budget without sacrificing quality
■ Transform master home plans to suit your design needs and unique personal style

All of our design options and prices are impressively affordable. A detailed quote is available for a $50 consultation fee. Plan modification is an interactive service. Our skilled team of designers will guide you through the customization process from start to finish making recommendations, offering ideas, and determining the feasibility of you changes. This level of service is offered to ensure the final modified plan meets your expectations. If you use our service the $50 fee will be applied to the cost of the modifications.

You may purchase the customization consultation before or after purchasing a plan. In either case, it is necessary to purchase the Reproducible Plan Package and complete the accompanying license to modify the plan before we can begin customization.

Customization Consultation $50

TOOLS TO WORK WITH YOUR BUILDER

Two Reverse Options For Your Convenience – Mirror and Right-Reading Reverse (as available)

Mirror reverse plans simply flip the design 180 degre e s keep in mind, the text will also be flipped. For a minimal fee you can have one or all of your plans shipped mirror reverse, although we recommend having at least one regular set handy. Right-reading reverse plans show the design flipped 180 degrees but the text reads normally. When you choose this option, we ship each set of purchased blueprints in this format.

Mirror Reverse Fee (indicate the number of sets when ordering) $55
Right Reading Reverse Fee (all sets are reversed) $175

A Shopping List Exclusively for Your Home – Materials List

A customized Materials List helps you plan and estimate the cost of your new home, outlining the quantity, type, and size of materials needed to build your house (with the exception of mechanical system items). Included are framing lumber, windows and doors, kitchen and bath cabinetry, rough and finished hardware, and much more.

Materials List . . . .$85 each
Additional Materials Lists (at original time of purchase only) . . $20 each

Plan Your Home-Building Process – Specification Outline

Work with your builder on this step-by-step chronicle of 166 stages or items crucial to the building process. It provides a comprehensive review of the construction process and helps you choose materials.
Specification Outline . . . .$10 each

Get Accurate Cost Estimates for Your Home – Quote One® Cost Reports

The Summary Cost Report, the first element in the Quote One" package, breaks down the cost of your home into various categories based on building materials, labor, and installation, and includes three grades of construction: Budget, Standard, and Custom. Make even more informed decisions about your project with the second element of our package, the Material Cost Report. The material and installation cost is shown for each of more than 1,000 line items provided in the standard-grade Materials List, which is included with this tool. Additional space is included for estimates from contractors and subcontractors, such as for mechanical materials, which are not included in our packages.

Quote One® Summary Cost Report $35
Quote One® Detailed Material Cost Report $140*
***Detailed material cost report includes the Materials List**

Learn the Basics of Building – Electrical, Plumbing, Mechanical, Construction Detail Sheets

If you want to know more about building techniques and deal more confidently with your subcontractors we offer four useful detail sheets. These sheets provide non-plan-specific general information, but are excellent tools that will add to your understanding of Plumbing Details, Electrical Details, Construction Details, and Mechanical Details.

Electrical Detail Sheet $14.95
Plumbing Detail Sheet $14.95
Mechanical Detail Sheet $14.95
Construction Detail Sheet $14.95
SUPER VALUE SETS:
Buy any 2: $26.95; Buy any 3: $34.95; Buy All 4: $39.95

▲ **Best Value**

MAKE YOUR HOME TECH-READY – HOME AUTOMATION UPGRADE

Building a new home provides a unique opportunity to wire it with a plan for future needs. A Home Automation-Ready (HA-Ready) home contains the wiring substructure of tomorrow's connected home. It means that every room—from the front porch to the backyard, and from the attic to the basement—is wired for security, lighting, telecommunications, climate control, home computer networking, whole-house audio, home theater, shade control, video surveillance, entry access control, and yes, video gaming electronic solutions.

Along with the conveniences HA-Ready homes provide, they also have a higher resale value. The Consumer Electronics Association (CEA), in conjunction with the Custom Electronic Design and Installation Association (CEDIA), have developed a TechHome™ rating system that quantifies the value of HA-Ready homes. The rating system is gaining widespread recognition in the real estate industry.

Developed by CEDIA-certified installers, our Home Automation Upgrade package includes everything you need to work with an installer during the construction of your home. It provides a short explanation of the various subsystems, a wiring floor plan for each level of your home, a detailed materials list with estimated costs, and a list of CEDIA-certified installers in your local area.
Home Automation Upgrade $250

GET YOUR HOME PLANS PAID FOR!

IndyMac Bank, in partnership with Hanley Wood, will reimburse you up to $600 toward the cost of your home plans simply by financing the construction of your new home with IndyMac Bank Home Construction Lending.

IndyMac's construction and permanent loan is a one-time close loan, meaning that one application—and one set of closing fees—provides all the financing you need.

Apply today at www.indymacbank.com, call toll free at 1-800-847-6138, or ask a Hanley Wood customer service representative for details.

DESIGN YOUR HOME – INTERIOR AND EXTERIOR FINISHING TOUCHES

Be Your Own Interior Designer! – Home Furniture Planner
Effectively plan the space in your home using our Hands-On Home Furniture Planner. It s fun and easy no more moving heavy pieces of furniture to see how the room will go together. The kit includes reusable peel-and-stick furniture templates that fit on a 12"x18" laminated layout board enough space to lay out every room in your house.
Home Furniture Planning Kit $15.95

Enjoy the Outdoors! – Deck Plans
Many of our homes have a corresponding deck plan, sold separately, which includes a Deck Plan Frontal Sheet, Deck Framing and Floor Plans, Deck Elevations, and a Deck Materials List. A Standard Deck Details Package, also available, provides all the how-to information necessary for building any deck. Get both the Deck Plan and the Standard Deck Details Package for one low price in our Complete Deck Building Package. See the price tier chart below and call for deck plan availability.
Deck Details (only) $14.95
Deck Building Package . . . . Plan price + $14.95

Create a Professionally Designed Landscape – Landscape Plans

Many of our homes have a front-yard Landscape Plan that is complementary in design to the house plan. These comprehensive Landscape Blueprint Packages include a Frontal Sheet, Plan View, Regionalized Plant & Materials List, a sheet on Planting and Maintaining Your Landscape, Zone Maps, and a Plant Size and Description Guide. Each set of blueprints is a full 18" x 24" with clear, complete instructions in easy-to-read type. Our Landscape Plans are available with a Plant & Materials List adapted by horticultural experts to eight regions of the country. Please specify your region when ordering your plan see region map below. Call for more information about landscape plan availability and applicable regions.

LANDSCAPE & DECK PRICE SCHEDULE

PRICE TIERS	1-SET STUDY PACKAGE	5-SET BUILDING PACKAGE	8-SET BUILDING PACKAGE	1-SET REPRODUCIBLE*
P1	$25	$55	$95	$145
P2	$45	$75	$115	$165
P3	$75	$105	$145	$195
P4	$105	$135	$175	$225
P5	$175	$205	$305	$405
P6	$215	$245	$345	$445

PRICES SUBJECT TO CHANGE — * REQUIRES A FAX NUMBER

TERMS & CONDITIONS

OUR 90-DAY EXCHANGE POLICY

BUY WITH CONFIDENCE!

Hanley Wood is committed to ensuring your satisfaction wit your blueprint order, which is why a we offer a 90-day exchange policy. With the exceptio of Reproducible Plan Package orders, we will exchange your entire first order for an equa or greater number of blueprints from our plan collection within 90 days of the origina order. The entire content of your original order must be returned before an exchange wi be processed. Please call our customer service department at 1-888-690-1116 for your retur authorization number and shipping instructions. If the returned blueprints look used, redlined or copied, we will not honor your exchange. Fees for exchanging your blueprints are as follows: 20% of th amount of the original order, plus the difference in cost if exchanging for a design in a higher price bracket o less the difference in cost if exchanging for a design in a lower price bracket. (Because they can be copied Reproducible blueprints are not exchangeable or refundable.) Please call for current postage and handlin prices. Shipping and handling charges are not refundable.

ARCHITECTURAL AND ENGINEERING SEALS

Some cities and states now require that a licensed architect or engineer review and "seal" a blueprint, or officially approve it, prior to construction. Prior to application for a building permit or the start of actual construction, we strongly advise that you consult your local building official who can tell you if such a review is required.

LOCAL BUILDING CODES AND ZONING REQUIREMENTS

Each plan was designed to meet or exceed the requirements of a nationally recognized model building code in effect at the time and place the plan was drawn. Typically plans designed after the year 2000 conform to the International Residential Building Code (IRC 2000 or 2003). The IRC is comprised of portions of the three major codes below. Plans drawn before 2000 conform to one of the three recognized building codes in effect at the time: Building Officials and Code Administrators (BOCA) International, Inc.;

the Southern Building Code Congress International, (SBCCI) Inc.; the International Conference of Building Officials (ICBO); or the Council of American Building Officials (CABO).

Because of the great differences in geography and climate throughout the United States and Canada, each state, county, and municipality has its own building codes, zone requirements, ordinances, and building regulations. Your plan may need to be modified to comply with local requirements. In addition, you may need to obtain permits or inspections from local governments before and in the course of construction. We authorize the use of the blueprints on the express condition that you consult a local licensed architect or engineer of your choice prior to beginning construction and strictly comply with all local building codes, zoning requirements, and other applicable laws, regulations, ordinances, and requirements. Notice: Plans for homes to be built in Nevada must be redrawn by a Nevada-registered professional. Consult your local building official for more information on this subject.

TERMS AND CONDITIONS

These designs are protected under the terms of United States Copyright Law and may not be copied or reproduced in any way, by

any means, unless you have purchased Reproducible Plan Package and signed th accompanying license to modify and cop the plan, which clearly indicates your righ to modify, copy, or reproduce. We authoriz the use of your chosen design as an aid the construction of ONE (1) single- or mu tifamily home only. You may not use th design to build a second dwelling or mu tiple dwellings without purchasing anoth blueprint or blueprints or paying addition design fees. Multi-use fees vary designer—please call one of experience sales representatives for a quote.

DISCLAIMER

The designers we work with have put substan tial care and effort into the creation of the blueprints. However, because we cannot pr vide on-site consultation, supervision, and co trol over actual construction, and because the great variance in local building requir ments, building practices, and soil, seismi weather, and other conditions, WE MAK NO WARRANTY OF ANY KIN EXPRESS OR IMPLIED, WITH RESPEC TO THE CONTENT OR USE OF TH BLUEPRINTS, INCLUDING BUT NO LIMITED TO ANY WARRANTY OF MEF CHANTABILITY OR OF FITNESS FOR PARTICULAR PURPOSE. ITEMS, PRICE TERMS, AND CONDITIONS ARE SU JECT TO CHANGE WITHOUT NOTIC

CALL TOLL-FREE
1-800-521-6797
OR VISIT
EPLANS.COM

IMPORTANT COPYRIGHT NOTICE

From the Council of Publishing Home Designers

Blueprints for residential construction (or working drawings, as they are often called in the industry) are copyrighted intellectual property, protected under the terms of the United States Copyright Law and, therefore, cannot be copied legally for use in building. The following are some guidelines to help you get what you need to build your home, without violating copyright law:

1. HOME PLANS ARE COPYRIGHTED

Just like books, movies, and songs, home plans receive protection under the federal copyright laws. The copyright laws prevent anyone, other than the copyright owner, from reproducing, modifying, or reusing the plans or design without permission of the copyright owner.

2. DO NOT COPY DESIGNS OR FLOOR PLANS FROM ANY PUBLICATION, ELECTRONIC MEDIA, OR EXISTING HOME

It is illegal to copy, change, or redraw home designs found in a plan book, CDROM or on the Internet. The right to modify plans is one of the exclusive rights of copyright. It is also illegal to copy or redraw a constructed home that is protected by copyright, even if you have never seen the plans for the home. If you find a plan or home that you like, you must purchase a set of plans from an authorized source. The plans may not be lent, given away, or sold by the purchaser.

3. DO NOT USE PLANS TO BUILD MORE THAN ONE HOUSE

The original purchaser of house plans is typically licensed to build a single home from the plans. Building more than one home from the plans without permission is an infringement of the home designer's copyright. The purchase of a multiple-set package of plans is for the construction of a single home only. The purchase of additional sets of plans does not grant the right to construct more than one home.

4. HOUSE PLANS IN THE FORM OF BLUEPRINTS OR BLACKLINES CANNOT BE COPIED OR REPRODUCED

Plans, blueprints, or blacklines, unless they are reproducibles, cannot be copied or reproduced without prior written consent of the copyright owner. Copy shops and blueprinters are prohibited from making copies of these plans without the copyright release letter you receive with reproducible plans.

5. HOUSE PLANS IN THE FORM OF BLUEPRINTS OR BLACKLINES CANNOT BE REDRAWN

Plans cannot be modified or redrawn without first obtaining the copyright owner's permission. With your purchase of plans, you are licensed to make non-structural changes by red-lining the purchased plans. If you need to make structural changes or need to redraw the plans for any reason, you must purchase a reproducible set of plans (see topic 6) which includes a license to modify the plans. Blueprints do not come with a license to make structural changes or to redraw the plans. You may not reuse or sell the modified design.

6. REPRODUCIBILE HOME PLANS

Reproducible plans (for example sepias, mylars, CAD files, electronic files, and vellums) come with a license to make modifications to the plans. Once modified, the plans can be taken to a local copy shop or blueprinter to make up to 10 or 12 copies of the plans to use in the construction of a single home. Only one home can be constructed from any single purchased set of reproducible plans either in original form or as modified. The license to modify and copy must be completed and returned before the plan will be shipped.

7. MODIFIED DESIGNS CANNOT BE REUSED

Even if you are licensed to make modifications to a copyrighted design, the modified design is not free from the original designer's copyright. The sale or reuse of the modified design is prohibited. Also, be aware that any modification to plans relieves the original designer from liability for design defects and voids all warranties expressed or implied.

8. WHO IS RESPONSIBLE FOR COPYRIGHT INFRINGEMENT?

Any party who participates in a copyright violation may be responsible including the purchaser, designers, architects, engineers, drafters, homeowners, builders, contractors, sub-contractors, copy shops, blueprinters, developers, and real estate agencies. It does not matter whether or not the individual knows that a violation is being committed. Ignorance of the law is not a valid defense.

9. PLEASE RESPECT HOME DESIGN COPYRIGHTS

In the event of any suspected violation of a copyright, or if there is any uncertainty about the plans purchased, the publisher, architect, designer, or the Council of Publishing Home Designers (www.cphd.org) should be contacted before proceeding. Awards are sometimes offered for information about home design copyright infringement.

10. PENALTIES FOR INFRINGEMENT

Penalties for violating a copyright may be severe. The responsible parties are required to pay actual damages caused by the infringement (which may be substantial), plus any profits made by the infringer commissions to include all profits from the sale of any home built from an infringing design. The copyright law also allows for the recovery of statutory damages, which may be as high as $150,000 for each infringement. Finally, the infringer may be required to pay legal fees which often exceed the damages.

hanley▲wood

BLUEPRINT PRICE SCHEDULE

PRICE TIERS	1-SET STUDY PACKAGE	5-SET BUILDING PACKAGE	8-SET BUILDING PACKAGE	1-SET REPRODUCIBLE*
A1	$465	$515	$570	$695
A2	$505	$560	$615	$755
A3	$570	$625	$685	$860
A4	$615	$680	$745	$925
C1	$660	$735	$800	$990
C2	$710	$785	$845	$1055
C3	$775	$835	$900	$1135
C4	$830	$905	$960	$1215
L1	$920	$1020	$1105	$1375
L2	$1000	$1095	$1185	$1500
L3	$1105	$1210	$1310	$1650
L4	$1220	$1335	$1425	$1830
SQ1				$0.40/SQ. FT.
SQ3				$0.55/SQ. FT.
SQ5				$0.80/SQ. FT.
SQ7				$1.00/SQ. FT.
SQ9				$1.25/SQ. FT.
SQ11				$1.50/SQ. FT.

PRICES SUBJECT TO CHANGE

* REQUIRES A FAX NUMBER

PLAN #	PRICE TIER	PAGE	MATERIALS LIST	QUOTE ONE®	DECK	DECK PRICE	LANDSCAPE	LANDSCAPE PRICE	REGIONS
HPK2700174	C2	6							
HPK2700296	SQ1	10	Y						
HPK2700001	A1	16	Y						
HPK2700002	A2	17							
HPK2700003	A3	18	Y						
HPK2700004	A3	19	Y						
HPK2700005	A4	20	Y						
HPK2700006	A3	20	Y						
HPK2700007	A2	21							
HPK2700008	A2	21	Y						
HPK2700009	A3	22							
HPK2700010	A3	22							
HPK2700011	A3	23							
HPK2700012	A4	23							
HPK2700013	A3	24	Y						
HPK2700014	A3	24	Y						
HPK2700015	A3	25							
HPK2700016	A3	25	Y						
HPK2700017	A3	26							
HPK2700018	A3	26							
HPK2700019	A4	27	Y						
HPK2700020	A3	27							
HPK2700021	A3	28	Y						
HPK2700022	A4	28							
HPK2700023	A3	29							
HPK2700024	A4	29	Y	Y					
HPK2700025	A4	30	Y						
HPK2700026	A4	30							
HPK2700027	A4	31	Y						
HPK2700028	C1	31							
HPK2700029	A3	32	Y			OLA001	P3	123568	
HPK2700030	A4	32	Y						
HPK2700031	A3	33	Y						
HPK2700032	A3	33	Y						
HPK2700033	A3	34	Y						
HPK2700034	C1	34							
HPK2700035	A3	35							
HPK2700036	C1	35				OLA024	P4	123568	
HPK2700037	A3	36							
HPK2700038	A4	36	Y	Y					
HPK2700039	A4	37							
HPK2700040	C1	37	Y						
HPK2700041	C1	38							
HPK2700042	C1	38							
HPK2700043	A4	39	Y						

PLAN #	PRICE TIER	PAGE	MATERIALS LIST	QUOTE ONE®	DECK	DECK PRICE	LANDSCAPE	LANDSCAPE PRICE	REGIONS
HPK2700044	C1	39							
HPK2700045	A3	40	Y						
HPK2700046	A4	40	Y						
HPK2700047	A4	41	Y	Y					
HPK2700048	C1	41							
HPK2700049	C1	42	Y						
HPK2700050	C1	42	Y						
HPK2700051	C1	43	Y						
HPK2700052	C1	43	Y						
HPK2700053	A3	44	Y						
HPK2700054	A4	44							
HPK2700055	C2	45							
HPK2700056	C1	45							
HPK2700057	A4	46							
HPK2700058	A4	46							
HPK2700059	A3	47							
HPK2700060	A4	47	Y						
HPK2700061	A3	48	Y	Y		OLA010	P3	1234568	
HPK2700062	A3	48	Y						
HPK2700063	A3	49	Y						
HPK2700064	C1	49				OLA024	P4	123568	
HPK2700065	C1	50	Y						
HPK2700066	A4	50							
HPK2700067	A3	51	Y			OLA001	P3	123568	
HPK2700068	A4	51							
HPK2700069	C1	52							
HPK2700070	A3	52							
HPK2700071	A4	53	Y	Y					
HPK2700072	A4	53	Y						
HPK2700073	C1	54							
HPK2700074	C1	54	Y						
HPK2700075	A3	55	Y						
HPK2700076	A3	55	Y						
HPK2700077	A3	56							
HPK2700078	A3	56	Y						
HPK2700079	A3	57	Y						
HPK2700080	C1	57	Y						
HPK2700081	A4	58	Y		ODA011	D1	OLA083	P3	12345678
HPK2700082	C1	58	Y						
HPK2700083	C1	59	Y						
HPK2700084	C1	59	Y						
HPK2700085	A4	60	Y						
HPK2700086	A4	60							
HPK2700087	A4	61	Y						
HPK2700088	A2	61	Y						

ORDER BLUEPRINTS ANYTIME AT EPLANS.COM OR 1-800-521-679

PLAN #	PRICE TIER	PAGE	MATERIALS LIST	QUOTE ONE®	DECK	DECK PRICE	LANDSCAPE	LANDSCAPE PRICE	REGIONS
HPK2700089	A4	62							
HPK2700090	A4	62							
HPK2700091	A3	63	Y	Y	ODA014	D1	OLA021	P3	123568
HPK2700092	C1	63	Y				OLA017	P3	123568
HPK2700093	A4	66							
HPK2700094	A4	67							
HPK2700095	C2	68							
HPK2700096	A4	69	Y						
HPK2700097	A4	70	Y	Y			OLA035	P3	1234567
HPK2700098	C1	71	Y						
HPK2700099	C2	72							
HPK2700100	C1	73							
HPK2700101	A3	74							
HPK2700102	C1	75	Y						
HPK2700103	A4	76	Y						
HPK2700104	C2	77							
HPK2700105	C1	78	Y						
HPK2700106	C2	79							
HPK2700107	C1	80	Y						
HPK2700108	A4	81	Y						
HPK2700109	A4	82							
HPK2700110	C2	83	Y						
HPK2700111	C2	84							
HPK2700112	C1	85	Y						
HPK2700113	C1	86							
HPK2700114	C1	87	Y						
HPK2700115	C2	88							
HPK2700116	A4	89	Y						
HPK2700117	C2	90							
HPK2700118	C2	91							
HPK2700119	C2	92							
HPK2700120	C1	93	Y						
HPK2700121	C2	94	Y	Y			OLA010	P3	1234568
HPK2700122	C1	95							
HPK2700123	C1	96	Y						
HPK2700124	C2	97							
HPK2700125	A4	98							
HPK2700126	A4	99	Y						
HPK2700127	C2	100							
HPK2700128	C1	101							
HPK2700129	C1	102							
HPK2700130	A4	103	Y	Y					
HPK2700131	A4	104	Y						
HPK2700132	C1	105	Y						
HPK2700133	C1	106	Y						
HPK2700134	C1	107							
HPK2700135	A4	108	Y						
HPK2700136	A4	109							
HPK2700137	C2	110							
HPK2700138	A4	111	Y						
HPK2700139	C2	112							
HPK2700140	C3	113							
HPK2700141	C2	114							
HPK2700142	A4	115							
HPK2700143	A4	116	Y						
HPK2700144	C1	117	Y	Y	ODA001	D1	OLA001	P3	123568
HPK2700145	C3	118							
HPK2700146	C1	119	Y	Y	ODA006	D1	OLA023	P3	123568
HPK2700147	C2	120	Y						
HPK2700148	C2	121	Y						
HPK2700149	C2	122							
HPK2700150	C2	123							
HPK2700151	C1	124							
HPK2700152	C1	125	Y						
HPK2700153	C2	126	Y						
HPK2700154	C2	127	Y	Y			OLA024	P4	123568
HPK2700155	C2	128							
HPK2700156	C1	129							
HPK2700157	C1	130							
HPK2700158	A4	131	Y						
HPK2700159	A4	132	Y						
HPK2700160	C3	133							
HPK2700161	C1	134							
HPK2700162	C1	135							
HPK2700163	A4	136	Y						
HPK2700164	C2	137	Y						
HPK2700165	C1	138							
HPK2700166	C1	139							
HPK2700167	C3	140							
HPK2700168	A4	141							
HPK2700169	C1	142							
HPK2700170	A4	143	Y						
HPK2700171	C2	144	Y						
HPK2700172	C2	145					OLA001	P3	123568
HPK2700173	C1	146							
HPK2700174	C2	147							
HPK2700175	A4	148	Y						
HPK2700176	C1	149							
HPK2700177	A4	150							
HPK2700178	C1	151	Y						
HPK2700179	C1	152							
HPK2700180	A4	153							
HPK2700181	C1	154	Y						
HPK2700182	C1	155	Y						
HPK2700183	C1	156	Y						
HPK2700184	C1	157	Y				OLA001	P3	123568
HPK2700185	C1	160							
HPK2700186	C1	161							
HPK2700187	C2	162	Y						
HPK2700188	C1	163	Y						
HPK2700189	C1	164	Y	Y			OLA008	P4	1234568
HPK2700190	C2	165	Y						
HPK2700191	C2	166	Y						
HPK2700192	C3	167							
HPK2700193	C2	168	Y						
HPK2700194	C2	169							
HPK2700195	C2	170	Y						
HPK2700196	C2	171	Y						
HPK2700197	C3	172							
HPK2700198	C1	173	Y						
HPK2700199	C3	174	Y	Y			OLA083	P3	12345678
HPK2700200	C3	175	Y						
HPK2700201	C1	176	Y						
HPK2700202	C2	177	Y						
HPK2700203	C2	178	Y						
HPK2700204	C3	179	Y						
HPK2700205	C1	180							
HPK2700206	C1	181	Y						
HPK2700207	C2	182	Y						
HPK2700208	C1	183	Y						
HPK2700209	C1	184	Y						
HPK2700210	C1	185	Y				OLA001	P3	123568
HPK2700211	C2	186	Y	Y	ODA012	D2	OLA024	P4	123568
HPK2700212	C1	187							
HPK2700213	C1	188							
HPK2700214	C1	189	Y	Y			OLA008	P4	1234568
HPK2700215	C1	190							
HPK2700216	C2	191							
HPK2700217	C2	192	Y						
HPK2700218	C2	193	Y						
HPK2700219	C3	194					OLA010	P3	1234568
HPK2700220	C3	195							
HPK2700221	C1	196							
HPK2700222	C1	197							
HPK2700223	C3	198	Y	Y			OLA014	P4	12345678
HPK2700224	C1	199							
HPK2700225	C1	200	Y						
HPK2700226	C1	201	Y						
HPK2700227	C1	202	Y				OLA091	P3	12345678
HPK2700228	C1	203	Y						
HPK2700229	C3	204							
HPK2700230	C1	205	Y						
HPK2700231	C3	206	Y						
HPK2700232	C2	207							
HPK2700233	C4	208							
HPK2700234	C1	209							
HPK2700235	C1	210							
HPK2700236	C4	211							
HPK2700237	C3	212							
HPK2700238	C3	213							
HPK2700239	C2	214	Y						
HPK2700240	C1	215							
HPK2700241	C2	216	Y						
HPK2700242	C3	217							
HPK2700243	C1	218	Y						
HPK2700244	C1	219	Y						
HPK2700245	C2	220	Y						
HPK2700246	C1	221					OLA010	P3	1234568

PLAN #	PRICE TIER	PAGE	MATERIALS LIST	QUOTE ONE®	DECK	DECK PRICE	LANDSCAPE	LANDSCAPE PRICE	REGIONS
HPK2700247	C3	222	Y						
HPK2700248	SQ1	223							
HPK2700249	C2	224	Y						
HPK2700250	C4	225							
HPK2700251	C1	226							
HPK2700252	C1	227	Y						
HPK2700253	C3	228	Y						
HPK2700254	C3	229							
HPK2700255	C2	230							
HPK2700256	C2	231	Y						
HPK2700257	C2	232							
HPK2700258	C3	233	Y						
HPK2700259	C1	234							
HPK2700260	C2	235	Y						
HPK2700261	C3	236							
HPK2700262	C2	237	Y						
HPK2700263	C3	238							
HPK2700264	C2	239							
HPK2700265	C1	240							
HPK2700266	C1	241	Y			OLA014	P4		12345678
HPK2700267	C2	241	Y						
HPK2700268	C3	244	Y						
HPK2700269	C2	245							
HPK2700270	C2	246							
HPK2700271	C4	247							
HPK2700272	C2	248							
HPK2700273	C2	249	Y						
HPK2700274	C4	250	Y						
HPK2700275	SQ1	251	Y						
HPK2700276	C3	252	Y						
HPK2700277	C3	253	Y	Y		OLA038	P3		7
HPK2700278	C3	254	Y						
HPK2700279	C3	255	Y						
HPK2700280	C2	256	Y						
HPK2700281	C4	257	Y						
HPK2700282	C4	258							
HPK2700283	C3	259	Y						
HPK2700284	C2	260	Y						
HPK2700285	C2	261							
HPK2700286	C4	262							
HPK2700287	C2	263	Y	Y		OLA008	P4		1234568
HPK2700288	C2	264							
HPK2700289	C2	265							
HPK2700290	C3	266	Y						
HPK2700291	SQ1	267	Y						
HPK2700292	C4	268							
HPK2700293	C2	269							
HPK2700294	C2	270	Y						
HPK2700295	C4	271							
HPK2700296	SQ1	272	Y						
HPK2700297	C4	273							
HPK2700298	C2	274							
HPK2700299	C3	275	Y						
HPK2700300	C2	276				OLA017	P3		123568
HPK2700301	C3	277	Y	Y		OLA008	P4		1234568
HPK2700302	C4	278	Y						
HPK2700303	SQ1	279	Y						
HPK2700304	SQ1	280							
HPK2700305	C4	281	Y						
HPK2700306	C4	282							
HPK2700307	C4	283	Y						
HPK2700308	SQ1	284	Y			OLA008	P4		1234568
HPK2700309	C3	285	Y						
HPK2700310	C3	286				OLA008	P4		1234568
HPK2700311	C3	287	Y						
HPK2700312	C3	288							
HPK2700313	C4	289	Y						
HPK2700314	C4	290							
HPK2700315	C4	291	Y						
HPK2700316	L1	292							
HPK2700317	L1	293							
HPK2700318	C2	294							
HPK2700319	SQ1	295							
HPK2700320	L1	296							
HPK2700321	SQ1	297	Y						
HPK2700322	C4	298							
HPK2700323	L1	299	Y			OLA008	P4		1234568
HPK2700324	L1	300							
HPK2700325	L1	301							
HPK2700326	L1	302							
HPK2700327	SQ1	303	Y						
HPK2700328	C4	304	Y						
HPK2700329	SQ7	305							
HPK2700330	C4	306	Y						
HPK2700331	L2	307							
HPK2700332	SQ1	308							
HPK2700333	L1	309	Y	Y					
HPK2700334	SQ1	310							
HPK2700335	SQ1	311							
HPK2700336	L1	312	Y						
HPK2700337	L1	313	Y						
HPK2700338	L1	314							
HPK2700339	SQ1	315	Y						
HPK2700340	SQ7	316							
HPK2700341	SQ1	317							
HPK2700342	L1	318	Y						
HPK2700343	L1	319							
HPK2700344	L1	320	Y						
HPK2700345	SQ1	321	Y			OLA017	P3		123568
HPK2700346	L1	322							
HPK2700347	SQ1	323	Y	Y		OLA028	P4		12345678
HPK2700348	SQ7	324							
HPK2700349	SQ7	325	Y						
HPK2700350	SQ1	326	Y						
HPK2700351	SQ1	327							
HPK2700352	P5	330	Y						
HPK2700353	P5	330	Y						
HPK2700354	P4	330	Y						
HPK2700355	P4	330	Y						
HPK2700356	P4	330	Y						
HPK2700357	P4	330	Y						
HPK2700358	P5	330	Y						
HPK2700359	P4	330	Y						
HPK2700360	P5	330	Y						
HPK2700361	P5	331	Y						
HPK2700362	P5	331	Y						
HPK2700363	P4	331	Y						
HPK2700364	P4	331	Y						
HPK2700365	P5	331							
HPK2700366	P6	331	Y						
HPK2700367	P6	331	Y						
HPK2700368	P5	331	Y						
HPK2700369	P2	332							
HPK2700370	P4	332							
HPK2700371	P2	332							
HPK2700372	P2	332							
HPK2700373	P2	332							
HPK2700374	P4	332							
HPK2700375	P4	332							
HPK2700376	P1	332							
HPK2700377	P1	332							
HPK2700378	P2	333							
HPK2700379	P1	333							
HPK2700380	P1	333							
HPK2700381	P2	333							
HPK2700382	P1	333							
HPK2700383	P1	333							
HPK2700384	P1	333							
HPK2700385	P3	334							
HPK2700386	P3	336							
HPK2700387	P2	338							
HPK2700388	P2	340							
HPK2700389	P2	342							
HPK2700390	P3	344							
HPK2700391	P3	346							
HPK2700392	P4	348							
HPK2700393	P3	350							
HPK2700394	P3	352							
HPK2700395	P3	354							
HPK2700396	P3	356							
HPK2700397	P3	358							
HPK2700398	P3	360							
HPK2700399	P3	362							
HPK2700400	P3	364							
HPK2700401	P2	366							
HPK2700402	P4	368							
HPK2700403	P4	370							
HPK2700404	P3	372							